英文 **東京紹介事典**

トウキョウペディア

Phrase Book on Tokyo

まえがき

　東京は何度も歴史の曲がり角に立った街です。
　入江と沼、草原と森が広がっていた関東平野の一角に江戸城が建設されて以来、江戸幕府の創設、明治維新、第二次世界大戦という激動を経て、その後は経済復興をした日本の首都となり、今は未来に向けて変化する文化の発信地の一つとして人々が常に見つめる大都会になっています。

　それだけに、東京は多様で多彩です。
　日本の表玄関の顔、下町や歓楽街の顔、そして歴史の残り香があるかと思えば、21世紀を牽引するアートや技術を生み出す顔。さらに、ファインアートからサブカルチャー、伝統的な和食から、世界のシェフが集まるグルメの数々、ファーストフードから神社のそばで売られている昔ながらの和菓子まで、東京ほど多くの顔を持ち、それぞれに規模感や深みのある都市は多くはありません。

　東京を英語で説明するには、そんな多様な東京への理解も必要です。
　伝統を感じさせる東京駅の赤レンガのそばには、高層ビルが林立し、その向こうには皇居があります。そこは17世紀からずっと一般の人が立ち入れない巨大な森閑たる城郭でした。そして、駅の逆側には町人の街が広がり、周囲のビジネス街を越えてゆけば、鉄道のガードのそばに飲み屋や、蕎麦屋、寿司屋などが広がる庶民が集う街が広がります。

そんな街には最近アジア各地からやってきた人たちの開いたレストランや店舗のネオンも混ざっています。
　でも、東京駅周辺は東京の一つのセンターにすぎません。無数のセンターがそれぞれの顔を持って旅人を迎えるのが、東京の特徴です。

　英語は片言でも、そんな素顔の東京を海外の人と一緒に歩けば、きっと素晴らしい旅の思い出をプレゼントすることができるはずです。*Tokyopedia* は、そんな東京の人々、そして外国人と交流したいと思う広い読者に向けて作成しました。大都市のメカニズムや、そこに根付く文化をどのように説明するか。この試みは、日常の外国人との一つ一つの交流の積み重ねによって育まれます。

　ぜひ、そんなコミュニケーションというブロックを地道に積み上げながら、東京を世界に紹介するという壮大な事業に参加してみましょう。
　本書の姉妹版に、日本を短文の英語で紹介する書籍 *Japapedia* があります。そちらと合わせて、ぜひ英語を楽しみながら、訪日する人々との交流を深めるツールとして本書を活用してください。

2016年　夏
IBC パブリッシング編集部

目次

まえがき　　　　　　　2
東京中心部マップ　　　10

1部　東京ジェネラル　Tokyo General Information

1-01 東京とは　　14
Tokyo City

ワンセンテンスで説明する東京
Tokyo in Single Sentences

東京とは　　　　　　　　　　18
東京ライフ　　　　　　　　　20
東京の位置　　　　　　　　　23
東京の行政組織　　　　　　　24
東京の主要地域と都市の構造　25
東京の主要施設　　　　　　　28
東京の商店街　　　　　　　　29
東京とその周辺　　　　　　　30
東京の気候　　　　　　　　　32

1-02 東京の交通と移動　　34
Tokyo Transportation and Access

東京の通勤電車／東京のJR・私鉄・地下鉄／山手線／都電荒川線／東京モノレール・ゆりかもめ／東京のバス・タクシー／通勤ラッシュ／新幹線／リニアモーターカー／成田空港／羽田空港

ワンセンテンスで説明する東京
Tokyo in Single Sentences

東京の交通全般　　　　　　　54

東京の地下鉄　　　　　　　　58
東京の鉄道ネットワーク　　　62
東京の駅　　　　　　　　　　63
山手線・中央線・京浜東北線・
　総武線　　　　　　　　　　64
切符の購入　　　　　　　　　66
PASMOとSuica　　　　　　　66
東京のターミナル駅　　　　　70
成田空港と羽田空港　　　　　72
成田空港／羽田空港への交通　73
東京の歩き方　　　　　　　　76
東京の通勤常識とマナー　　　77

1-03 東京サバイバル　　80
Tokyo Survival Tips

安全と警察／キャッシングなど／ホテル・宿泊

ワンセンテンスで説明する東京
Tokyo in Single Sentences

東京の便利情報　　　　　　　84
英語でのコミュニケーション　86
安全と警察　　　　　　　　　88
地震　　　　　　　　　　　　90

Contents

緊急時の電話番号	90
郵便・キャッシング・クレジットカード	91
宿泊施設	92

1-04 東京で食べる・見る・遊ぶ　94
Tokyo Dining, Sightseeing and Entertainment

コンビニ／自動販売機／トイレ／喫煙／居酒屋／ラーメン屋／回転寿司／東京の百貨店／デパ地下／家電量販店／パチンコ屋／カラオケ

ワンセンテンスで説明する東京
Tokyo in Single Sentences

東京の食事	110
東京のランチ	115
カフェ・ベーカリー	116
日本料理	118
江戸前寿司	119
東京のショッピング体験	121
美術館	125
博物館	127

2部　東京観光　Tokyo Sightseeing

2-01 皇居とその周辺　130
Around the Imperial Palace

江戸城／皇居／二重橋／大手門／二の丸公園／桜田門／田安門と北の丸公園／霞ヶ関

ワンセンテンスで説明する東京
Tokyo in Single Sentences

江戸城	142
皇居	142
霞ヶ関と永田町	145

2-02 大手町・日本橋とその周辺　146
Around Otemachi, Nihonbashi

東京駅／八重洲／大手町／日本橋（橋）／日本橋（地名）／三越百貨店／小伝馬町

ワンセンテンスで説明する東京
Tokyo in Single Sentences

東京駅とその周辺	156
大手町・日本橋とその周辺	158

2-03 銀座とその周辺 162
Around Ginza

銀座／和光ビル／銀座すずらん通り／歌舞伎座／築地／新橋／有楽町／三菱一号館ミュージアム

ワンセンテンスで説明する東京
Tokyo in Single Sentences

伝統芸術	174
銀座とその周辺	175
新橋と有楽町、そして日比谷	177

2-04 浅草とその周辺 180
Around Asakusa

浅草／浅草寺／合羽橋商店街／東京スカイツリー

ワンセンテンスで説明する東京
Tokyo in Single Sentences

浅草	186
浅草寺	189
東京スカイツリー	191

2-05 新宿とその周辺 194
Around Shinjuku

新宿／新宿でのショッピング／新宿ゴールデン街／新宿西口商店街／新大久保／新宿御苑／バスタ新宿

ワンセンテンスで説明する東京
Tokyo in Single Sentences

新宿とその周辺	202
新宿御苑	204
新宿	206
新大久保	212
高田馬場	213
東京で楽しむ世界の料理	214
中野	216
高円寺	217
吉祥寺	218

2-06 渋谷・六本木とその周辺 220
Around Shibuya and Roppongi

渋谷／ハチ公／六本木／六本木ヒルズ／東京ミッドタウン／麻布十番／恵比寿・広尾

Contents

ワンセンテンスで説明する東京
Tokyo in Single Sentences

渋谷	232
六本木	235
恵比寿	237
広尾	239

2-07 原宿・表参道・青山とその周辺 240
Around Harajuku, Omotesando, Aoyama

原宿／明治神宮／表参道／根津美術館／太田記念美術館／赤坂見附

ワンセンテンスで説明する東京
Tokyo in Single Sentences

原宿・表参道	250
青山	253
赤坂	254

2-08 神田・秋葉原とその周辺 256
Around Kanda, Akihabara

神田／神田明神／神田古本屋街／秋葉原／湯島聖堂／浅草橋（人形問屋街）

ワンセンテンスで説明する東京
Tokyo in Single Sentences

東京の「麺」	264
秋葉原	265
神保町	268
漫画喫茶	270

2-09 上野・谷中とその周辺 272
Around Ueno, Yanaka

上野／寛永寺／上野公園／東京国立博物館／アメヤ横丁／谷中・根津／谷中霊園

ワンセンテンスで説明する東京
Tokyo in Single Sentences

上野	282
谷中・根津・千駄木（谷根千）	285
銭湯体験	288

2-10 月島・深川とその周辺 290
Around Tsukishima, Fukagawa

下町／隅田川／月島（もんじゃ焼き）／門前仲町・富岡八幡宮／江戸東京博物館／国技館／深川／亀戸／亀戸天神／清澄庭園／柴又

ワンセンテンスで説明する東京
Tokyo in Single Sentences

深川とその周辺	306
下町の食	307

2-11 池袋・巣鴨とその周辺 310
Around Ikebukuro, Sugamo

池袋／巣鴨／染井町／六義園／旧古河庭園

ワンセンテンスで説明する東京
Tokyo in Single Sentences

六義園	318
池袋	319
巣鴨	320

2-12 品川・海浜とその周辺 322
Around Shinagawa, Kaihin

品川／お台場／浜離宮／旧芝離宮恩賜公園／増上寺・芝公園／東京タワー

ワンセンテンスで説明する東京
Tokyo in Single Sentences

目黒	332
品川	333
浜離宮	334
お台場・東京湾	336
東京タワー	338

2-13 後楽園・神楽坂とその周辺 340
Around Korakuen, Kagurazaka

東京ドーム／小石川後楽園／小石川植物園／矢来能楽堂／神楽坂／靖國神社／椿山荘

ワンセンテンスで説明する東京
Tokyo in Single Sentences

後楽園（庭園）	350
神楽坂	351

2-14 東京から日帰りできる観光名所 355
Day Trips from Tokyo

東海道／東京ディズニーランド／成田山／横浜／鎌倉／奥多摩／富士五湖／日光／伊豆／箱根／熱海／伊豆・小笠原諸島／川越

ワンセンテンスで説明する東京
Tokyo in Single Sentences

近郊へのアクセス	370
軽井沢	371
温泉	373

Contents

3部 江戸と東京の歴史と文化
History and Culture of Edo and Tokyo

3-01 江戸と東京の歴史と文化 378
History and Culture of Edo and Tokyo

江戸時代／江戸幕府／明暦の大火／ペリー来航／明治維新／義理と人情・勧善懲悪／将軍／旗本・御家人／士農工商／文明開化／関東大震災／東京大空襲／高度成長／バブル景気

ワンセンテンスで説明する東京
Tokyo in Single Sentences

江戸時代以前	406
江戸時代	407
明治時代	413
大正から昭和	416
戦後から現在	417
2020年	419

装 幀＝斉藤 啓
英文作成＝David Satterwhite
編集協力＝Robb Satterwhite
写 真＝IBC編集部
ナレーション＝Howard Colefield
録音スタジオ＝株式会社巧芸創作

東京中心部マップ

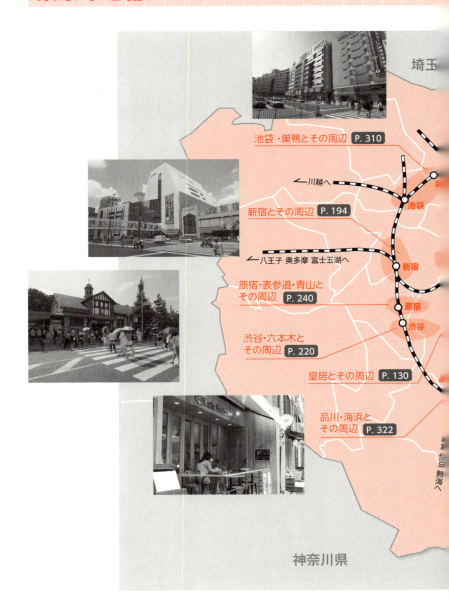

1部　東京ジェネラル
Tokyo General Information

東京とは
東京の交通と移動
東京サバイバル
東京で食べる・見る・遊ぶ

1-01 東京とは

　東京について、まず思い浮かべることは何ですか？ 世界クラスの大都市、日本の首都、そして2020年オリンピック・パラリンピック開催地？ そのすべてが当てはまるのですが、それだけではないのです。それではもっと見てみましょう。

　世界最大の都市の一つとして、東京都23区には900万人超の人が住み（23区は東京都の中でそれぞれが独立した地区として治められています）、東京が位置する関東平野の隣接する都市まで数えると、首都圏は世界で最も人口の多い大都市となり、その合わせた人口は3500万人を超えます。

　もちろん一夜にしてこのような大都市が生まれたわけではありません。なにせ東京の歴史は1400年以上も遡れるのです（初の仏教寺院である浅草の浅草寺は645年に建立されました）。当時の東京は今よりもかなり小さかったのですが、そのころの日本の統治者である徳川家康が江戸に幕府を開き、1603年から現在に至るまで、410年以上にわたって日本の首都であり続けてきたのです。

　300年以上も平穏が続いた江戸時代には、歌舞伎や他の演劇をはじめ、浮世絵など多くの芸術的な様式

Tokyo City

What comes to mind when you think of Tokyo? A big, world-class city, the capital of Japan, and the host of the Olympic and Paralympic Games to be held in 2020? It is all of these, and more. Let's take a closer look.

As one of the world's largest cities, Tokyo is home to over 9 million people in the city's 23 wards (each of the 23 is governed as a separate city within Tokyo), and if we count the adjacent cities in the Kanto Plain, where Tokyo is located, Greater Tokyo is the most populous metropolitan center in the world, with a combined population of over 35 million.

This did not happen overnight, of course, as Tokyo traces its history back over 1,400 years (its first major Buddhist temple, Senso-ji in Asakusa, was founded in 645 AD). Although the city was much smaller then, it has served as Japan's capital continuously since 1603 — over 410 years — when the ruler of Japan, Tokugawa Ieyasu, opened Edo Bakufu in Edo, present-day Tokyo.

The Edo era saw the flowering of Japanese culture, including kabuki and other forms of theater, ukiyo-e

を含めて、日本文化が繁栄しました。

　東京は20世紀に2度復興を遂げました。1923年の関東大震災と第2次世界大戦による荒廃の後です。しかしながら今日の東京は、日本全域を治める政庁所在地としてだけではなく、主要な経済センターとしても機能しています。なんと、「フォーチュン・グローバル500社」のうち50社以上（世界中でどの都市よりも多い）が東京にあるのです。東京は世界で最も住みやすい都市（2014年）としてだけではなく、世界で最も安全な都市にもランクされました。

　この国際的な都市の文化的な側面を見ても、東京には数千に及ぶレストランがあり、世界各国の料理が楽しめ、かつ世界の他のどの都市よりも多くの星をミシュランガイドから獲得しているのです。

　東京は1964年にアジア初のオリンピック開催都市となりました。そして、2020年のオリンピック・パラリンピック開催地にも選ばれました。東京を訪れ体験しようと決めたからには、東京のすべてを探求し、歴史、経済的な躍動感、文化遺産、素晴らしい料理から、魅力的なファッションや革新的な技術、そして若者たちが打ち出す新しいトレンドなどを楽しんでほしいと思います。

　ようこそ、日本へ。ようこそ、東京へ！

woodblock printing, and many other artistic forms in over three centuries of peace.

Tokyo has been rebuilt twice in the last century, after suffering the Great Kanto Earthquake in 1923 and then being largely destroyed during World War II. Today, however, it is not only the seat of government for all of Japan, but it is a major economic center as well, with over fifty of the world's Fortune Global 500 companies, more than any other city in the world. It has been ranked not only as the world's Most Livable City (2014), but the World's Safest City.

And as a measure of how cosmopolitan it is in a cultural sense, among its thousands of restaurants and its global cuisine the Michelin Guide has awarded more Michelin stars to Tokyo than any other city in the world.

Tokyo hosted the first Olympic Games ever held in Asia, in 1964, and it has been awarded the Olympic and Paralympic Games to be held in 2020 as well. Now that you've chosen to visit and experience Tokyo, we hope you will explore all it has to offer, and will enjoy its rich history, its economic dynamism, its cultural legacies, its fabulous cuisine, and its attractive trends in fashion, innovation, and youth-oriented new directions.

Welcome to Japan, welcome to Tokyo!

▶▶▶ ワンセンテンスで説明する東京

東京とは

Track 01

東京は日本の首都です。
- [ ] Tokyo is the capital of Japan.

東京は、日本の首都で、行政、立法、司法の中心地です。
- [ ] Since Tokyo is the capital of Japan, it is the center of government, the legislature and the judiciary.

東京は、日本の政治、経済、文化の中心地です。
- [ ] Tokyo is the political, economic and cultural center of Japan.

東京は、日本だけでなく、世界でも有数の文化都市です。
- [ ] Tokyo is one of the leading cultural capitals of the world, not just Japan.

東京を中心とした首都圏と、大阪を中心とた京阪神が、日本の経済・文化の二大中心地です。
- [ ] The Tokyo Metropolitan Area, centered on Tokyo, and the Kyoto-Osaka-Kobe Metropolitan Area, centered on Osaka, are Japan's main economic and cultural centers.

東京は日本列島の中央にある、日本で最も大きな都市です。
- [ ] Tokyo is located in the middle of the Japanese archipelago, and it is Japan's largest city.

Tokyo in Single Sentences

東京は日本で最も人口の多い都市です。
- [ ] Tokyo is the most populous city in Japan.

東京都の面積はおよそ2187平方キロメートルです。
- [ ] Tokyo covers 2,187 square kilometers.

フランスのパリのように、東京には多くの文化活動が集中しています。
- [ ] Like Paris, Tokyo has a concentration of many cultural activities.

東京を中心とした一帯は首都圏と呼ばれています。
- [ ] Tokyo and its surrounding region are collectively referred to as the Tokyo Metropolitan Area.

東京には、1300万人の人が住んでいます。
- [ ] There are 13 million people living in Tokyo.

東京とその周辺を合わせると、3000万人の人が住んでいます。
- [ ] There are 30 million people living in the greater Tokyo area.

KEY WORD

- [ ] capital — 首都
- [ ] Tokyo Metropolitan Area — 首都圏
- [ ] Japanese archipelago — 日本列島

▶▶▶ ワンセンテンスで説明する東京

東京都の経済規模は、都市としては世界一です。

☐ Tokyo's economy is the largest of any city in the world.

東京都の中心部は 23 の区に別れています。

☐ Tokyo's central city is divided into 23 wards.

東京は 23 の区からなる、いわゆる特別区と、その他の市町村による地域からできています。

☐ Tokyo is made up of 23 so-called special wards plus a collection of sub-cities, towns and villages.

太平洋にある伊豆諸島と小笠原諸島も東京都の一部となります。

☐ The Izu and Ogasawara archipelagos, which lie in the Pacific Ocean, are also part of Tokyo.

東京都の都内総生産は約 92 兆 9000 億円です。

☐ Tokyo's GDP is around 92.9 trillion yen.

東京都の経済規模は、カリフォルニア州の約半分です。

☐ Tokyo's economy is about half the size of California's economy.

東京ライフ

Track 02

東京は眠ることのない都市です。

☐ Tokyo is a city that doesn't sleep.

Tokyo in Single Sentences

東京の都心への通勤ラッシュは午前8時頃から9時頃までがピークで、公共交通は大変混み合います。

- [ ] During peak commuting rush hour, roughly between 8 am and 9 am, public transportation heading in to Tokyo is terribly crowded.

東京の人は、ラッシュ時に地下鉄などに押し込まれ、体と体をくっつけながら通勤することに慣れています。

- [ ] Tokyoites are used to being pushed onto subway trains and standing so close to other commuters as to be touching.

東京の午後のラッシュアワーは、5時頃にはじまって夜遅くまで続きます。というのも、多くの人が、残業したり、仕事終わりに仲間と飲んだりしているからです。

- [ ] Tokyo's evening rush hour starts around 5 pm and continues late into the night, since many people work overtime or socialize after work.

東京では、通常の勤務時間は午前9時から午後5時までで、週休二日制です。しかしながら、多くの人が残業しています。

- [ ] In Tokyo, standard working hours are 9 am to 5 pm, with two days off a week. However, many people work overtime.

KEY WORD ✓

☐ 23 wards	23区
☐ Ogasawara archipelago	小笠原諸島
☐ commuting rush hour	通勤ラッシュ
☐ public transportation	公共交通
☐ Tokyoite	東京(の)人

▶▶▶ ワンセンテンスで説明する東京

東京のビジネスマンは、ランチは比較的早く切り上げ、重要な打ち合わせや会食は夕食時に行います。

☐ In Tokyo, most businesspeople have a relatively brief lunch, and leave important business matters and socializing for dinnertime.

東京の若者の多くは共働きですが、専業主婦もまだかなりいます。

☐ In Tokyo, there are a lot of young working couples, but there are still a lot of full-time housewives as well.

東京では、共働きの親のための託児所の不足が社会問題になっています。

☐ In Tokyo, the lack of childcare for working parents is a problem.

東京ではキャリアを見据えて、結婚や出産を断念する女性が増えています。

☐ In Tokyo, the number of women who choose to focus on their careers and forsake marriage and motherhood is increasing.

東京の子どもたちの多くは、放課後も塾などで勉強を続け、高校受験、大学受験に備えます。

☐ After school, lots of kids in Tokyo continue studying at prep schools to prepare for high school and college entrance exams.

東京では、夜に子どもだけで地下鉄に乗っていることがあります。

☐ In Tokyo, you can see kids traveling alone on the subway in the evening.

Tokyo in Single Sentences

東京の位置

東京は、アメリカのオクラホマシティ、イランのテヘランと同じ緯度に位置しています。

☐ Tokyo is at the same latitude as Oklahoma City in the U.S. and Tehran in Iran.

東京は、関東地方の南に位置しています。

☐ Tokyo is located in the southern part of the Kanto region.

東京は東京湾に面しています。

☐ Tokyo faces Tokyo Bay.

東京は、西は山岳地帯に面し、東は東京湾に面しています。

☐ Tokyo faces mountains to the west and Tokyo Bay to the east.

KEY WORD ✓

☐ working couple	共働き
☐ full-time housewife	専業主婦
☐ childcare	託児所
☐ prep school	塾
☐ latitude	緯度
☐ Kanto region	関東地方

東京の行政組織

東京は正式には東京都と呼ばれ、日本の他の県と同様の行政機関を持っています。

☐ Tokyo is officially called Tokyo Metropolis, and it has a government similar to that of Japan's prefectures.

東京都の行政の長は東京都知事です。

☐ The head of Tokyo's government is called the Governor of Tokyo.

東京都知事は4年ごとに、一般投票によって選ばれます。

☐ The Governor of Tokyo is elected every four years by popular vote.

東京都庁は新宿にあり、そこには都議会も併設されています。

☐ Tokyo City Hall, which includes the Metropolitan Assembly, is in Shinjuku.

東京都の年間予算は約13兆円です。

☐ Tokyo's annual budget is around 13 trillion yen.

東京23区にはそれぞれ区議会があり、区長が一般投票で選ばれます。

☐ Each of Tokyo's 23 wards has an assembly and a ward mayor elected by popular vote.

Tokyo in Single Sentences

東京23区以外の市町村では、他の県と同様に、議会と行政の長が選挙されます。

☐ Outside Tokyo's 23 central wards, the city's sub-cities, towns and villages have elected assemblies and mayors just like in Japan's other prefectures.

東京の主要地域と都市の構造

東京都心の西側一帯は「山手」と呼ばれ、比較的新しい住宅地や商業施設が集まっています。

☐ The area on the west side of central Tokyo, called "*Yamanote*," is a comparatively new residential and commercial area.

山手の主要なビジネス街は、渋谷、新宿、池袋です。

☐ Major business districts in *Yamanote* include Shibuya, Shinjuku and Ikebukuro.

東京都心の東側一帯は「下町」と呼ばれ、古い情緒の残る、庶民が日常生活する地域です。

☐ The area on the east side of central Tokyo, called "*Shitamachi*," has a more old-fashioned atmosphere, and is a place where ordinary people go about their daily life.

KEY WORD ✓

☐ Tokyo Metropolis	東京都
☐ Governor of Tokyo	東京都知事
☐ popular vote	一般投票

上野や浅草といった商業地区が、下町を代表する二大エリアです。

☐ The commercial centers of Ueno and Asakusa are two major *Shitamachi* neighborhoods.

東京湾に接する地域は、ほとんどが埋め立て地です。

☐ The neighborhoods bordering Tokyo Bay are mostly built on reclaimed land.

都心の北端は荒川を境とし、西端は多摩川を境としています。

☐ Central Tokyo is bordered to the north by the Arakawa River and to the west by the Tamagawa River.

山手線と呼ばれる東京の環状線沿いには、商業、ビジネス、文化の中心が集まっています。

☐ The Yamanote line is a railway loop line in Tokyo, and several commericial, business and cultural hubs are located at stations along the line.

東京23区のうち、千代田区には国の行政機関や金融機関が集まっています。

☐ One of Tokyo's 23 wards, Chiyoda Ward, is home to many of the country's government and financial institutions.

港区には、麻布や六本木といった国際色豊かな繁華街があり、東京を代表する商業の中心地です。

☐ Minato Ward, which includes the cosmopolitan commercial centers of Azabu and Roppongi, is one of Tokyo's business centers.

Tokyo in Single Sentences

都心の中央部には皇居があり、そこから放射状に都市が拡がっています。

☐ The Imperial Palace is located near the middle of central Tokyo, with the rest of the city radiating out around it.

皇居の正門から広い道路を少し行くと東京駅があり、そこから地方へ無数の鉄道網が伸びています。

☐ A wide boulevard leads from the Imperial Palace to Tokyo Station, where numerous rail lines connect Tokyo to the provinces.

皇居から放射状にのびる幹線道路や、山手線に接続する数え切れない鉄道路線が、都心と郊外を結んでいます。

☐ Central Tokyo is connected to its suburbs by several major thoroughfares, radiating out from the Imperial Palace, and by numerous train lines connecting to the Yamanote loop line.

東京には、新宿、渋谷、池袋、上野、品川といった繁華街があり、それらの駅では膨大な数の乗客が乗り降りしています。

☐ In Tokyo, several business centers are served by train stations that draw large numbers of passengers. These include Shinjuku, Shibuya, Ikebukuro, Ueno and Shinagawa.

KEY WORD ✓

☐ reclaimed land	埋立地
☐ loop line	環状線
☐ finanacial institution	金融機関
☐ commercial center	商業中心地

東京とは｜東京の主要地域と都市の構造

▶▶▶ ワンセンテンスで説明する東京

東京の主要施設

東京都庁は、新宿副都心という高層ビル街の一画を成しています。

☐ Tokyo City Hall is part of the skyscraper district called Shinjuku Sub-Center.

東京ビッグサイトは、東京で最も大きな国際展示場です。

☐ Tokyo Big Sight is Tokyo's largest international convention center.

東京の代表的なスポーツ施設は、1964年の東京オリンピックのために造られました。

☐ Tokyo's signature sports facilities were created for the Tokyo 1964 Olympic Games.

東京ドームと神宮球場が東京の二大野球場です。

☐ Tokyo Dome and Jingu Baseball Stadium are two large baseball stadiums located in Tokyo.

かつて江戸城であった皇居は、東京の中心にあります。

☐ The Imperial Palace, which used to be Edo Castle, is located in the center of Tokyo.

東京には国会議事堂や各省庁の建物をはじめ、国の主要機関が集中しています。

☐ Japan's major institutions, such as the Diet Building and government agencies, are intensively concentrated in Tokyo.

Tokyo in Single Sentences

東京の商店街

東京のほとんどの地域にスーパーマーケットがあります。

☐ Supermarkets can be found in most Tokyo neighborhoods.

東京の多くの地域にはショッピングストリートがあり、「商店街」と呼ばれています。

☐ Many Tokyo neighborhoods have a dedicated shopping street, called a *shotengai*.

商店街には、お米、お茶、家庭用電化製品などを扱う小規模の店が軒を連ねています。

☐ Along the *shotengai* are many small shops that specialize in items like rice, tea, and household electronics.

東京の中心街には、大型家電量販店があります。

☐ Huge consumer-electronics stores can be found in Tokyo's major centers.

とくに、東京でも比較的古い地区には、家族経営の店を今でもよく見かけます。

☐ Small "mom-and-pop" stores are still common in Tokyo, especially in older neighborhoods.

KEY WORD ✓

☐ Tokyo City Hall　　　　　東京都庁
☐ Diet　　　　　　　　　　国会議事堂
☐ huge consumer-electronics store　大型家電量販店

東京とその周辺

東京都に隣接して大都市がいくつかあります。

☐ Several other large cities are located near Tokyo.

東京都と神奈川県は多摩川で隔てられています。

☐ The Tama River separates Tokyo from Kanagawa Prefecture.

埼玉県は東京の北に位置し、東京へ通勤する人が多く住んでいます。

☐ Saitama Prefecture, located to the north of Tokyo, is home to many people who commute to Tokyo.

東京の東にある千葉県も東京湾に面しています。

☐ To the east of Tokyo is Chiba Prefecture, which also faces Tokyo Bay.

八王子市や立川市などの中核市街地は、東京23区の外に位置しています。

☐ Major sub-cities such as Hachioji and Tachikawa are located outside Tokyo's 23 central wards.

首都圏の中で、東京の次に規模が大きいのが横浜市です。

☐ Yokohama is the next-largest city in the Tokyo metropolitan area, after Tokyo itself.

東京の南西28キロに位置する横浜の人口は、約370万人です。

☐ Yokohama is located 28 kilometers southwest of Tokyo, and has a population of around 3.7 million people.

Tokyo in Single Sentences

東京と横浜は、日本と海外を結ぶ二大港湾都市です。

☐ Tokyo and Yokohama are two of Japan's major port cities, connecting Japan to the world.

横浜と千葉は首都圏の一部です。

☐ Yokohama City and Chiba Prefecture are part of the Tokyo Metropolitan Area.

富士山は、東京の西にあります。

☐ Mt. Fuji is located to the west of Tokyo.

東京の西は、富士山などで有名な山岳地帯に面しています。

☐ To the west, Tokyo faces several mountains, the most famous of which is Mt. Fuji.

富士山は、東京都内にはありませんが、晴れた日には東京から見ることができます。

☐ Mt. Fuji isn't located in Tokyo, but on a clear day you can see it from Tokyo.

東京の気候

東京は、春と秋は温暖です。

☐ Tokyo has mild weather in the spring and fall.

東京では、桜は４月初旬に一斉に開花します。

☐ Cherry blossoms bloom in Tokyo at the beginning of April.

６月から７月にかけて、東京は梅雨という雨期になります。

☐ In June and July Tokyo has a rainy season, which is called *tsuyu*.

東京は、夏の間ときどき台風に見舞われます。

☐ Tokyo occasionally has typhoons during the summer months.

東京は、夏に予期せぬ土砂降りに見舞われることがあります。

☐ Tokyo sometimes gets unexpected downpours during the summer.

東京の夏はとても蒸し暑いです。

☐ Tokyo summers are hot and humid.

エアコンが一因で、東京の夏の気温は摂氏40度を超えることがあります。

☐ Partially due to the effect of air conditioners, summertime temperatures in Tokyo can sometimes exceed 40 degrees Celsius.

Tokyo in Single Sentences

東京の冬はどちらかというと穏やかです。

☐ Tokyo winters are relatively gentle.

東京の冬はとても乾燥します。

☐ Tokyo winters are very dry.

東京に雪が降るのは一冬に多くても数回ですが、雪に慣れていないので、多くの都市機能に影響がでます。

☐ Tokyo sees snow a few times at most each winter, and since Tokyo isn't accustomed to regular snowfall, many city functions can be disrupted when it snows.

東京とは

東京の気候

KEY WORD ✓

☐ Cherry blossom	桜
☐ rainy season	梅雨
☐ typhoon	台風
☐ downpour	土砂降り

東京の交通と移動

　地図なしで東京を歩き回るのは大変です。住人にとってさえ、東京は案内するのが難しいのです。たとえば、多くの東京の通りには名前がついていません。東京の住所は通り名ではなく、区画ごとの番号で決まっているのです。ですから、携帯電話のGPSアプリは東京を歩き回るとき役に立ちます。

　日本人に英語で話しかけると、驚いたりパニックになったように見えるかもしれません。それは、あなたのせいではありません。なぜそうなってしまうのかというと、あなたが出会う日本人のほとんどは、英語を話さないからなのです。たまには、英語が上手で、手助けしてくれるような風変わりな日本人に出会うかもしれませんが……。

東京の通勤電車

　東京には非常に効率的な地下鉄や通勤電車のネットワークがあります。それに清潔で静かです。しかし、ラッシュアワー時は、東京の電車は大変混雑します。他の人に接近して立っているといった、今まで感じたことのないような空間かもしれません。

Tokyo Transportation and Access

It is very hard to get around Tokyo without a map. Even for locals, Tokyo is a hard city to navigate. For example, most streets in Tokyo don't have names. Instead of using street names, Tokyo addresses are determined by block numbers. Therefore, a GPS application for your mobile phone is useful for getting around Tokyo.

If you speak to a Japanese person in English they might look surprised or panicked. Don't take it personally. It happens because, unfortunately, most Japanese you meet won't speak English. Occasionally you may meet a stranger who speaks good English and offers to help you.

Tokyo commuter trains

Tokyo has a very effective subway and commuter train network. Plus, Tokyo subway cars are clean and quiet. However, Tokyo trains are very crowded during rush hour. You may find yourself standing very close to other people. In other words, you may feel a different sense of space.

東京の駅には出口がたくさんあります。駅には、目的地別にどの出口が便利かを示す案内が掲示されています。非常に広い駅もあるので、正しい出口を見つけるようにしましょう。さもないと、目的地まで長い道のりになってしまうかもしれません。

電車の切符は自動販売機で買うことができます。たとえ料金が違う切符を買ったとしても、改札口の手前に「精算機」があります。駅を出るには切符か定期券が必要です。

東京のJR・私鉄・地下鉄

線路が地上でも地下でも交差している東京という都市を思い描いてみてください。世界中のどの都市よりも交通網が縦横に行き渡っているのです。

JRとして知られる東日本鉄道には主要な路線がいくつかあります。東京を一周する線（山手線）や東京を東西に駆け抜ける線（総武線と東京駅から西の高尾までを繋ぐ中央線）、南北に横浜からさらにその先の駅まで、北は大宮からさらにその北の駅までを東京と結びつける路線もあります。

このような東日本鉄道網に加えて、池袋・新宿・渋谷・目黒・品川といったJRの各駅から東西南北にわたって郊外に枝分かれする私鉄の路線網があり、さらに東京の中心部から大都市エリアを縦横に駆け抜ける地下鉄網が12路線以上もあるのです。

Train stations in Tokyo can have many exits. There are maps in the train station to show you which exits are convenient for which destinations. Because some train stations are so big, it is a good idea to pick the correct exit, or you could be a long way from your destination.

Train tickets are purchased from vending machines. If you buy a ticket for the wrong fare, you can use the "fare adjustment machine" before the exit gates. You need your train ticket or pass to exit the train station.

Tokyo JR, other railways, subways

Imagine the city of Tokyo crisscrossed with train lines both above and below ground, with the most extensive transportation network of any city in the world.

East Japan Railway (known as "JR East" or just "JR"), has major lines circling the city (the Yamanote line), crossing the city from east to west (the Sobu line, and the Chuo line from Tokyo to Takao in the west), as well as north-south, connecting Tokyo to Yokohama and points farther south, and Omiya and other destinations farther north.

In addition to these JR lines, there are other rail lines branching out to the suburbs from such JR stops as Ikebukuro, Shinjuku, Shibuya, Meguro and Shinagawa, and over a dozen subway lines, also connecting the center of Tokyo to destinations throughout the metropolitan area.

地下鉄網は最初は複雑に思われるかもしれませんが、路線ごとに色分けされ、駅ごとにナンバーが振られており、車両や駅には英語（中国語や韓国語でも）の表示がついています。迷ったときは、改札口にいる駅員に尋ねるのがいちばんいいでしょう。英語の地図を用意していて、正しい方向を教えてくれますよ。

山手線

山手線は、東京の都心部の拠点をリンクする環状の鉄道です。1925年に環状線としての旅客運送が始まりました。1923年に起きた関東大震災で廃墟と化してたった2年後のことです。

山手線が開業したことで、当時まだ東京の郊外であった渋谷や新宿、そして池袋の都市化が急激に進み、今では東京の副都心と呼ばれるほどに成長しました。

山手線の山手とは、東京の都市部のうち西側を指す言葉で、ニューヨーク風にいえばアップタウンとなります。それに対して、もともと江戸時代から商業地として発展した東京の東側は下町と呼ばれます。山手線はこの二つの地

The subway system might seem confusing at first, but it is color-coded, each station has a number, and signage on the trains and stations includes English (as well as Chinese and Korean). If you are confused, it is best to ask one of the station crew at the ticket wickets for assistance — they are prepared with maps in English and will point you in the right direction.

Yamanote line

The Yamanote train is a circular loop line linking major sub-centers around the metropolitan core of Tokyo. It began passenger service circling Tokyo in 1925, just two years after the devastation caused by the Great Kanto Earthquake of 1923.

Until the Yamanote began operations, the sub-centers of Shibuya, Shinjuku and Ikebukuro, among others, were seen as being on the edge of the city, although they were growing rapidly. Today, of course, these are each known as highly developed, important core areas of Tokyo.

The term *Yamanote* in the train line's name refers to the western side of the city, somewhat akin to the way a New Yorker might refer to uptown. In contrast to this, the eastern part of Tokyo, where commercial activities were centered from the time of the Edo era, is known as the downtown (*shitamachi*). With this as background, the Yamanote line

域を環状にリンクしたわけです。

　また、山手線沿線の拠点となる多くの駅には、もうひとつ別の役目があります。東京と郊外を結ぶ何本もの地下鉄や私鉄が、山手線の駅にリンクしていて、多くの通勤客のための乗換駅としても機能しているのです。

都電荒川線

　早稲田から、三ノ輪橋にいたる12.2キロを走る都電荒川線は、東京都に唯一残る市街電車です。一両編成の電車で、都民の生活の場をぬって走ります。三ノ輪橋からは浅草もそう遠くありません。

東京モノレール・ゆりかもめ

　東京をあらゆる方向に駆け抜け、郊外と連結する、無数の鉄道網や地下鉄網とは別に、JR山手線の浜松町駅から羽田空港まで伸びる東京モノレールがあります。また新橋(やはり山手線です)からは、レインボーブリッジを渡って、新しい街であるお台場や有明まで、ゴムタイヤ式の高架線であるゆりか

can be seen as having linked these divergent sectors of the city together for the first time.

Furthermore, the many stations on the Yamanote line play another important function, as many subway and rail lines link these stations to suburban areas throughout the whole metropolis, enabling millions of people to commute to work through the connections the Yamanote makes possible.

Toden Arakawa line

Running along a stretch of tracks only 12.2 km in length, the Toden Arakawa line connecting Waseda with Minowabashi is only one remaining streetcar lines in all of Tokyo. With its single-car form, this serves the special purpose of connecting people's daily lives in the neighborhood it runs through, even though the distance it covers is not so great.

Tokyo Monorail, Yurikamome train

Separate from the train and subway lines serving a multitude of destinations and suburbs in and around Tokyo, there is also a monorail line running to Haneda Airport (from Hamamatsucho station on the JR Yamanote line), and a rubber-wheeled, elevated line from Shinbashi station (also on the JR Yamanote line) crossing the Rainbow Bridge to the newer areas of Odaiba and Ariake (on landfill extensions

もめが、地下鉄有楽町線の終点、豊洲駅までをつなげています。現在、東京の繁華街、築地にある世界最大の魚市場は豊洲に移転することになっています（2016年11月の予定）。

東京のバス・タクシー

　電車や地下鉄が東京を縦横に交差し、都内から近郊までどこへでも運んでくれるのですが、場所によっては近くに駅がない場合もあります。しかし、そんなときには民営か都営によるバスが多く走っています。

　ほとんどのバス路線はJR（あるいは私鉄）の主要駅から発車するので、電車や地下鉄からバスに乗り換え目的地に向かう際に、継ぎ目のない旅を可能にしてくれます。バスには電車ほど英語による表示がないので、どのバスに乗り、どこへ向かうのか、そしてなんというバス停で降りればいいのかを事前に聞いておくのがベストです。

　夜遅くなるとバスの運行が終わりますので、気をつけてください。都内、または電車の駅に戻る最終バスをチェックしておきましょう。午後9時半か10時に終わることがあります。

　電車、地下鉄、モノレール、バス以外にもタクシーがあり、雨が降ったり、暑かったり、あるいは荷物がかさむなど、歩くにはすこし距離があるというときに便利です。駅や人の集まるビルの近くには、「タ

of Tokyo), and finally connecting to Toyosu station at the other end, on the Yurakucho subway line. Toyosu is the new location (from November, 2016), of the world's largest fish market, previously located at Tsukiji in downtown Tokyo.

Tokyo buses and taxis

Although train and subway lines crisscross the city, carrying you to numerous destinations in Tokyo and its surrounding suburbs, for locations not served by nearby train stations there are also many bus lines, operated either by private companies or by Tokyo's metropolitan government.

Most bus lines originate at key train stations, allowing for seamless travel when you change from the train or subway to a bus line to your destination. Less of the signage for buses than for trains is in English, so it is best to ask in advance about which bus you need, which destination it should be headed for, and which stop you should get off at.

Note that few of the bus lines operate late at night, so be certain to check the last bus from your destination back to the city center or train station, as it may be as early as 9:30 or 10:00 pm.

In addition to trains, subways, monorail, and bus lines, you will find taxi service for a ride too far to walk in the rain or heat, or with luggage. At train stations and near major buildings you will find signs indicating "Taxi Stand,"

クシー乗り場」という表示があり、よく数台のタクシーが乗客を待っています。街中にいるときは、フロントガラス越しに見える赤い文字や、屋根の上についているランプを見てください。両方とも、そのタクシーが空車であり、お客さんを探していることを示しています。

　すべてのタクシーには公認の料金メーターが設置され、運行距離や時間(渋滞してしまうこともあります!)に従って加算される料金が表示されます。タクシー料金が夜の11時から上がることも覚えておきましょう。従って、同じ距離であっても昼間とは違って午後11時以降は深夜料金となり、帰宅するにもホテルへ戻るにも、それだけお金がかかってしまいます。

通勤ラッシュ

　東京のような大都市では、数百万人が朝夕の通勤をしています。通勤ラッシュの電車や地下鉄がどれほど混むか、これは体験した人でないと想像がつかないほどのものです。

　もっとも混む時間帯には、電車の許容量を超えた人数が詰め込まれ、ときには「押し屋」と呼ばれる係の人が乗客の手足や書類かばんを、閉まる扉の内側に押し込みます。これはまったく本当の話です。とくに新宿駅などの、何本もの路線が乗り入れて毎日何千本もの電車が発着し、数百万人が通過したり、

often with several taxis waiting for fares. When out in town, though, look for the red letters in the taxi-cab's front window, or the illuminated light on the cab's roof, both of which will indicate that the taxi is empty and available.

All taxis operate with official fare meters, which will show the fare as it increases based both on distance and time (in case your cab is stuck in traffic). Note, too, that taxi fares increase from 11:00 pm at night, so the same distance you might travel during daylight hours and evenings before 11:00 pm may cost more for the late-night ride back home or to your hotel.

Rush hour

In a city as large as Tokyo, with millions commuting to and from work each weekday morning and evening, you can only imagine how crowded the trains and subways are during rush hour — unless you experience it yourself.

In peak hours, trains are filled beyond their official capacity, sometimes with "pushers" ensuring that arms, legs, and briefcases are inside the closing doors. This is particularly true at the major stations, where several lines converge and thousands — in some cases such as Shinjuku, millions — of commuters pass through or change trains every day.

乗り換えを行ったりするような主要な駅においては。

日々の人間関係の中で人々は周囲の人と「社会的距離」をとって生活していますが、満員電車に乗ると乗客同士の距離は「ゼロ」になってしまい、全員が密着して押し合いへし合いすることになります。このラッシュ時の過密状態を解消するため、近年では都市や多くの会社が「フレックス制」を推奨していますが、古くからの習慣を改めるのは難しいもので、東京のラッシュアワーは依然として通勤客で非常に混雑しています！

新幹線

新幹線は東京を起点に北部全域（長野、新潟、金沢、仙台、盛岡、青森、そして今や北海道まで）をカバーし、西部方面は名古屋、京都、大阪、神戸、広島から列島南部の主要な島である九州の地までに至っています。

新幹線に乗車するときは、自分に割り当てられた乗車券の列車番号、出発時刻、車両番号を必ず確認してください。東京から他の主要駅へは数分おきに新幹線が出ていますので、たとえ自分が乗るべき正しいホームであったとしても5分あるいは10分前に乗り込んでしまうと、それは1本前の新幹線で、違うところに行ってしまうかもしれません。

In a society that maintains a "socially-acceptable distance" in day-to-day relations, the rush-hour ride reduces the space between commuters to zero, as everyone is squished together closely. The city and many firms are now promoting flex-time in order to reduce the congestion at peak times, but old habits are difficult to change, and rush hour in Tokyo is still a very crowded time to be commuting to or from work!

Bullet trains

The Shinkansen bullet train lines originate in Tokyo for all points north (to the cities of Nagano, Niigata, Kanazawa, Sendai, Morioka, Aomori, and now to Hokkaido as well), and to all points west of Tokyo, including the cities of Nagoya, Kyoto, Osaka, Kobe, Hiroshima, and destinations in the southern major island of Kyushu.

When you prepare to board the Shinkansen, be certain to check your ticket for the train number, departure time, and car number you have been assigned. With departures every few minutes from Tokyo and other major terminals, if you board a train at the right track even five or ten minutes early it may be an earlier train, going to a different destination.

さらに新幹線の中には、限られた駅にしか止まらないものもありますので、目的の駅を通り過ぎてしまうかもしれません。また一方で、各駅に停車するものもあり、遠くの目的地に行くには時間がかかってしまいます。ほとんどの新幹線は指定席ですが、時折、1～3号車までは自由席というものもあります。

最後に、新幹線の中には途中の駅で分離して、一部の車両は最初の目的地にそのまま向かいますが、他の車両は別のところへ行ってしまいますので、乗車券に記載された車両番号に必ず乗ってください。さもないと、思いもよらないところへ行きついてしまうかもしれませんよ。

リニアモーターカー

東京と日本全国の都市を結ぶ「弾丸列車」新幹線は、十分に速いと思っていることでしょう。しかし、日本が1964年に世界初の高速鉄道である新幹線を開業させた当時と同じように、「リニアモーターカー」と呼ばれる磁気浮上（マグレブ）技術に関しても、日本は世界の先端を走ってきました。

東京の品川駅と、日本の中央に位置する名古屋とを結ぶ路線の、2027年開通を目指す工事が始められています（2045年には大阪まで開通予定）。286キロメートルの距離を、名古屋までは40分、大阪まで67分で走ります。2015年に行われた、

In addition, some Shinkansen trains stop at only a limited number of stations, possibly bypassing your intended station, and others stop at every stop along the way, which would take you a longer time to reach your intended station far away. Although most Shinkansen seats are reserved, there are occasionally 1–3 train cars with non-reserved seats.

Finally, as some Shinkansen lines diverge, with part of the train proceeding to one destination and the other half of the train heading to a different destination, be certain to ride in the train car indicated on your ticket, or you may be in for a surprise!

Maglev trains

You might think that the Shinkansen "bullet train" is fast enough, connecting Tokyo to many cities in Japan. However, just as Japan was the first in the world to launch the high-speed, designated-track Shinkansen in 1964, Japan has been a leader in magnetic levitation (maglev) technology, called the Linear Motor Car in Japan.

Construction has begun on a route between Shinagawa Station in Tokyo and Nagoya in central Japan, scheduled to open in 2027 (continuing on to Osaka by the year 2045), covering the 286 kilometers to Nagoya in 40 minutes, and to Osaka in 67 minutes total. The L0 Series maglev train

名古屋までを結ぶL0系リニアモーターカーの試験走行で、時速606キロメートル（375マイル毎時）の世界新記録を出しましたが、実際の運用にあたっては、それよりは「控えめな」時速505キロメートル（314マイル毎時）に抑える予定です。それでも信じられないほどの速度で、すこしも「控えめ」とは思えませんが！

成田空港

　成田国際空港は東京の中心部から50km離れたところに位置しているので、自分が搭乗する旅客機の指定されたチェックイン時間に間に合うように空港に着くには、周到な準備が必要です。幸いなことに成田まで行くには、JRの成田エクスプレス（新宿、品川、横浜、東京駅経由）、京成線（上野、日暮里駅経由）、浅草線（都内では地下鉄の一つの路線ですが、なかには成田空港と羽田空港間を往復するものもあります）、そして多数のバス路線などがあります。

　"使い勝手のよい"エアポートリムジンバスは主要なホテルとの間を往復し、そのうえ主要な駅にも停車します。他にも民営のバスが近くの駅から発着しています。事前にホテルのコンシェルジュや旅行代理店に、成田空港まで行くのに電車がいいのか、バスがいいのか、もっとも信頼できる方法を聞いておくのがベストでしょう。

planned for the Nagoya route set a world speed record in 2015 of 606 km/hr (375 mph), but is scheduled to operate at a more "modest" speed of 505 km/hr (314 mph). That seems incredibly fast, and is not "modest" at all!

Narita Airport

The Narita New Tokyo International Airport is located over 50 km away from the center of Tokyo, so it requires careful planning to reach the airport in time for your designated airline check-in time. Fortunately, there are several ways to reach Narita, including the JR Narita Express line (with trains from Shinjuku, Shinagawa, Yokohama and Tokyo stations), the Keisei Line (with trains from Ueno and Nippori stations), the Asakusa line (which serves as a subway line in town, and has some trains directly from Narita Airport to and from Haneda Airport), and numerous bus lines.

The "Friendly" Airport Limousine bus line operates to and from major hotels, in addition to stops at major railway stations, and other private bus lines originate or terminate near train stations as well. It is best to inquire in advance from your hotel concierge desk or travel agency for the most reliable mode of train or bus travel to Narita Airport.

最後に、成田空港には2つの主要なターミナルがあるので、正しいターミナルで電車やバスから降りるように確認してください。もし間違ったターミナルに降り立ったとしても、無料のシャトルバスがもう一方のターミナルまで出ています。しかし、余分な時間がかかってしまい、すこし分かりにくいかもしれません。

　成田空港は24時間体制ではないので、深夜に最終電車やバスを逃してしまうと、空港近くのホテルに泊まり、翌朝東京に出向くことになってしまいます。

羽田空港

　羽田空港は長年の間、国内線だけに使われていました。しかし、新たに国際線のターミナルが完成し、羽田にはいまや多くの国際線が乗り入れており、国際線から国内線への乗り継ぎがますます便利になりました。羽田空港は成田空港よりも東京や横浜の繁華街に近く、さらに24時間体制という利点もあります。

　羽田は成田空港より、東京都心や横浜に距離的に近く、その上、24時間営業しているという利点もあります。東京、横浜、その他の中心市街からのアクセスが簡単で、京成線、浜松町と結ぶモノレール、そしておびただしい数のリムジンバスも、主要ホテルと空港を往復しています。

Finally, note that there are two main terminals at Narita, so be certain to get off your train or bus at the correct terminal. You can find a free shuttle bus to the other terminal if you have gotten off at the wrong one, but this will take additional time and can be a bit confusing.

Narita does not operate as a 24-hour airport, so if your airplane has arrived later than scheduled, it may be necessary to stay at a hotel close to Narita and ride into Tokyo the next morning if you have missed the last trains or buses leaving Narita late at night.

Haneda Airport

Haneda Airport was, for many years, used almost exclusively for domestic flights within Japan. With its new International Terminal, however, Haneda now has many scheduled international flights, and provides the added convenience of transfers to and from overseas flights to domestic flights within Japan.

Haneda is closer to central Tokyo or Yokohama than Narita Airport, and it has the additional advantage of operating as a 24-hour airport. It is accessible from Tokyo, Yokohama, and other city-centers by the Keisei train line, a monorail line from Hamamatsucho, and numerous limousine bus lines, either to and from major hotels.

東京の交通全般

東京の交通網は複雑です。
- [ ] Tokyo's transit network is complex.

東京の交通網は複雑ですが、とても便利です。
- [ ] Tokyo's transit network is complex, but it is very convenient.

都心部の移動には、公共交通機関が便利です。
- [ ] Public transportation is convenient for getting around the center city.

渋滞を考えれば、東京での移動は鉄道や地下鉄がおすすめです。
- [ ] Considering the traffic, the best way to get around the city is by train or subway.

東京ではほとんどの人が公共交通を使って都内を行き来します。
- [ ] In Tokyo, most people travel around the city using public transportation.

多くの企業が従業員に交通費を支給しています。
- [ ] Companies often pay the commuting fees of their employees.

東京では車を持っていない人は珍しくありません。
- [ ] It's not unusual for many Tokyo people to not own a car.

Tokyo in Single Sentences

東京では車の維持費がとても高いのです。

☐ It is very expensive to keep a car in Tokyo.

東京では駐車場を借りるのに、月に数百ドルもかかることがあります。

☐ It can cost several hundred dollars a month to rent a parking space in Tokyo.

東京には免許証を持ってはいるものの運転を忘れてしまったいわゆるペーパードライバーが多くいます。

☐ Tokyo has many so-called "paper drivers"—people who have driver's licenses but don't remember how to drive.

主婦たちは自転車でお遣いにいったり、子どもを保育園や幼稚園に連れていきます。

☐ Housewives use bicycles to run errands and to take kids to preschool.

東京にはバスのネットワークがあります。

☐ Tokyo is served by a network of buses.

KEY WORD ✓

☐ transit network	交通網
☐ get around	あちこち移動する
☐ commuting fee	交通費
☐ run errands	お遣いに行く
☐ preshool	保育園、幼稚園

▶▶▶ ワンセンテンスで説明する東京

東京都が運営する都営バスが都内を走っています。

☐ Toei Bus is the name of the main municipal bus system serving central Tokyo.

昔は東京にも路面電車が縦横に走っていました。

☐ In the past, a network of streetcars crisscrossed the city.

かつては縦横に走っていた都電ですが、現在残っているのは一路線だけです。

☐ There is only one remaining line still in service from the once-extensive *Toden* streetcar system.

都電荒川線は、早稲田と下町の三ノ輪橋を結んでいます。

☐ The Toden Arakawa line connects Waseda with Minowabashi in *Shitamachi*.

タクシーはメーター制なので、過剰に請求されることはありません。

☐ Taxi fares are based on a metered system, so you don't have to worry about being overcharged.

タクシーは、一部の地区を除いて、どこでも手をあげて呼び止めることができます。

☐ Except for a few areas, you can hail a taxi anywhere by waving your hand.

タクシーの初乗り料金は730円です。

☐ The base fare for taxis is 730 yen.

Tokyo in Single Sentences

ほとんどのタクシーではクレジットカードも利用できます。

- [ ] Most taxis take credit cards.

銀座などでは、タクシー乗り場にタクシーが並んでいます。

- [ ] In places like Ginza, taxis line up in front of taxi stands.

深夜になると公共交通の運行は終了するので、その替わりにタクシーを使います。

- [ ] Late at night, public transportation stops running so people take taxis instead.

KEY WORD ✓

☐ streetcar	路面電車
☐ metered system	メーター制
☐ overcharge	過剰請求する
☐ hail	呼び止める
☐ base fare	初乗り料金
☐ taxi stand	タクシー乗り場

東京の地下鉄

都心部は地下鉄網が張り巡らされています。

- [ ] Central Tokyo is served by an extensive subway system.

東京には、地下鉄が 13 路線あります。

- [ ] There are thirteen subway lines in Tokyo.

東京の 13 の地下鉄路線は、東京メトロと都営地下鉄が別々に運営しています。

- [ ] Tokyo's thirteen subway lines are run by two different operators, Tokyo Metro and Toei Subway.

東京メトロの入り口は「M」のマークが表示されています。

- [ ] Subway entrances for the Tokyo Metro are marked with an "M."

東京の地下鉄と通勤電車は直接つながっているので、大変便利です。

- [ ] Tokyo's subway lines connect directly to commuter lines, which is very convenient.

地下鉄の料金は 160 円からで、乗車距離によって高くなります。

- [ ] Subway tickets start at 160 yen and increase in price depending on how far you travel.

Tokyo in Single Sentences

東京の交通と移動 / 東京の地下鉄

Suicaも PASMOも地下鉄で使用できます。

☐ You can use Suica and PASMO prepaid cards on the subway.

東京の地下鉄で最も古いのは銀座線で、1927年に開業しました。

☐ Tokyo's oldest subway line is the Ginza Line, which was completed in 1927.

銀座線は、浅草から銀座を通って渋谷まで行く、日本で一番古い地下鉄です。

☐ The Ginza Line runs from Asakusa to Shibuya by way of Ginza, and it is Japan's oldest subway line.

地下鉄副都心線に乗れば、そのまま東横線で乗り換えなしに横浜まで行くことができます。

☐ The Fukutoshin Line is connected to the Toyoko line, so you can ride all the way to Yokohoma on the Toyoko Line without changing trains.

東西線は、千葉県と都心を結び、さらに中央線、総武線へと乗り入れています。

☐ The Tozai Line connects Chiba Prefecture with central Tokyo, and then continues on to the Chuo and Sobu train lines.

KEY WORD ✓

☐ commuter line   通勤電車
☐ by way of   〜を通って

丸の内線は池袋から大手町、東京、銀座を経由して、新宿までぐるりとまわっていく便利な地下鉄です。新宿から西へ、荻窪、方南町に伸びています。

☐ The Marunouchi Line is a useful subway line that runs in a loop from Ikebukuro to Shinjuku by way of Otemachi, Tokyo Station and Ginza; from Shinjuku it continues west to Ogikubo and Honancho.

丸ノ内線は、池袋と荻窪、または方南町を結ぶ地下鉄です。

☐ The Marunouchi Line is a subway line that runs from Ikebukuro to Ogikubo and Honancho.

千代田線は JR 常磐線からの直通運転で運行されている地下鉄です。皇居の前を通り、代々木上原という駅で、小田急線に乗り入れています。

☐ The Chiyoda Line is a subway line that runs as a continuation of the JR Joban train line; it runs past the front of the Imperial Palace and then to Yoyogi Uehara, where it continues as the Odakyu train line.

日比谷線は、北は東武伊勢崎線、南は東急東横線と直通運転している地下鉄です。

☐ The Hibiya Line is a subway line that continues on from the Tobu Isesaki Line in the north and the Tokyu Toyoko Line in the south.

有楽町線は、西武池袋線や東武東上線と直通運転している地下鉄です。池袋から永田町や銀座を経て東京湾に近い新木場まで運行しています。

☐ The Yurakucho Line is a subway line that continues on from the Seibu Ikebukuro Line and the Tobu Tojo Line in the north; it runs from Ikebukuro to Shin-Kiba, on Tokyo Bay, by way of Nagatacho and Ginza.

Tokyo in Single Sentences

半蔵門線は、東は東武伊勢崎線と直通運転している地下鉄です。都心を経由したあと、西は渋谷から東急田園都市線に乗り入れています。

☐ The Hanzomon Line is a subway line that continues on from the Tobu Isesaki Line in the east; it runs through central Tokyo and continues on as the Tokyu Denentoshi Line west of Shibuya.

南北線は、西は東急目黒線に乗り入れている地下鉄です。都心を南北に横断したあと、埼玉県へとのびています。

☐ The Nanboku Line is a subway line that continues on from the Tokyu Meguro Line in the west; it runs from south to north through central Tokyo and continues up to Saitama Prefecture.

都営三田線は、三田駅から有楽町や大手町を経て、高島平という住宅街へのびる地下鉄です。

☐ The Toei Mita Line is a subway line that runs from Mita north to the residential area of Takashimadaira by way of Yurakucho and Otemachi.

都営新宿線は、東は総武線とつながる地下鉄です。千葉から都心を経て、新宿から京王線に乗り入れています。

☐ The Toei Shinjuku Line is a subway line that connects with the Sobu Line in the east; it runs from Chiba through central Tokyo and joins the Keio Line at Shinjuku, running to the residential area of Tama in the west.

▶▶▶ ワンセンテンスで説明する東京

都営新宿線は、京王線と連結して、多摩地区と呼ばれる住宅地へとのびています。

☐ The Toei Shinku Line joins the Keio Line, which runs to the residential area of Tama.

都営大江戸線は、都心部を周回して光が丘につながる環状地下鉄です。

☐ The Toei Oedo Line is a loop subway line that runs around central Tokyo, with one spur running northwest to an area called Hikarigaoka.

東京の鉄道ネットワーク

Track 12

東京都内と近郊の都市との間には、数多くの通勤電車が走っています。

☐ There are a great number of commuter trains running between Tokyo and the suburbs.

東京には50以上の通勤電車の路線があり、何社か異なる会社が経営しています。

☐ There are over fifty commuter rail lines in Tokyo, run by several different companies.

多くの通勤電車は、地下鉄と相互に乗り入れています。

☐ Most of the commuter train lines connect directly to subway lines.

東京の通勤電車は、朝夕は混雑します。

☐ Tokyo's commuter trains are crowded in the mornings and evenings.

Tokyo in Single Sentences

東京の駅

_{Track 13}

東京近郊のほとんどの地域は、電車や地下鉄の駅が中心になっています。

- [ ] Train and subway stations are at the heart of most Tokyo neighborhoods.

東京では、電車や地下鉄の駅が多くの人の日常生活の拠点になっています。

- [ ] The train or subway station is at the center of daily life for many people in Tokyo.

駅の中や周辺にはたくさんの店や飲食店があります。

- [ ] Many shops and restaurants are located in and around train stations.

山手線にある大きな駅には、駅の中にも店や食べるところがあります。

- [ ] Many large train stations, like those on the Yamanote Line, have shops and restaurants inside the station.

駅の周りには多くの店や施設が密集しているので、東京での生活はとても便利です。

- [ ] Because so many shops and services are clustered around train stations, life in Tokyo is very convenient.

KEY WORD ✓

☐ suburb	郊外
☐ be clustered	群がる

山手線・中央線・京浜東北線・総武線

都内を環状運転する電車を山手線といいます。
- [ ] The train line that runs in a loop around the city is called the Yamanote Line.

山手線は、都心の主要駅をつなぐ環状線です。
- [ ] The Yamanote Line is a loop line that connects major train stations in central Tokyo.

山手線沿線の主要駅は、東京、上野、池袋、新宿、渋谷、品川などです。
- [ ] The major stops on the Yamanote Line are Tokyo, Ueno, Ikebukuro, Shinjuku, Shibuya and Shinagawa.

山手線は、元国鉄のJR東日本が運営する路線です。
- [ ] The Yamanote Line is a train line run by the East Japan Railway Company (JR East), formerly part of the national railway.

JRの主要駅では、私鉄や地下鉄に乗り換えることができます。
- [ ] At major JR stations you can transfer to other railways and the subway.

東京駅と新宿駅は、中央線や地下鉄で結ばれています。
- [ ] Tokyo Station and Shinjuku Station are connected by the Chuo Line and the subway.

Tokyo in Single Sentences

中央線は、新宿駅から西に伸び、甲府や松本を経て、名古屋へつながっています。

- [ ] The Chuo Line runs west from Shinjuku Station through Kofu and Matsumoto to Nagoya.

中央線の快速電車は、東京駅から新宿を経て、八王子や高尾まで行きます。

- [ ] Rapid trains on the Chuo Line run from Tokyo Station via Shinjuku Station to Hachioji and Takao.

京浜東北線は、大宮、東京、横浜、さらに大船を結ぶJR路線で、昼間は一部快速運転をしています。

- [ ] During the daytime, rapid trains on the JR Keihin Tohoku Line connect Omiya, Tokyo, Yokohama and Ofuna.

総武線は、三鷹から新宿、秋葉原を経て千葉を結ぶJRの路線です。

- [ ] The Sobu Line is a JR line that runs from Mitaka to Chiba by way of Shinjuku and Akihabara.

山手線と京浜東北線は田端から東京駅を経て、品川まで並走しています。

- [ ] The Yamanote Line and the Keihin Tohoku Line run parallel to each other from Tabata through Tokyo to Shinagawa.

山手線、京浜東北線、中央線、総武線は、頻繁に電車がくるので、長い間待つことはありません。

- [ ] Trains on the Yamanote Line, Keihin Tohoku Line, Chuo Line and Sobu Line run so frequently that you seldom need to wait long for a train.

東京の交通と移動

山手線・中央線・京浜東北線・総武線

▶▶▶ ワンセンテンスで説明する東京

切符の購入

JR の料金は 160 円からです。

☐ Tickets for JR trains start at 160 yen.

電車に乗るには、駅の自動券売機で切符を買います。

☐ To take the train, buy a ticket from one of the vending machines at the station.

長距離列車の場合は、特別な自動券売機か、みどりの窓口という切符売り場を利用します。

☐ To take a long-distance train, buy a ticket from one of the special vending machines or from a "*Midori no Madoguchi*" ticket window.

PASMO と Suica

公共交通を定期的に利用する場合、Suica や PASMO などのプリペイドカードを購入すると便利です。

☐ If you take public transportation regularly, it is convenient to buy a prepaid pass called either Suica or PASMO.

Suica や PASMO は自動券売機で購入できます。

☐ You can buy Suica and PASMO cards from ticket vending machines.

Tokyo in Single Sentences

Suicaと PASMO は、発行している会社は違いますが、どちらもほとんどの交通機関で使用できます。

☐ Suica and PASMO cards are issued by different companies, but they can both be used on almost all transit lines.

PASMOとSuicaは、東京中の交通機関や買い物に使える大変便利なプリペイドカードです。

☐ Both PASMO and Suica cards are very convenient prepaid cards, widely used throughout Tokyo for transportation and for many purchases.

海外から来た人も駅のキオスクや切符を予約する「緑の窓口」で、500円の預かり金を払って、PASMOやSuicaを購入できます。

☐ Visitors from abroad may also purchase PASMO and Suica cards at station kiosks and at the "Green Window" ticket reservation windows at most stations, paying a 500-yen deposit.

KEY WORD ✓

☐ ticket vending machine	自動券売機
☐ long-distance train	長距離列車
☐ ticket window	切符売り場
☐ deposit	預かり金

東京の交通と移動 ● 切符の購入 ● PASMOとSuica

67

▶▶▶ ワンセンテンスで説明する東京

500円の預かり金とカードの残額は、カードを返却すれば返金してくれます。ただし、残金が220円以下の場合は、手数料がかかり返金できません。

☐ The 500-yen deposit and the remaining balance will be returned to you when you return the card. However, a fee will be charged if the balance is below 220 yen.

PASMOとSuicaは、東京の地下鉄、電車、バスなどの交通機関で使用できるほか、コンビニでの支払いもできます。

☐ PASMO and Suica cards can be used not only on subways, railway lines and buses in Tokyo, but they can also be used to pay in convenience stores.

PASMOやSuicaでの買い物は、少額のお釣りをもらわずにすむので、とても便利です。

☐ PASMO and Suica cards are convenient because you don't have to be bothered with receiving small change when you make a purchase.

PASMOとSuicaは、それぞれ別の会社が発売するカードですが、どちらも同じように使用できます。

☐ Although PASMO and Suica cards are issued and sold by separate companies, they can be used interchangeably.

PASMOとSuicaは、上限2万円までチャージできます。

☐ PASMO and Suica cards may be charged to hold up to 20,000 yen in prepaid value.

Tokyo in Single Sentences

電車や地下鉄の駅の自動券売機やコンビニなど、カードを扱っている場所であれば、どこでもチャージできます。

- [ ] They can be charged at locations with terminals that handle them, such as at convenience stores and at vending machines in train and subway stations.

PASMO や Suica のチャージの方法は、駅やコンビニで聞けば簡単に教えてくれます。

- [ ] If you ask at a station or convenience store, they can explain how to charge your PASMO or Suica card.

大阪などの大都市には、PASMO や Suica と同じようなプリペイドカードがあります。

- [ ] There are similar prepaid cards used throughout Japan in major cities such as Osaka.

PASMO と Suica は東京地区だけではなく、東京以外の大都市でも使用できます。

- [ ] You can use PASMO and Suica cards in other large cities as well; they are not limited to the Tokyo area.

KEY WORD	
☐ remaining balance	残額
☐ small change	少額の釣銭

▶▶▶ ワンセンテンスで説明する東京

東京のターミナル駅

Track 17

東京駅は、東京の鉄道の中央駅です。

☐ Tokyo Station is Tokyo's central train station.

全ての新幹線は、東京駅から発着します。

☐ All bullet trains depart from and arrive at Tokyo Station.

東京駅から、新幹線が日本の主要都市に向けて出発します。

☐ From Tokyo Station, bullet trains depart for major cities across Japan.

東海道新幹線に乗れば、東京から2時間半で京都に行くことができます。

☐ If you take the Tokaido bullet train, you can ride from Tokyo to Kyoto in two and a half hours.

東京駅から、東北新幹線で、仙台、盛岡、青森、そして最北の北海道へと旅ができます。

☐ If you take the Tohoku bullet train from Tokyo Station, you can travel to Sendai, Morioka, Aomori and all the way north to Hokkaido.

東北新幹線は、山形新幹線、秋田新幹線に分かれるので、山形や秋田を含めた東北の主だった都市へと旅ができます。

☐ The Tohoku bullet train line splits into the Yamagata bullet train and the Akita bullet train, so you can travel to all major cities in Tohoku, including Yamagata and Akita.

Tokyo in Single Sentences

東京駅から上越新幹線に乗れば、高崎から山間部を経て新潟へと旅ができます。

☐ If you take the Joetsu bullet train from Tokyo Station, you can travel through Takasaki and the mountains to Niigata.

東京駅から北陸新幹線に乗れば、長野を経て金沢を訪ねることができます。

☐ If you take the Hokuriku bullet train from Tokyo Station, you can travel all the way to Kanazawa via Nagano.

東京と大阪間は、新幹線で2時間40分かかります。

☐ It takes two hours and forty minutes to travel by bullet train between Tokyo and Osaka.

新宿駅からは、山梨県や長野県などに向かう列車が出ています。

☐ From Shinjuku Station, trains depart for Yamanashi and Nagano prefectures.

上野駅からは、列車は北に向かいます。

☐ From Ueno Station, trains head north.

東京の交通と移動 — 東京のターミナル駅

KEY WORD ✓

☐ bullet train	新幹線
☐ depart from and arrive	発着する

▶▶▶ ワンセンテンスで説明する東京

上野駅は、新幹線を含む北に向かう列車が発着する、東京の北の玄関です。

☐ Ueno Station is Tokyo's gateway to the north; it is where bullet trains and other trains depart for northern areas.

品川から、名古屋や大阪に向かうリニアモーターカーの工事がはじまりました。

☐ Construction has started on a maglev train line from Shinagawa Station to Nagoya and Osaka.

リニアモーターカーが完成すれば、東京・大阪間が、約1時間になると報じられています。

☐ When the maglev train line is completed, it reportedly will be possible to travel from Tokyo to Osaka in one hour.

成田空港と羽田空港

Track 18

東京には羽田と成田の二つの国際空港があります。

☐ Tokyo has two international airports, Haneda and Narita.

羽田空港は東京にあり、国内線と国際線が発着しています。

☐ Haneda Airport is located in Tokyo and is served by domestic and international routes.

成田空港は、東京の北東約80キロの位置にあります。

☐ Narita Airport is located 80 kilometers to the northeast of Tokyo.

Tokyo in Single Sentences

羽田空港では、国内便が発着します。

☐ Domestic flights arrive at and depart from Haneda Airport.

羽田空港では、国内線や一部の国際線が発着します。

☐ Domestic flights and some international flights arrive at and depart from Haneda Airport.

東京の国際線の玄関口は主に成田空港です。

☐ Tokyo's international gateway is mainly Narita Airport.

成田空港 / 羽田空港への交通

Track 19

成田空港には、鉄道でのアクセスが可能です。

☐ It is possible to get to and from Narita Airport by train.

成田空港へは、京成上野駅と日暮里駅から出る京成スカイライナーという電車が便利です。

☐ The Keisei Skyliner train, which departs from Keisei Ueno and Nippori stations, is a convenient way to get to Narita Airport.

KEY WORD ✓

☐ gateway to the north	北の玄関
☐ maglev train	リニアモーターカー
☐ domestice flight	国内線

東京都内から成田空港まで、京成スカイライナーで約 40 分かかります。

☐ It takes 40 minutes to get from Tokyo to Narita Airport by the Keisei Skyliner.

東京駅からは成田エクスプレスという特急列車が成田空港に向かっています。

☐ From Tokyo Station, there is a limited express train called the Narita Express that goes to Narita Airport.

東京駅から成田空港まで、成田エクスプレスで約 1 時間かかります。

☐ It takes about one hour to get from Tokyo to Narita Airport by the Narita Express.

成田エクスプレスは、東京駅と都内の主な駅からも利用できます。

☐ The Narita Express stops at Tokyo Station and other major stations around the city.

東京には箱崎というバスターミナルがあり、成田空港までのリムジンバスが発着しています。

☐ Limousine buses run from the Hakozaki Bus Terminal in Tokyo to Narita Airport.

東京の主要ホテルから成田空港へはリムジンバスが運行しています。

☐ Limousine buses depart from Tokyo's major hotels for Narita Airport.

成田空港へのバスでの所要時間は、渋滞がなければ 80 分前後です。

☐ Without traffic, it takes about 80 minutes to get to Narita Airport by limousine bus.

Tokyo in Single Sentences

羽田空港へは浜松町駅からモノレールが出ています。

☐ A monorail runs from Hamamatsucho Station to Haneda Airport.

浜松町から羽田空港までの所要時間は約 30 分です。

☐ It takes 30 minutes to get to Haneda Airport from Hamamatsucho.

東京から羽田空港には京急電鉄でも行くことができます。

☐ You can also get to Haneda Airport from Tokyo by the Keikyu Railway.

京急電鉄は都営浅草線と相互に乗り入れています。

☐ The Keikyu Railway connects directly with the Toei Asakusa Line.

京急電鉄の急行に乗れば、都心から約 30 分で羽田空港に着きます。

☐ If you take an express train on the Keikyu Railway, you can get from central Tokyo to Haneda Airport in 30 minutes.

KEY WORD ✓

☐ limited express train	特急列車
☐ limousine bus	リムジンバス
☐ monorail	モノレール
☐ express train	急行列車

東京の交通と移動 / 成田空港 / 羽田空港への交通

東京の歩き方

東京の住所表示は最初はわかりにくいのですが、一度慣れてしまえば理解できます。

- [ ] The Tokyo address system sounds confusing at first, but it makes sense once you get used to it.

東京の道案内をするのは大変なので、ホテルやレストラン、そしてショップなどはウエブサイトに地図を載せています。

- [ ] Because Tokyo is difficult to navigate, many hotels, restaurants and shops include maps on their websites.

歩道や駅には、地面に突起した黄色い帯状の通路がありますが、これは目の不自由な人を手助けするものです。

- [ ] On sidewalks and in train stations, you can see raised yellow strips on the ground, which are there to help blind people.

交差点にもよりますが、信号が変わるときに音楽が流れるところがあります。これは目の不自由な人に渡るタイミングを教えているのです。

- [ ] Some intersections play music when the light changes to help blind people know when to cross the street.

Tokyo in Single Sentences

東京の通勤常識とマナー

電車に乗っている人の大半は礼儀正しく行動します。

☐ The majority of people riding on the train behave politely.

ほとんどの人は携帯電話をながめて通勤・通学の時間をつぶしています。

☐ Most people spend their commute staring at their mobile phones.

ラッシュの時間帯には、女性専用車両があり、ピンク色の目印が貼られています。

☐ During rush hour, there are women-only cars marked with pink signs.

車両の端の座席は障害者、高齢者、妊婦のための優先席です。

☐ Some seats at the ends of train cars are reserved for handicapped, elderly and pregnant people.

電車の中で眠っている人がいて、驚くかもしれません。

☐ You may be surprised to see people sleeping on the train.

東京は比較的に治安がいいので、人々は安心して車内で眠ります。

☐ Because Tokyo is relatively safe, people feel comfortable sleeping on the train.

通勤・通学時間が長い人も大勢いて、そういう人たちは電車内で寝るのです。

☐ Because many people have long commutes, they often sleep on the train.

▶▶▶ ワンセンテンスで説明する東京

寝ている人があなたの肩にもたれかかってきたら、その人を起こしても構いません。

- [ ] If someone falls asleep on your shoulder, you can wake him or her up.

ときには、電車内で酔っぱらいを見かけることもあるでしょう。

- [ ] Sometimes you see people drunk on the train.

日本人は電車内の酔っ払いなどは無視する傾向があります。

- [ ] Japanese people tend to ignore things like drunken people on the train.

電車内に、無視できないほどの問題を起こす人がいたら、駅員に知らせましょう。

- [ ] If you see someone causing a serious problem on the train, you can tell the staff at the train station.

ほとんどの駅にはエスカレーターとエレベーターが設置されています。

- [ ] There are escalators and elevators in most train stations.

駅のホームには、エスカレーターやエレベーターの位置を示す表示があります。

- [ ] There are maps on the train platform to show you where the escalators and elevators are.

電車内で大声で話をするのはマナー違反です。

- [ ] It is impolite to talk in a loud voice on the train.

Tokyo in Single Sentences

電車内で携帯電話で会話するのはマナー違反です。

☐ It is impolite to talk on a mobile phone on the train.

ものを食べながら通りを歩くのはマナー違反です。

☐ It is impolite to eat while walking down the street.

日本人はおとなしく列に並びます。

☐ Japanese people are very good about waiting in line.

電車を待つ人がたくさんいるときは、車両ドアの両側に分かれて一列に並びます。

☐ If there are many people waiting for a train, they will form lines on either side of the train doors.

東京の人は、エスカレーターでは左側に立ちます。

☐ In Tokyo, people stand on the left side of the escalator.

東京はたくさんの人であふれていますが、押し合いへし合いすることはありません。

☐ Even though Tokyo is a very crowded city, there is no pushing.

東京の交通と移動 / 東京の通勤常識とマナー

KEY WORD ✓

☐ drunken people	酔っ払い
☐ impolite	マナー違反である
☐ mobile phone	携帯電話
☐ wait in line	列に並ぶ

東京サバイバル

安全と警察

これほどの大都会にしては、東京は比較的安全ですが、それでも注意を怠らないことです。東京でよくある3大盗難品は、雨傘・自転車・下着です。東京でスリに遭うことは滅多にありませんが、起こりうることは確かです。通常、東京では女性の夜の一人歩きも安全とされています。

緊急時に呼び出す警察の番号は「110」番です。東京ではあらゆるところに「交番」という警察の派出所があります。そこには24時間警官がいるのですが、残念ながら英語を話してくれるのはごくわずかです。

キャッシングなど

日本の銀行のATM機では海外のATMカードは使えませんが、代わりに郵便局やコンビニでは海外のカードを受け付けます。郵便局のATM機には英語で使い方が書かれています。クレジットカードは多くの場所で使えますが、それでも多少の現金は持っておくと安心です。小さい古くからのレストランや店では、クレジットカードが使えないからです。

Tokyo Survival Tips

Safety, police

Tokyo is relatively safe for a large city, but you should still be careful. In Tokyo, the three most common thefts are umbrellas, bicycles and underwear. Pickpocketing is rare in Tokyo, but it can happen. It is also generally safe for women to walk alone at night in Tokyo.

In the case of an emergency, the number for the police is #110. There are police boxes, called "*koban*," in every neighborhood in Tokyo. Many police boxes are staffed 24 hours a day. Unfortunately, very few police officers speak English.

ATMs

The ATMs at Japanese banks do not accept foreign ATM cards. However, ATMs in post offices and in some convenience stores accept foreign ATM cards. Post office ATMs have instructions in English. Even though many places accept credit cards, it is still a good idea to carry some cash because many small or older restaurants and shops still don't accept credit cards.

日本のほとんどの店では、価格が決まっているので値引き交渉はできませんが、青空市場や蚤の市では可能です。百貨店や家電販売店のなかには免税で買い物ができます。免税で買い物したいときは、パスポートを店に持っていく必要があります。

ホテル・宿泊

　国際的な高級ホテルを除くと、東京のホテルの部屋はかなり狭いことでしょう。しかし、ホテル側は必要なものをすべて提供してくれます。実際、ほとんどの部屋には綿製のローブ、スリッパ、歯ブラシ、インターネットをつなぐWi-Fiが備えられています。

　東京には実に多様なホテルがあります。一泊20ドルの手ごろな共同寝室タイプから、一泊1000ドル以上もする贅沢なスイートタイプまでさまざまです。

　「ビジネスホテル」は、狭くても清潔な部屋で、基本的な設備が付いています。カプセルホテルとは、ユースホステルの共同寝室のようなものですが、それよりもプライバシーが守られています。多くのカプセルホテルは男性用ですが、なかには女性用のフロアがあるところもあります。カプセルホテルに宿泊するのも日本文化を楽しむひとつの方法です。

　ラブホテルはカップル用で、一泊することもできれば、午後の数時間だけを過ごすこともできます。

In almost every store in Japan, prices are fixed and you cannot bargain, although it is possible to bargain at outdoor markets and flea markets. Some department stores and electronics stores offer duty-free shopping. If you want to shop duty-free, you need to bring your passport to the store.

Hotels and other accommodations

Except in expensive international hotels, hotel rooms in Tokyo can be very small. However, they provide everything you need. Actually, most hotel rooms provide a cotton robe, slippers, a toothbrush and Wi-Fi internet.

There are a huge variety of hotels in Tokyo. You can get a cheap dorm room for $20 a night or a suite in a luxury hotel for more than $1,000 a night.

A "business hotel" is a hotel with small, cheap rooms and basic amenities. A capsule hotel is kind of like a hostel dormitory, except you get more privacy. Most capsule hotels are just for men, but some capsule hotels have a floor for women. Staying in a capsule hotel is a fun way to experience Japanese culture.

A love hotel is a hotel for couples. At a love hotel, you can stay for the whole night or just for a few hours in the afternoon.

東京の便利情報

日中、東京を歩き回るには公共交通がはるかに便利です。安い、早い、そして安全です。

☐ During the daytime, public transportation is by far the best way to get around central Tokyo; it's cheap, fast and very safe.

東京にあるキリスト教の教会、モスク、シナゴーグの情報を入手したければ、事前に調べておくとよいでしょう。

☐ If you need information about Tokyo's churches, mosques and synagogues, it's a good idea to look it up beforehand.

寿司は一般的に高価な食べ物と思われていますが、回転寿司なら良心的な値段の寿司が楽しめます。

☐ Sushi is generally thought of as an expensive food, but at "revolving sushi" restaurants, called "*kaiten-zushi*," you can enjoy very affordable sushi.

東京では、水道の水は飲んでも問題はありません。

☐ It is safe to drink the tap water in Tokyo.

東京も含め、日本中どこでもチップの習慣はありません。

☐ In Tokyo, as well as in the rest of Japan, there is no custom of tipping.

Tokyo in Single Sentences

チップを渡そうとすれば、相手はそれを返そうとするでしょう。

☐ If you try to tip someone, they might try to return the money to you.

東京はインターネット環境は充実していますが、どこでもWi-Fiが利用できるわけではありません。

☐ Tokyo is a very wired city, but you still can't get Wi-Fi everywhere.

東京では、東洋医学を体験することができます。針、お灸、そして指圧は疲労や筋肉痛によく効きます。

☐ In Tokyo you can experience traditional Oriental Medicine; accupuncture, moxibustion, and *shiatsu* work well against fatigue and muscle pain.

東京でもジョギングは人気で、5キロの皇居周回コースを走る人をよく見かけます。

☐ In Tokyo jogging is popular, especially along the five-kilometer course around the Imperial Palace.

KEY WORD ✓

☐ revolving sushi	回転寿司
☐ affordable	良心的な値段
☐ tap water	水道の水
☐ tip	チップを渡す
☐ wired	（インターネットに）つながる
☐ Oriental Medicine	東洋医学

東京サバイバル

東京の便利情報

テレビやラジオでは多言語放送も行っています。日本語のニュースを英語に切り替えて視聴することもできます。

☐ There are television and radio broadcasts in multiple languages, and it is often possible to switch the Japanese news to English.

東京の通勤時間帯、人々はとても早足で、その波にのるのは大変です。

☐ During rush hour people in Tokyo walk fairly quickly, and it can be hard to keep up.

英語でのコミュニケーション

東京は、英語の読み書きはできても、会話のできる人はそう多くはありません。

☐ People in Tokyo may be able to read and write English but not many can actually speak English.

英語が話せる日本人でも、外国人と向かい合うと気後れしてしまうのです。

☐ Some Japanese can speak English but lose their nerve when they meet a foreign person.

英語で話をするときは、できるだけゆっくり話し、時には筆談などを交えると効果的です。

☐ When you speak English, it is best to speak as slowly as possible, and it can also be useful to write down what you want to say.

Tokyo in Single Sentences

残念ながら、ほとんどのタクシー運転手は英語を話しません。

☐ Unfortunately, most taxi drivers don't speak English.

宿泊するホテルの名刺があれば、タクシー運転手に見せることもできます。

☐ You should carry a business card from your hotel to show to the taxi driver.

東京では、タクシー会社によって、英語のサービスを行っている会社があります。ウエブサイトで、Tokyo, Taxi, English といれて検索してみてください。

☐ In Tokyo, there are some taxi companies that offer services in English; you can try searching for "Tokyo," "taxi," and "English" on the web.

東京観光情報センターに行けば、外国語で旅行の情報を取得できます。

☐ The Tokyo Tourist Information Center offers travel information in foreign languages.

東京では、英語の通じる病院がいくつかあります。Tokyo, Hospital, English でウエブ検索してみてください。

☐ There are a few hospitals in Tokyo where English is spoken; try searching for "Tokyo," "hospital," and "English" on the web.

KEY WORD ✓

☐ multiple languages broadcast   多言語放送
☐ lose one's nerve   気後れする

東京サバイバル

東京の便利情報 ● 英語でのコミュニケーション

87

▶▶▶ ワンセンテンスで説明する東京

東京の標識は日本語と英語が併記されています。

☐ Street signs in Tokyo are in Japanese and English.

東京の電車や地下鉄の標識は英語でも書かれています。

☐ Train and subway signs in Tokyo are in English as well.

地下鉄の停車駅は英語でもアナウンスされます。

☐ Stops on the subway are announced in English.

インターネットで検索をすれば、英語による外国人向けの東京情報が多数出てきます。

☐ If you search on the internet, you can find lots of information about Tokyo for foreigners in English.

安全と警察

Track 24

世界中の他の都市と比べても、東京は犯罪率が低く、安全と言えます。

☐ Compared to other cities around the world, Tokyo has a low crime rate and is fairly safe.

交番という警察官が待機している詰所があり、緊急のときに助けてくれます。

☐ There are police boxes called *koban*, and they can help you in the event of an emergency.

Tokyo in Single Sentences

東京は、かなり安全な街ですが、貴重品の管理など、常識的な配慮は必要です。

☐ Tokyo is relatively safe, but you should still use common sense and guard your valuables.

何かトラブルがあったら、交番に行きましょう。

☐ If you have any trouble, you should go to a police box.

失くし物をしたときは、交番に行きましょう。

☐ If you lose something, you should go to a police box.

もし、道に迷ったら交番で道順を尋ねしましょう。

☐ If you are lost, you can ask for directions at a police box.

警察官は街を自転車でパトロールしています。

☐ Police officers patrol the city on bicycles.

KEY WORD ✓

☐ street sign	標識
☐ crime rate	犯罪率
☐ police box	交番
☐ valuables	貴重品

東京サバイバル 英語でのコミュニケーション●安全と警察

地震

東京は地震が多いので、常に地震への備えをしています。

☐ Tokyo experiences a lot of earthquakes and is always preparing for the next one.

東京は、何世紀にもわたって無数の地震に見舞われています。

☐ Countless earthquakes have occurred in Tokyo over the centuries.

緊急時の電話番号

東京、あるいは日本で救急車や消防車を呼ばなければならないときは、119番に電話しましょう。

☐ In Tokyo, as well as in the rest of Japan, dial 119 if you need to call an ambulance or the fire department.

東京、あるいは日本で警察に連絡をしなければならないときは、110番に電話しましょう。

☐ In Tokyo, as well as in the rest of Japan, dial 110 if you need to call the police.

東京、あるいは日本で電話番号を知りたいときは、104番に電話しましょう。

☐ In Tokyo, as well as in the rest of Japan, the number for information is 104.

Tokyo in Single Sentences

郵便・キャッシング・クレジットカード　Track 27

日本の銀行の ATM の中には、外国発行のカードが使えないところがあります。

☐ Some of the ATMs at Japanese banks do not accept foreign-issued cards.

郵便局やコンビニの ATM は、外国発行のカードも使えます。

☐ The ATMs in post offices and in some convenience stores accept foreign-issued ATM cards.

日本では郵便局に ATM があります。

☐ In Japan, post offices have ATMs.

東京の都市部では、クレジットカードを使える場所が増えましたが、海外と比べるとまだ現金社会です。

☐ More and more places in Tokyo accept credit cards, but it's still a cash society compared to other countries.

東京は比較的治安がいいので、多くの現金を持ち歩いても大丈夫です。

☐ Because Tokyo is relatively safe, it is okay to carry a large amount of cash.

東京サバイバル　地震●緊急時の電話番号●郵便・キャッシング・クレジットカード

▶▶▶ ワンセンテンスで説明する東京

郵便局は月曜日から金曜日まで、朝9時から夕方5時まで営業しています。

☐ Most post offices are open Monday through Friday, from 9 am to 5 pm.

東京のいくつかの区には中央郵便局があり、24時間営業を行っています。

☐ Some Tokyo wards have central post offices that are open 24 hours a day.

郵便局のATMは営業時間終了後も使えますが、24時間使えるわけではありません。

☐ Post office ATMs have longer hours, but are not available 24 hours a day.

宿泊施設

新宿、渋谷、上野などの交通の要所には、ビジネスホテルがあります。

☐ You can find business hotels in all the major hubs, such as Shinjuku, Shibuya and Ueno.

ビジネスホテルにはシングルとダブルの部屋があります。

☐ Business hotels have single and double rooms.

東京では、カプセルホテルで夜を過ごすこともできます。

☐ In Tokyo, you can spend the night in a capsule hotel.

Tokyo in Single Sentences

カプセルホテルの部屋は、ベッドひとつ分の広さで、上半身を起こして座れるくらいの高さです。

☐ In a capsule hotel you get a space just big enough to fit a bed, and just tall enough to sit up in.

実際のところ、背の高い人だと、カプセルホテルでは上体を起こして座れないかもしれません。

☐ Actually, if you are tall, you may not be able to sit up in a capsule hotel.

カプセルホテルの各カプセルの入口は、カーテンで仕切られていて、それなりにプライバシーが守られています。

☐ Capsule hotels offer some privacy, because there is a curtain at the opening of each capsule.

カプセルホテルでは、他の客に眠りを妨げられないように耳栓をもらえます。

☐ Capsule hotels provide earplugs so the other guests don't disturb you.

渋谷の道玄坂や新宿の歌舞伎町界隈にはラブホテルがたくさんあります。

☐ The Dogenzaka neighborhood of Shibuya and the Kabukicho neighborhood of Shinjuku have many love hotels.

KEY WORD ✓

☐ central post offices　中央郵便局
☐ open 24 hours a day　24時間営業

東京サバイバル　郵便・キャッシング・クレジットカード ● 宿泊施設

東京で食べる・見る・遊ぶ

コンビニ

　東京には無数のコンビニがあり、たいてい近くのコンビニまでは5分もかかりません。コンビニでは、サンドイッチ、おにぎり、弁当という箱詰めの食事などが売られています。コンビニでは、ボールペン、歯ブラシ、電池といった日常品も売っています。

　手ごろな価格のコーヒーをコンビニで買うこともできます。ほとんどのコンビニには、ATM機やコピー機があります。コンサート、演劇、スポーツイベントのチケットまでコンビニで買うことができます。その上、年中無休です。

自動販売機

　東京には数えきれない自動販売機があります。自動販売機は通りや電車のプラットホームに置かれています。ほとんどの自動販売機ではお茶やコーヒーといった飲み物を売っています。冬場の自動販売機では温かい飲み物を売っています。アイスクリーム、新聞、雨傘や他の日常品を売っているものもあります。

Tokyo Dining, Sightseeing and Entertainment

Convenience stores

Tokyo has thousands of convenience stores. You are usually never more than five minutes away from a convenience store. Convenience stores sell food such as sandwiches, rice balls, and boxed meals called *bento*. Convenience stores sell useful items like pens, toothbrushes and batteries.

You can get inexpensive hot coffee at convenience stores. Most convenience stores have ATMs and photocopy machines. You can buy tickets for concerts, shows and sporting events from convenience stores. Most convenience stores are open 24 hours a day, seven days a week.

Vending machines

In Tokyo, there are thousands of vending machines. You can find vending machines on the street and on train platforms. Most vending machines sell drinks such as tea and coffee. In winter, vending machines have hot drinks. You can also find vending machines selling ice cream, newspapers, umbrellas and other unusual items.

トイレ

　東京にはタイプの異なるトイレがいくつもあります。伝統的な和式トイレはしゃがんで使いますが、東京の公衆トイレには洋式が、少なくとも１つは備わっているのでご安心を。たいていの駅にはトイレがありますし、コンビニも客用のトイレがあります。

　ホテル、レストラン、百貨店では「ウォシュレット」というモダンな電気式のトイレに出くわすことがあります。ウォシュレットにはビデ機能が付いており、便座を温めてくれるものもあります。ウォシュレットのコントロールパネルには、各機能を示すアイコンが表記されたボタンが付いています。

　公衆トイレにはペーパータオルやハンドドライヤーがないところもあるので注意してください。日本では、手を拭くために小さなタオルやハンカチを持ち歩くのが習慣なのです。

喫煙

　東京では公衆の場での喫煙は違法です。歩きながらの喫煙も違法です。タバコを吸いたいときは、決められた喫煙エリアへ行かなければなりません。ほとんどの駅の外側には喫煙エリアがあります。しかし東京では、喫煙禁止の表示がなければ、レストランやバーのなかで喫煙することができます。

Toilets

In Tokyo, you will see many different kinds of toilets. Traditional Japanese toilets are squat toilets. Most public restrooms in Tokyo have at least one Western-style toilet. Most train stations have public restrooms. Some of convenience stores also have restrooms for customers.

In hotels, restaurants and department stores you may encounter modern, electric toilets called "washlets." Washlets have bidet functions and sometimes heated toilet seats. They have control panels with many buttons that have icons explaining their functions. Once you try a washlet you will be converted.

Be careful, as many public restrooms do not have paper towels or hand dryers, and it is customary in Japan to carry a small towel or handkerchief to dry your hands.

Smoking

In Tokyo, it is illegal to smoke in public areas. It is also illegal to smoke while walking down the street. If you want to smoke, you have to go to a designated smoking area. There are designated smoking areas outside most train stations. In Tokyo, however, it is legal to smoke inside restaurants and bars unless you see a no-smoking sign.

居酒屋

　西洋では、勤勉な勤め人たちは、毎日の仕事帰りにバーやパブに立ち寄り、同僚たちと一緒に軽いつまみでお酒を飲みます。日本では、居酒屋がこれにあたります。日本にも、帰宅を阻む愉しみがあるのです。

　その居酒屋というのは、内装は伝統的な和風のあつらえで、木製のカウンターを備えているところが多く、おひとり様でも二人連れでも飲むことができます。グループ用のテーブルと椅子もあれば、畳敷きの席もあります（テーブルの下が足を伸ばすための掘りごたつになっている席だと快適です！）。

　飲み物のメニューは、すぐにサーブされる生ビールはもちろん、その他にも幅広く取り揃えられていますが、日本酒や焼酎に特化した居酒屋もあります。焼酎とは、芋や麦などから作るアルコール度数が25～30％の蒸留酒です。ある居酒屋に定期的に通えば「常連」と認識され、仕事終わりに他の常連客たちの輪に入って会話を楽しむこともできます。

ラーメン屋

　急いでランチを食べたいときや、友人たちと飲んだ楽しい夜の最後の締めとしても、日本人にとってラーメンは欠くことのできないものです。ラーメン

Izakayas

In Western countries hard-working office staff might stop into a bar or pub on their way home from a day's work, sharing a drink and light snacks with colleagues. In Japan, the equivalent is an *izakaya*, and here, too, the journey home is pleasantly interrupted.

An *izakaya* will typically have traditional decor, usually with a wooden counter for those sipping alone or in pairs, tables and chairs for those in groups, and sometimes tatami mats, some of which will have sunken floors under the tables for people to comfortably place their legs.

The selection of beverages is often fairly broad, and normally includes beer on tap. Some *izakaya* specialize in Japanese sake, and others in *shochu*, a distilled drink made from potatoes, rye or other ingredients with an alcohol content of 25–30%. If you go to an *izakaya* regularly, you may become known as a *joren* (regular customer), encountering other regulars and falling easily into post-work conversations.

Ramen noodle shop

Whether for a quick bite of lunch or a final meal at the end of a pleasant evening out drinking with friends, ramen is one of Japan's staple forms of pasta, served in a hot bowl

は日本人の主食ともいえる麺類で、熱いスープをはった丼にさまざまな具がのっています。うどん、そば、きしめん、素麺などの他の伝統的な麺類とは異なり、ラーメンの麺の食感は硬めです。ラーメンは主に4種に分類ができ、それは日本の地域によって特徴が出るのですが、スープや材料の種類は増えていく一方です。

　古典的なラーメンといえば、白髪ネギとチャーシューが1〜2枚のせられているものですが、新たなスタイルとして、「４種類のチーズ入りラーメン」などが創作され、ユニークなラーメンの選択肢が広がっています。新横浜駅近くにはラーメン博物館というものまであって、1950年代の雰囲気、多彩なつくり方、ラーメンの地域ごとの違いを見ることができます。

回転寿司

　和食が世界の無形文化遺産として認定されたころには、「回転寿司」のレストランが、世界に知られた飲食業界の頂点に立つとは、想像されていませんでした。しかし「寿司」そのものは明らかに評価されていました。伝統的な寿司屋へ入ると、厚い木製のカウンターの席に着き、タネごとに対で出される寿司を前に、職人と会話するというのが一般的な流れです。

　残念なことに、この体験をするのにはお金がかか

of broth and complemented by a variety of toppings. With a consistency different from Japan's other traditional noodles — such as udon, soba, *kishimen*, or *somen* — ramen noodles have a slightly tougher texture. There are four main varieties of ramen, often associated with particular regions of Japan, but the range of types of broth and ingredients continues to expand.

Traditional ramen was topped with fine strips of leek and a slice or two of *chashu* pork, but newer styles include inventions like "four-cheese ramen" and other unique variations that provide a broad choice. There is even a ramen museum close to the Shin-Yokohama Station, offering a taste of the 1950s, a variety of preparations, and an explanation of ramen's regional differences.

Conveyor-belt sushi restaurants

When Japanese cuisine achieved World Heritage status, the idea of conveyor-belt sushi restaurants was likely not at the top of the list of celebrated food services. Sushi, however, clearly was. To step into a traditional sushi restaurant usually meant being seated at a big wooden counter and talking with the chef as you watched your sushi being prepared piece-by-piece in pairs.

Unfortunately, this experience was also expensive,

ります。特別な日のためであるとか、お金持ちでない限り、家族みんなでお手軽に寿司を楽しむということはなかなかできません。

「回転寿司」では、皿に乗った低価格の寿司がずらりと並んで回転しており、客は手軽に好きな寿司ダネを選ぶことができます。これによって、この伝統的な酢飯と生魚の料理は、日本人にとって身近なものになりました。ベルトコンベアー寿司は、現在では世界的な事象となっており、世界の人々に世界無形文化遺産の料理を送り届けています。

東京の百貨店

東京には数多くの百貨店があります。百貨店は、多くの人が集まってくる銀座や日本橋の周辺地域、さらには膨大な数の通勤客が通り過ぎる新宿、渋谷、池袋、そして上野などの駅周辺に集中しています。

百貨店は日本ならではのサービスを充実させていて、顧客への応対には日本の伝統的なおもてなしの精神が息づいています。

百貨店の地下では、日本の伝統的なお惣菜から、日本が誇る高級和牛やワインまで、ありとあらゆる食材や食品が並んでいます。百貨店自体が、東京の重要な観光資源といっても差し支えないでしょう。

reserved for special occasions or the well-heeled, and it was not easy for ordinary people to enjoy sushi with their families at an affordable price.

"*Kaiten-zushi*" — with a revolving array of sushi plates priced economically, let customers choose their favorite sushi at affordable rates, bringing Japan's traditional vinegared rice and raw fish closer to more of Japan's population. Conveyer-belt sushi is now a global phenomenon, bringing a World Heritage cuisine to people worldwide.

Department stores

There are quite a few department stores in Tokyo. These are concentrated in areas of the city where many people gather, such as in Ginza and Nihonbashi, and also near stations with large numbers of commuters passing through, including Shinjuku, Shibuya, Ikebukuro and Ueno.

Department stores embody the essence of service found only in Japan, where a spirit of the nation's traditional hospitality lives and breathes in the manner in which each customer is taken care of by attentive staff.

Moreover, in department-store basements you can find a wide assortment of food and cooking ingredients, ranging from prepared dishes to wine and Japan's famous *wagyu*. Department stores have become destination spots.

デパ地下

　デパートの地下フロアは、「デパ地下」と呼ばれます（文字通りデパートの地下を略したものです）。そこでは、日本全国また世界各地からのさまざまな食品や酒類を買うことができます。伝統的な和菓子や洋菓子も購入することができます。デパ地下は、伝統的な日本料理の材料を調達するのにも絶好の場所です。

　すぐに食べられる食品の中には高級惣菜もあり、忙しい人は夕飯のメインディッシュをデパ地下で買うこともあります。季節ごとの贈答品も豊富で、有名デパートのデパ地下で買い求めたギフトは喜ばれます。

家電量販店

　電化製品だけを専門に販売する大規模店舗は、日本以外にもあるとはいえ、日本の店は、想像し得る限りありとあらゆる家電を、整然と陳列して販売するというアイデアが申し分なく表現されているようです。

　日本全国に展開するチェーンの家電量販店が販売するのは、冷蔵庫、洗濯機、乾燥機、炊飯器といった定番商品だけでなく、季節ごとの家電、例えばこたつ（足を温めてくれるヒーター付きの机）、ホット

Department store basements

The basement floors of department stores are called "*depa-chika*" (literally a shortened way to say "department store basement"). There you can purchase a wide variety of food and alcohol from Japan and around the world, including traditional Japanese and Western sweets. The *depa-chika* floor of department stores is also the best place to find ingredients for traditional Japanese cuisine.

Because many foods are ready to eat and are prepared to high standards, busy people often purchase the main-dish items for their dinner from the *depa-chika*. Seasonal gifts, too, are appreciated when they have been bought and sent from the *depa-chika* of a name-brand department store.

Household appliance stores

Although Japan is not alone in having large stores that specialize in household electrical appliances, it seems to have perfected the idea of being able to shop for virtually any imaginable household appliance in one well-organized retail outlet.

Several chains of these retail appliance shops operate all over Japan, offering not only standard items such as refrigerators, washing machines, driers, and rice cookers, but seasonal electrical appliances such as *kotatsu* (tables with

カーペット、エアコンなども揃えています。チェーン店ごとにポイント還元システムがあり、顧客はポイントを稼ぐために店へ通い、得たポイントは次回の買い物で割引に使うことができます。

パチンコ屋

ギャンブルを禁じている国で、許されているもののひとつが「パチンコ」です。もともとパチンコは、バネのレバーを引いてパチンコ玉をはじき出して遊ぶ純粋な遊技機でした。何本もの釘を打たれたガラス張りの立板に沿って、パチンコ玉が下まで転がり落ちていきます(この場合、配当はありません)。運がいいと途中の穴に玉が落ちて、よりたくさんの玉を得ることができ、ゲームに勝つ可能性が高まります。

しかし1920年代に生まれたこの元祖パチンコは、国民的娯楽へと進化を遂げ、国中にパチンコ屋が建てられるようになりました。単なる娯楽から、広く普及した合法的なギャンブルへ進化したパチンコは、よりハイテクな電子機器になり、勝った人への配当は高額になりました。あくまで「賭博ではない」という体裁を保つため、勝った人は別の区画まで行って、パチンコ店とは別の窓口で景品を換金しなければなりません。

heating elements to keep your feet warm), electric heated carpets, and air conditioners. Each chain offers a loyalty point system, enticing customers back to accrue points, from which they can earn discounts on future purchases.

Pachinko pinball stores

In a country that officially prohibits gambling, one form that is permitted is *pachinko*. Originally *pachinko* was a purely mechanical game of pinballs being launched from a spring lever, tumbling down a glass-enclosed vertical board with pins, until the pinball would reach the bottom (with no payout), or more luckily fall into a hole that would win the customer more pinballs, and possibly a winning game.

From its origins in the 1920s, however, *pachinko* has evolved into a national pastime, with *pachinko* parlors located throughout the country. From a more simple form of entertainment, it has evolved into a widespread form of legalized gambling, with the *pachinko* machines much more high-tech and electronic, and the payoffs quite high for winners. To maintain the facade of not gambling, however, winners must still go around the block to another window to exchange their winnings.

カラオケ

「空のオーケストラ」これが「カラオケ」という語の意味です。日本で発祥し、世界的に人気となった娯楽のひとつです。有名な人気曲の楽器の演奏のみのバージョンを、歌詞を表示するビデオ映像と共に流して、それに合わせて心ゆくまで歌うことができるというものです。

音が合っていようと外れていようと声はマイクで増幅されますが、カラオケルームは防音仕様なので周囲からは隔絶されており、好きなだけ大きな声で歌うことができます。カラオケは長年、グループで楽しまれており、恥ずかしがり屋には歌うように勧めてみたりしながら、全員で気兼ねなく好きな曲を歌うことで、グループの団結心を高める効果もあります。

Karaoke

"An empty orchestra" — that is the meaning of the word *karaoke* — a form of entertainment originating in Japan that has become popular worldwide. Popular songs familiar to many people have been recorded in instrumental versions, their lyrics displayed on a video script that lets the customer sing along to their heart's content.

Customers can sing as loudly as they wish, their voices amplified whether they can sing on key or not, as the resulting noise is insulated from the neighbors by soundproof *karaoke* rooms. *Karaoke* has been a form of group entertainment for many years, as even shy participants are urged to sing, and group morale is built by everyone singing their favorite songs without hesitation.

東京の食事

東京では外食文化が発達してます。
- [ ] Tokyo has a big culture of eating out.

東京の生活はペースが速く、そのため頻繁に外食します。
- [ ] Because life in Tokyo is so fast-paced, people often eat out.

よく仕事の後に友人や同僚と夕食を食べたりお酒を飲んだりします。
- [ ] It is common for friends and co-workers to meet for dinner or drinks after work.

仕事終わりの友人や同僚との夕食や飲み会で、ストレスを解消するのです。
- [ ] Friends and co-workers meet for dinner or drinks after work to blow off steam.

週を通して毎晩満席になるレストランも珍しくありません。
- [ ] It is common to see restaurants full every night of the week.

年配の人たちはざっくばらんな焼き鳥屋を好みます。
- [ ] Many older people prefer to go to casual *yakitori* restaurants.

若い世代はおしゃれなダイニングバーを好みます。
- [ ] Many younger people prefer to go to stylish dining bars.

Tokyo in Single Sentences

居酒屋とは、日本式の伝統的なパブのことです。

☐ An *izakaya* is a traditional Japanese-style pub.

東京の飲食店の多くが非常に狭いので驚くかもしれません。

☐ You may be surprised to find that many Tokyo restaurants are very small.

東京には、十数人分の席しかないようなレストランもあります。

☐ Some Tokyo restaurants have only a dozen seats.

東京の家賃は高いので、飲食店も狭いのです。

☐ Rent is high in Tokyo, so restaurants are often very small.

レストランにはたいてい、高級店でも、カウンター席があります。

☐ Many restaurants, even expensive ones, have counter seats.

料理人との会話を楽しむために、カウンター席を好む人もいます。

☐ Some people prefer to sit at the counter so they can chat with the chefs.

KEY WORD ✓

☐ culture of eating out	外食文化
☐ blow off steam	ストレスを解消する
☐ stylish	おしゃれな
☐ chat	おしゃべりする

東京で食べる・見る・遊ぶ

東京の食事

▶▶▶ ワンセンテンスで説明する東京

カウンター席は一人で夕食をとるのにぴったりです。

☐ Counter seats are especially good for solo diners.

東京では、一人で外食するのはごく普通のことです。

☐ It is perfectly normal to eat out by yourself in Tokyo.

東京の朝食文化はあまり発達していません

☐ Tokyo doesn't have much of a breakfast culture.

ほとんどの飲食店はランチからの営業です。

☐ Most restaurants are only open from lunchtime.

パン屋でさえ、開店は 10 〜 11 時が普通です。

☐ Even bakeries don't usually open until 10 or 11 am.

ファーストフード店やカフェチェーン店なら、朝食を食べられます。

☐ Fast food restaurants and chain cafés open for breakfast.

お祭りには、「屋台」がたくさん出ます。屋台で売っている代表的なものは、焼きそば、たこ焼き、たい焼きなどです。

☐ At festivals, you can see many food stalls, called *yatai*, typically serving dishes like fried noodles, octopus dumplings and bean jam cakes shaped like fish.

屋台は上野のアメヤ横丁でも見ることができます。

☐ You can also find *yatai* at Ueno's Ameya-yokocho market.

Tokyo in Single Sentences

屋台の食べ物はほんの数ドルです。

☐ Meals from a *yatai* cost only a few dollars.

「横丁」とは、たくさんの飲食店が密集している狭い通りのことです。

☐ A *yokocho* is a small alley where many restaurants can be found.

東京には、新宿の思い出横丁、恵比寿の恵比寿横丁といった、よく知られた横丁があります。

☐ Tokyo has several famous *yokocho*, such as Omoide-yokocho in Shinjuku and Ebisu-yokocho in Ebisu.

横丁を歩くと、50年前の東京を歩いているような気分になります。

☐ Walking through a *yokocho* feels like walking through Tokyo fifty years ago.

大きな店や飲食店は年中無休です。

☐ Major shops and restaurants are open seven days a week.

KEY WORD ✓

☐ solo	一人の
☐ food stall	食べ物の屋台
☐ fried noodle	焼きそば
☐ octopus dumpling	たこ焼き
☐ bean jam cake shaped like fish	たい焼き

ランチとディナーの間、一時的に店を閉めるレストランもあります。

☐ Some restaurants close between lunch and dinner service.

通常、ランチメニューの提供時間は11時半から2時までです。

☐ Lunch service is usually from 11:30 am to 2 pm.

通常、ディナーの提供時間は午後6時ごろからです。

☐ Dinner service usually begins at around 6 pm.

東京のバーやクラブには決まった閉店時間がありません。

☐ There is no fixed closing time for bars and clubs in Tokyo.

東京のバーやクラブの多くは朝まで営業しています。

☐ Many bars and clubs in Tokyo stay open until morning.

カラオケ店、漫画喫茶などは一晩中開いています。

☐ *Karaoke* parlors and manga cafés stay open all night.

娯楽に関して言えば、東京は24時間営業です。

☐ When it comes to entertainment, Tokyo is a 24-hour city.

東京のランチ

ビジネス街の飲食店にとって、お昼どきは大忙しの時間帯です。

☐ Lunchtime in business districts is a very busy time for restaurants.

とくにビジネス街のお昼どきは、他のお客さんを待たせないように早めに食べましょう。

☐ During lunchtime, especially in business districts, you should eat quickly so other customers don't have to wait.

東京のランチは非常にお得です。

☐ Lunch is a great bargain in Tokyo.

ディナーは高くても、ランチは手頃な価格で出しているというレストランがたくさんあります。

☐ Many restaurants that are quite expensive for dinner offer reasonably priced lunches.

10ドル以下のランチでお腹いっぱい食べられます。

☐ You can get a very filling lunch set for under $10.

KEY WORD ✓

☐ fixed closing time	決まった閉店時間
☐ great bargain	お得

▶▶▶ ワンセンテンスで説明する東京

ランチセットの定番を定食といい、メインディッシュひと皿に、ご飯、味噌汁、漬物という献立です。

- [ ] A typical lunch set is called a *teishoku*, and includes one main dish along with rice, *miso* soup and pickles.

お昼どきになると、移動式屋台がビジネス街に集まってきます。

- [ ] During lunch hour, food trucks gather in business districts.

カフェ・ベーカリー

Track 31

東京ではカフェは人気があります。

- [ ] Cafés are very popular in Tokyo.

東京は世界一スターバックスが多い都市です。

- [ ] Tokyo has more branches of Starbucks than any other city in the world.

一杯のコーヒーが5ドル以上するようなカフェもあります。

- [ ] At some cafés, a cup of coffee can cost over $5.

午前11時までは、多くのカフェがお得なモーニングセットを出しています。

- [ ] Before 11 am, many cafés offer a "morning set," which is a good deal.

コーヒー、トースト、ゆで卵というのが一般的なモーニングセットです。

- [ ] A "morning set" usually includes a cup of coffee, toast, and a hard-boiled egg.

Tokyo in Single Sentences

東京中どこにもパン屋があります。

☐ Most neighborhoods in Tokyo have bakeries.

パン屋にある典型的なパンといえば、バゲットやデニッシュです。

☐ Bakeries typically carry items like baguettes and danish pastries.

パン屋は日本にしかないようなパンも作っています。

☐ Bakeries also make some types of bread that are unique to Japan.

パン屋へ行ったら、カレーパンやメロンパンを食べてみてください。

☐ If you visit a bakery, you should try *curry-pan* or *melon-pan*.

カレーパンは、生地にカレーを入れて揚げたものです。

☐ *Curry-pan* is a deep-fried doughnut filled with curry sauce.

KEY WORD ✓

☐ food truck	移動式屋台
☐ pickle	漬物
☐ hard-boiled egg	ゆで卵

▶▶▶ ワンセンテンスで説明する東京

メロンパンとは、甘くてふわっとしたパンで、メロンのような形をしています。

☐ *Melon-pan* is a sweet and fluffy bun that kind of looks like a melon.

日本料理

東京では様々な日本食を体験することができます。

☐ You can sample all kinds of Japanese food in Tokyo.

高級な日本料理店では、一種類の料理に特化しています。

☐ Many of the best Japanese restaurants specialize in just one type of dish.

焼き鳥を食べたいのなら、焼き鳥の専門店に行くのがおすすめです。

☐ If you want to eat *yakitori*, you should go to a restaurant that specializes in *yakitori*.

有楽町には焼き鳥屋がたくさんあります。

☐ There are many *yakitori* restaurants in Yurakucho.

浅草や上野には伝統的な日本料理の店がたくさんあります。

☐ Asakusa and Ueno have many traditional Japanese restaurants.

Tokyo in Single Sentences

江戸前寿司

Track 33

寿司には色んな種類があります。

☐ There are many types of sushi.

握り寿司は、江戸の郷土料理です。

☐ The type of sushi native to Edo is called *nigiri-zushi*.

握り寿司とは、一口大の長方形に握った酢飯の上に、新鮮な生の魚介をのせたものです。

☐ *Nigiri-zushi* is a bite-sized rectangle of rice topped with fresh raw fish and seafood.

握り寿司は江戸前寿司ともいい、これは東京の旧称である江戸に由来しています。

☐ *Nigiri-zushi* is also called *Edo-mae* sushi, because Edo is the old name for Tokyo.

握り寿司は江戸時代、日本橋の旧魚市場周辺で発展しました。

☐ *Nigiri-zushi* developed during the Edo era around the old fish market in Nihonbashi.

KEY WORD ✓

☐ fluffy bun	ふわっとしたパン
☐ native to Edo	江戸生粋の
☐ bite-sized	一口大の
☐ fish market	魚市場

東京で食べる・見る・遊ぶ ● カフェ・ベーカリー ● 日本料理 ● 江戸前寿司

▶▶▶ ワンセンテンスで説明する東京

握り寿司はすぐに作れるので、江戸時代のファーストフードでした。

☐ *Nigiri-zushi* was the Edo era equivalent of fast food, because it didn't take long to make.

握り寿司は箸で食べても手で食べても構いません。

☐ You can eat *nigiri-zushi* with chopsticks or with your hands.

握り寿司の代表的なタネといえば、鮪、鮭、鯖、イカなどです。

☐ Some popular toppings for *nigiri-zushi* include tuna, salmon, mackerel and squid.

寿司屋では、セットメニューでも、一貫ずつでも注文することができます。

☐ At a sushi restaurant, you can order a set meal or one piece of sushi at a time.

皿に醤油を少し入れ、寿司をつけて食べます。

☐ Put a small amount of soy sauce in the dish and dip your sushi in it.

飯と魚の間には、たいていワサビという香辛料が少し入っています。

☐ In between the rice and the fish there is usually a small amount of spicy horseradish called *wasabi*.

ワサビが苦手ならば、寿司職人に伝えましょう。

☐ If you don't like *wasabi*, tell the chef.

Tokyo in Single Sentences

東京のショッピング体験

東京の小売店では、様々なショッピング体験を楽しめます。

- [ ] Tokyo offers a broad variety of fun shopping experiences at its many retail shops.

東京の主要駅の周辺にはいろいろな店があり、家電から、生活用品、家具、アイデア商品など、豊富な商品を販売しています。

- [ ] In the areas around major Tokyo train stations you can find a variety of retail shops specializing in electrical goods, everyday necessities, furniture, and creatively designed personal items.

東急ハンズなどの大型店には、生活や趣味のための様々なアイデア商品があふれています。

- [ ] At some particular retail shops, such as Tokyu Hands, you can find an amazing assortment of goods both for everyday life and for hobbies.

KEY WORD ✓

- [ ] one piece of sushi　　　一貫ずつ
- [ ] set meal　　　セットメニュー
- [ ] everyday necessity　　　生活用品

121

ビックカメラや山田電気、ヨドバシカメラといった「欲しいものはなんでもある」家電量販店では、海外ではみられないようなユニークな家電やその付属品を見つけることができます。

☐ We think you will encounter truly unique household electrical goods and accessories, of the sort you will not find anywhere overseas, at well-stocked electric-goods shops such as Bic Camera, Yamada Electrical and Yodobashi Camera.

一度は行ってみたい量販店チェーンのひとつドン・キホーテでは、数え切れない生活用品が、大特価で販売されています。

☐ One chain of retail shops you might want to see is called Don Quixote; they are known for their very affordable prices for countless household goods.

日本の文房具店には、様々な驚きのアイテムがあります。

☐ Japan's stationery stores stock an amazing, and inspiring, selection of items.

Tokyo in Single Sentences

秋葉原に行けば、オタク文化に関連した面白い商品があります。

☐ If you visit Akihabara you can find interesting goods associated with Japan's unique *otaku* culture.

浅草の合羽橋通り界隈には、家庭の台所やレストランで使用する料理用具を売る店が並んでいます。

☐ In the Kappabashi-dori neighborhood near Asakusa, the streets are lined with shops selling cooking utensils for both restaurants and home kitchens.

和食をつくるときに必要な高品質の和包丁や竹ざるなどの台所用品を購入できます。

☐ You can purchase high-quality Japanese kitchen knives and bamboo serving trays that are must-have items when you are preparing Japanese cuisine.

百貨店の地下を"デパ地下"（文字通り、デパートの地下を短縮したもの）と呼びます。

☐ The basement floors of department stores are called *depachika*, which is simply an abbreviation of "department store basement."

KEY WORD ✓

☐ bamboo serving tray	竹ざる
☐ must-have items	必携品
☐ cooking utensils	料理用具

> デパ地下では、日本をはじめ世界中のさまざまな食料品や酒類を購入できます。さらに、伝統的な和菓子や洋菓子も揃っています。

- [ ] *Depa-chika* are places where you can purchase a wide variety of food and alcohol from Japan and around the world, including traditional Japanese and Western-style sweets.

> 日本の伝統的な食材を探すにはデパ地下が最適です。

- [ ] The *depa-chika* floors of department stores are a good place to find ingredients for traditional Japanese cuisine.

> 浅草や上野のアメ横などには、日本の伝統的なお菓子や食材を売る店が多くあります。

- [ ] There are a large number of shops selling traditional Japanese sweets and cooking ingredients in Ameyoko in Ueno, and in Asakusa.

> 東京のほとんどの駅には、駅前商店街があって、昔ながらの伝統的なものを売る懐かしい趣の小売店が並んでいます。

- [ ] Many train stations in Tokyo have a traditional shopping street close to the station where you can find old-fashioned shops selling traditional items from a bygone era.

美術館

北の丸公園内にある国立近代美術館は、明治時代から今日までの、日本の芸術家による芸術作品を展示しています。

☐ The National Museum of Modern Art is in Kitanomaru Park, and it displays artworks by Japanese artists from the Meiji Period and onwards.

東京都現代美術館は木場公園の中にあり、戦後美術を概観できます。

☐ The Museum of Contemporary Art is in Kiba Park, and it displays artworks from 1945 and onwards.

国立西洋美術館は上野公園にあり、主に西洋の芸術家たちによる作品を展示しています。

☐ The National Museum of Western Art is in Ueno Park, and it displays artworks by mostly European artists.

根津美術館は青山にあり、日本および東アジアの古美術品を展示しています。

☐ The Nezu Museum is in Aoyama, and it displays classical works and objects from Japan and East Asia.

KEY WORD ✓

☐ cooking ingredient	食材
☐ bygone era	過ぎ去った時代

▶▶▶ ワンセンテンスで説明する東京

森美術館は六本木にあり、現代アートの展示を行っています。

- [ ] The Mori Art Museum is in Roppongi, and it hosts contemporary art exhibitions.

国立新美術館は乃木坂にあり、注目を浴びるような現代アートの展示を行っています。

- [ ] The National Art Center is in Nogizaka, and it hosts high-profile temporary exhibitions.

サントリー美術館は六本木にあり、装飾美術作品を展示しています。

- [ ] The Suntory Art Museum is in Roppongi, and it hosts exhibitions of decorative arts.

東京都写真美術館は恵比寿にあり、日本人および海外の写真家たちの作品を展示しています。

- [ ] The Metropolitan Museum of Photography is in Ebisu, and it displays works by Japanese and non-Japanese photographers.

博物館

国立科学博物館は上野公園にあり、自然科学史の展示を行っています。

☐ The National Science Museum is in Ueno Park, and it includes exhibits on science and natural history.

未来館の呼び名で親しまれている日本科学未来館は、お台場にあり、ロボット工学や IT 技術についての展示を行っています。

☐ The National Museum of Emerging Science, nicknamed *Miraikan*, is in Odaiba, and it includes exhibits on robotics and information technology.

下町風俗資料館は上野にあり、明治、大正、昭和初期の東京の生活についての展示をしています。

☐ The Shitamachi Museum is in Ueno, and it has exhibits on life in Tokyo during the Meiji, Taisho, and early Showa periods.

深川江戸資料館は深川にあり、江戸時代の東京の生活の様子を展示しています。

☐ The Fukagawa Edo Museum is in Fukagawa, and it has exhibits on life in Tokyo during the Edo period.

KEY WORD

☐ host	〜を主催する
☐ decorative arts	装飾美術
☐ exhibit	展示

TOKYO PEDIA

2部 東京観光
Tokyo Sightseeing

皇居とその周辺
大手町・日本橋とその周辺
銀座とその周辺
浅草とその周辺
新宿とその周辺
渋谷・六本木とその周辺
原宿・表参道・青山とその周辺
神田・秋葉原とその周辺
上野・谷中とその周辺
月島・深川との周辺
池袋・巣鴨とその周辺
品川・海浜とその周辺
後楽園・神楽坂とその周辺
東京から日帰りできる観光名所

皇居とその周辺

江戸城

　江戸城は、1457年に前身となる城が築城された地に、徳川家康が1590年に江戸を本拠地としたときから改築を進めた城郭です。内堀と外堀とを合わせると、東京の都心部をすっぽりと包み込むほどの、目を見張るように巨大な城でした。

　現在は都市化が進み、堀の多くが埋め立てられたり、高速道路の下に隠れたりしています。虎ノ門や浅草橋といった東京の地名の多くが、江戸城の施設の名前をその起源としています。1603年に徳川家康が将軍となり全国を支配するようになったあとは、江戸城は日本の中心としての行政本部の役割を担いました。

　1868年に徳川幕府が倒れたあとは、江戸城だったところには天皇一家が居住し、今では皇居となって、現在に至っています。

Around the Imperial Palace

Edo Castle

Built on the location where an earlier castle had been constructed in 1457, Edo Castle was reconstructed in earnest after Tokugawa Ieyasu made Edo his operational headquarters in 1590. If you include both the Inner Moat and the Outer Moat, this was an impressive, enormous castle, as most of central Tokyo fit into its perimeter.

Nowadays, with the march of urbanization, most of the moats have been covered over, or are hiding beneath the expressways. The origins of many of Tokyo's modern place names are, in fact, the names they had in relation to Edo Castle, such as Toranomon and Asakusa-bashi. From 1603 onwards, when Tokugawa Ieyasu became Shogun and took control of the whole nation, Edo Castle was the center of Japan, playing the role of the central administrative seat of power.

From 1868, following the collapse of the Tokugawa Bakufu, to the present day, the Imperial family has lived in what were the grounds of Edo Castle, now known as the Imperial Palace.

皇居

現在の皇居は、その昔は江戸城として知られていました。1603年から1868年まで、ここに徳川氏によって軍事的な江戸幕府がおかれ、日本を統治していました。江戸城には昔は大きな天守閣もありましたが、江戸時代の火事で焼け落ちてしまいました。

1868年以降は、江戸城跡には天皇が居住していることから、皇居として知られるようになりました。江戸城は、築城当初から内堀と外堀によって守られており、今でも多くの歴史的遺構が保存されています。

皇居のすぐ周辺にあるのが内堀です。そして現在の御茶ノ水から赤坂見附にかけて、外堀の一部が残っています。昔は、外堀と内堀の間に多くの大名や身分の高い武士の屋敷があったのです。

二重橋

二重橋とは、江戸城（皇居）の正面にある橋のことです。実際は前にある石橋の後ろの橋が二重橋なのですが、多くの人が、正面にある二重アーチの石橋

Imperial Palace

The present-day Imperial Palace was known in olden days as Edo Castle, and it is where the Edo-based military Shogunate — established by Tokugawa in 1603 — ruled over Japan until 1868. There once was a large fortress on the castle grounds, but it burned to the ground in fires during the Edo era.

Beginning in 1868 the castle grounds came to be known as the Imperial Palace, due to the fact that the Emperor resides there. From the time it was constructed, the castle was surrounded for protection by the Inner Moat and the Outer Moat, and to this day many historical elements and artifacts have been preserved.

Immediately surrounding the palace is the Inner Moat. Portions of the Outer Moat, in turn, can still be seen today, stretching from Ochanomizu to Akasaka-Mitsuke. In those olden days the residences of many feudal lords (*daimyo*) and the homes of relatively high-status samurai (*bushi*) were located between the Inner and Outer Moats.

Nijubashi bridge

This is a bridge located on the main, front side of Edo Castle — now the Imperial Palace. The real "Nijubashi" is actually located behind another bridge, but most people think that

を二重橋だと思っています。二重アーチ構造のため「二重」であると間違って解釈されているのです。

　二重アーチ構造の石橋の後方にある本物の二重橋は、もともとは1614年に建設され、その後1964年に再建されたものです。1945年8月15日には、昭和天皇が、第二次世界大戦を終えるための日本の無条件降伏をラジオで放送しました。その時、このラジオ放送を聞こうと、この橋の前の広場に多くの人が集まり、天皇ご自身の降伏を宣言する御声を耳にし、深い悲しみと驚きにうちひしがれたのです。

大手門

　皇居の東側一帯、大手町は、現在では日本の金融の中心地となっています。東に広がる大手町に面している大手門が、江戸城の正門です。ここから皇居の中にはいれば、江戸時代の石造りの城郭の跡を歩きながら見ることができます。

　今は、昔の江戸城の内郭は、皇居東御苑（こうきょひがしぎょえん）と呼ばれ、江戸時代から残る建物もいくつか見ることができます。皇居東御苑には、皇居の北東にある平川門からもはいることができます。

the double-arched bridge visible in front is Nijubashi, as the word "*niju*" can be mistakenly interpreted to mean "double" — in this instance, double-arched.

The real Nijubashi, located behind the double-arched bridge in the foreground, was originally built in 1614 and rebuilt in 1964. On August 15, 1945, when the Showa Emperor's unconditional surrender ending World War II was broadcast over the radio, thousands of citizens gathered in the large grounds in front of Nijubashi to hear the broadcast, and were overcome with grief and astonishment to hear the Emperor's own voice proclaiming Japan's surrender.

Otemon gate

The financial sector of Japan today is located in an area east of the Imperial Palace known as Otemachi, and Otemon, facing in this easterly direction, was considered to be the main gate of the castle grounds. If you enter the palace grounds from here, you can see the stone foundations of the Edo-era castle as you walk through the grounds.

Nowadays, in the inner area of the old castle, called the Eastern Imperial Gardens, you can see buildings that have been preserved from the Edo era. This area is also accessible from the Hirakawa Gate, located on the northeastern side of the Imperial Palace.

二の丸公園

二の丸公園は、皇居の中、皇居東御苑にある伝統的な日本式の公園です。

もともとこの場所には、江戸時代に造られた庭園がありましたが、その後荒廃していました。それを、当時の設計資料などをもとに整備し、1968年に公開したものです。今では伝統的な日本庭園の美しさを満喫できる、理想的な憩いの場所として親しまれています。

桜田門

江戸城の南の入り口として知られる桜田門（さくらだもん）は、1663年に建設されました。桜田門は、大名が徳川将軍に参詣する際、江戸城に登城するときに通る門だったのです。

1860年3月24日、雪が降る中、井伊直弼（いいなおすけ）という大名が、この門の前で水戸藩士によって暗殺されました。井伊は、当時徳川幕府の中で最も重要な役職についており、また日本と海外との通商を促進しようとしていたことから、彼の死は徳川幕府が近く滅亡する凶兆と解釈されています。その8年後に起きた明治維新で、265年つづいた徳川幕府が一掃されたことは注目に値するでしょう。

Ninomaru garden

The Ninomaru Gardens are a traditional Japanese park located in the Eastern Imperial Gardens inside the Imperial Palace.

Although these gardens were built during the Edo era, they had fallen into disrepair, but they were repaired with the help of documents chronicling their original design, and were opened to the public in 1968. They are now seen as an ideal place in which to fully enjoy the distinctive beauty of the traditional Japanese garden.

Sakuradamon gate

The gate located at the south end of Edo Castle is called Sakuradamon. It was constructed in 1663 as the gate through which the nation's feudal lords were to enter when they came to pay homage to the Tokugawa Shogunate.

On a snowy day in 1860, on March 24, a feudal lord named Ii Naosuke was assassinated in front of this gate by a samurai from the Mito domain. As Ii held the most important position in the Tokugawa Shogunate, and had been publicly promoting an opening of relations between Japan and foreign countries, his death has been interpreted as a crucial sign that the Shogunate was near collapse. It should be noted that the Meiji Restoration of 1868, just eight years

田安門と北の丸公園

田安門は、1638年に造られました。田安門は、江戸城の北側に位置し、田安門からは北の丸公園にアクセスできます。あまり知られていませんが、北の丸公園は一般公開されており、そこには江戸城の北の丸天守閣の礎の跡が残り、とても印象的です。

さらに、この公園には驚くほど広い芝生の広場があり、木々が茂った小道で囲まれ、天気がいい日にはゆっくりとピクニックや散歩をするのにうってつけです。

北の丸公園は都心にあるにもかかわらず、騒音も車の往来もなく、堅牢な城壁と内堀によって守られているのです。この特別な空間のこと他人にしゃべらないようにして、来園者の雑踏から、この素晴らしい静粛を守りましょう！

霞ヶ関

霞ヶ関は、日本の政治の中枢となる役所や司法機関などが集まっている場所です。もともとは大名の江戸屋敷が多くあった地域で、東側には日比谷公園があります。この日比谷公園には、江戸時代から残

later, swept away and replaced the 265-year-long Tokugawa Shogunate.

Tayasumon gate and Kitanomaru Park

The Tayasumon Gate was constructed in 1638. Located at the northern end of the Edo Castle, this entrance lets you access Kitanomaru Park. Open to the public, although not widely known, Kitanomaru Park contains the impressive foundations remaining from the Kitanomaru fortress tower of Edo Castle.

In addition, the park has an unusually broad lawn surrounded by wooded paths, allowing for a stress-free picnic or stroll when the weather is good.

The park is situated in the heart of the city but with none of its sounds or traffic, protected by the massive castle walls and the Inner Moat. Try to keep this special space a secret, so that it retains its idyllic quietude without the bustle of too many visitors!

Kasumigaseki

Kasumigaseki is the area in which many of the central government's administrative ministries and offices, as well as offices of the judicial branch, are located. This is the area in which many of the feudal *daimyo* maintained their

されている当時の石壁を見ることができます。

　今では「霞ヶ関」という言葉は、日本政府の役所を意味する代名詞として使われています。霞ヶ関の近くにある「永田町」も、国会議事堂や議員会館のある場所を指す言葉として使われています。

official residences in Edo, and it is bordered on the east side by Hibiya Park, where you can still see some original stone walls that have been preserved from the Edo era.

The word "Kasumigaseki" is now used as shorthand to mean Japan's governmental offices, and the neighboring area called "Nagatacho" is where the National Diet (Parliament) building and the offices of Members of Parliament are located.

皇居とその周辺

▶▶▶ ワンセンテンスで説明する東京

江戸城

徳川幕府の中心は江戸城でした。

- [ ] The center of the Tokugawa Shogunate was Edo Castle.

江戸城は日本最大の城郭で、現在の皇居の場所にありました。

- [ ] Edo Castle was Japan's largest fortress, and it was located where the Imperial Palace is today.

江戸城を囲む内堀と外堀は、今でも残っています。

- [ ] The inner moat, closest to Edo Castle, and the outer moat around it still exist.

江戸城を囲む内堀と外堀の間には、身分の高い武士が屋敷を構えていました。

- [ ] Located between the inner and outer moats of Edo Castle were the estates of the highest ranking warriors.

江戸城のそばには大名屋敷が並び、その外側には商人や職人が住む一画がありました。

- [ ] Estates of lords were located alongside the castle, and beyond this were the quarters of merchants and artisans.

皇居

皇居は日本の天皇家の住む所です。

- [ ] The Imperial Palace is the home of Japan's Imperial family.

Tokyo in Single Sentences

皇居は東京の真ん中にあります。

☐ The Imperial Palace is located in the center of Tokyo.

皇居は千代田区にあり、近くには東京駅があります。

☐ The Imperial Palace is located near Tokyo Station, in Chiyoda Ward.

皇居の下は地下鉄が通っていません。

☐ No subway lines pass under the Imperial Palace.

皇居の敷地面積は、ニューヨークにあるセントラルパークのおよそ３倍です。

☐ The Imperial Palace grounds are about three times the size of New York City's Central Park.

皇居とその敷地の大部分は一般に公開されていません。

☐ The Imperial Palace and its grounds are mostly closed to the public.

皇居東御苑だけは一般に公開されています。

☐ Only the Imperial Palace East Gardens are open to the public.

皇居とその周辺

江戸城 ● 皇居

KEY WORD ✓

☐ inner moat	内堀
☐ outer moat	外堀
☐ quarters	一画

▶▶▶ ワンセンテンスで説明する東京

無料の皇居参観ツアーもあります。

☐ A free tour of the Imperial Palace is available.

皇居参観ツアーに参加しても、天皇家の住居を見学することはできません。

☐ Even if you take a tour of the Imperial Palace grounds, you cannot see the residence of the Imperial family.

皇居は堀に囲まれています。

☐ The Imperial Palace is surrounded by moats.

皇居周辺に残る堀や櫓（やぐら）は、江戸城の時代にまでさかのぼります。

☐ The moats and watchtowers around the Imperial Palace date to the time of Edo Castle.

1月2日と、天皇誕生日である12月23日には、皇族は皇居で国民の前に姿を現します。

☐ On January 2 and December 23, the Emperor's birthday, the Imperial family makes a public appearance at the palace.

皇居の周りは人気のジョギングコースです。

☐ There is a popular jogging course around the Imperial Palace grounds.

霞ヶ関と永田町

永田町と霞ヶ関は隣り合っており、千代田区にあります。

☐ Nagatacho and Kasumigaseki are neighboring districts in Chiyoda Ward.

永田町には、地下鉄の半蔵門線と有楽町線が停まります。

☐ Nagatacho is a stop on the Hanzomon and Yurakucho subway lines.

霞ヶ関には地下鉄の日比谷線、千代田線、丸ノ内線が停まります。

☐ Kasumigaseki is a stop on the Hibiya, Chiyoda, and Marunouchi subway lines.

国会議事堂と首相官邸は永田町にあります。

☐ The Japanese Diet and the Prime Minister's residence are located in Nagatacho.

法務省や外務省といった日本の省庁は、霞ヶ関に置かれています。

☐ Offices for Japan's Cabinet ministries, such as the Ministry of Justice and the Ministry of Foreign Affairs, are located in Kasumigaseki.

選出された政府は永田町を本拠とし、官僚は霞ヶ関を本拠としています。

☐ Nagatacho is the home of the elected government while Kasumigaseki is the home of the bureaucracy.

日本の最高裁判所は永田町の近くにあります。

☐ The Supreme Court of Japan is located near Nagatacho.

2-02 大手町・日本橋とその周辺

東京駅

　皇居の正面に向かって立つ東京駅は、日本の鉄道の中心となる駅です。日本で最初の鉄道は、1872年に建設され、新橋と港湾都市である横浜との間を結びました。後にこの鉄道は、東京駅まで延長されたのです。

　皇居に面した現在の中央駅舎は、大正時代に完成し、第二次世界大戦で一度破壊された赤レンガの駅舎を復元したものです。赤レンガの駅舎のある西側を丸の内口といい、その反対の東側を八重洲口といいます。

　東京駅は地下、地上、高架、さらに新幹線の駅に加え、地下鉄なども乗り入れている巨大な交通施設に発展しています。

Around Otemachi, Nihonbashi

Tokyo station

Tokyo Station — facing towards the Imperial Palace — is the central point for the railroad system in Japan. In 1872 Japan's first railway line was constructed, connecting Shinbashi to the port city of Yokohama, after which the line was extended to Tokyo Station.

Its distinctive red-brick building facing the Imperial Palace was built in 1914, and the present-day reconstruction was modeled on that building after its destruction during World War II. The western side with this red-brick station building is referred to as the Marunouchi Entrance, and the opposite, eastern side is called the Yaesu Entrance.

Tokyo Station has evolved into a truly enormous transportation facility, encompassing underground tracks, above-ground lines, the Shinkansen bullet train terminus, and several subway lines.

八重洲

　東京駅の東側の地区は、八重洲とよばれています。八重洲という地名は、江戸時代初頭に、この地域に住んでいたオランダ人の貿易商、ヤン・ヨーステンに由来します。

　ヤン・ヨーステンは、イギリス人のウイリアム・アダムス等、数名の乗組員と共に、1600年に九州に漂着すると、1603年に徳川幕府の下、将軍として日本を統一した徳川家康に捕らえられます。すると、二振りの帯刀を許された数少ない異国人の一人として将軍に信任され、ヨーステンは故郷のアムステルダムの運河を取り入れ、江戸の都市計画に大きく貢献した人物として知られています。

　これは、日比谷や日本橋といった地域が、当時江戸湾のほとりにあたり、埋め立て計画によって町がさらに東に向けて拡張されていた頃のことです。現在の八重洲は、どちらかというと商人の町として知られていますが、JRの線路を越えた皇居に近い大手町一帯は金融の町となっています。

Yaesu

The area directly east of Tokyo Station is known as Yaesu, named after a pre-Edo-era Dutch trader known as Jan Joosten (as his name was written into Japanese as "*Yan Yosuten*," then "*Yayoosu*") who lived in this neighborhood.

Joosten's ship had gone aground in Kyushu in 1600, but with some other crewmates, including Englishman William Adams, he was taken in by Tokugawa Ieyasu, later the Shogun who unified Japan under the Tokugawa Bakufu in 1603. In addition to becoming one of the few non-Japanese to wear two swords as a samurai, serving as a direct retainer to the Shogun, Joosten is also credited with helping design the early Edo capital, taking the idea of canals from Amsterdam, his hometown.

This was at a time when parts of Edo such as Hibiya and Nihonbashi were at the edge of Edo Bay, and the town was expanding eastward into the bay through a landfill program. Yaesu today is known more as a merchant's part of Tokyo, in contrast to the financial district in Otemachi across the JR tracks, closer to the Imperial Palace.

大手町

　大手町は、皇居の正門前にある東京屈指のビジネス街、金融街です。大手町の名前は、（現在の皇居にあたる）江戸城の正門の名前が大手門であったことに由来しています。

　江戸時代には、この大手町一帯には全国の大名の屋敷がありました。徳川幕府の政策で、大名は江戸に住居を構えることとされており、また自らの領地に戻るときには、家族を江戸に残すことを求められていたのです。

　戦後の目覚ましい高度成長期に、多くの商社や金融機関がこの大手町周辺に本社をおきました。大手町駅には5本もの地下鉄が乗り入れていますし、日本の中心である東京駅や日本橋にも、地下通路が通じています。そうしたことからも、大手町がいかに重要な拠点であるかが理解できるでしょう。

日本橋（橋）

　日本橋として知られるようになる最初の橋は、1603年に架けられました。当時は木製の橋でした。江戸幕府を開いた徳川家康が、日本各地と江戸とを

Otemachi

Located in front of the Imperial Palace's main gates, Otemachi is famous as Tokyo's main business and financial center. It takes its name from the major "Otemon" gate to Edo Castle.

During the Edo era many of the feudal lords from across Japan maintained their official residences in the Otemachi area (as they were required to reside in Edo, or leave their families in Edo when the lords would return to their feudal domains, as a means of political control by the Tokugawa Shogunate).

It was during the years of Japan's rapid economic growth following World War II that many of the major trading houses and financial institutions set up their headquarters in this Otemachi district. You can get a sense of how important a hub it is, as five subway lines converge with stations in Otemachi, and there are underground passages leading to Japan's center — Tokyo Station and Nihonbashi — from Otemachi.

Nihonbashi (bridge)

The first bridge erected in what came to be known as Nihonbashi was built in 1603, and was constructed out of wood. In order to connect the new capital with the rest

結ぶために5つの街道の整備を命じました。日本橋はその起点となったところです。以来、現代まで日本橋は日本の道路網の起点となっています。現在の日本橋は、100年以上前の1911年に架けられたもので、1603年以来、11代目の橋となります。

日本橋（地名）

日本橋は、橋の名前とは別に、橋の周辺一帯の街を指す地名でもあります。日本銀行などの金融機関の多くがこの近くにあります。大手の百貨店や製薬会社などのオフィスも並んでいます。

この一帯は江戸時代以降、重要性が高まり、伝統的な小物を扱う店の他に、海苔や鰹節など、日本食には欠かすことのできない食材を扱う老舗も並んでいます。それは、1923年の関東大震災まで、橋のそばに魚市場があった名残でもあるのです。

of Japan, Tokugawa Ieyasu, who founded the military Shogunate, mandated that five major arterial routes be built. These five roads to and from the capital would all meet in Nihonbashi, and from that time to the present Nihonbashi has served as "Mile Zero" for any location in Japan. The present bridge — the eleventh in its location since 1603 — was constructed in 1911, more than 100 years ago.

Nihonbashi (place name)

In addition to being the name of the bridge itself, Nihonbashi also refers to the surrounding neighborhood. Quite a few financial institutions are located nearby, such as the Bank of Japan building. Large department stores are also here, as well as numerous office buildings that house some of Japan's major pharmaceutical firms and many other businesses.

As an outgrowth of the area's importance dating from the Edo era, there are quite a few shops that carry traditional Japanese goods, and numerous historical shops specializing in food products — such as seaweed and bonito fish flakes — that are essential ingredients in Japanese cuisine. This would explain why there was also a major fish market located next to the bridge, until it was destroyed in the Great Kanto Earthquake of 1923.

三越百貨店

　日本橋にある三越百貨店は、日本で最も伝統のある百貨店で、江戸時代は越後屋と呼ばれ、1673年に呉服屋として創業しました。

　三越は銀座をはじめ、日本全国にいくつかの店舗があるほか、海外の数ヵ国にも展開しています。三越はまさに日本橋を代表する百貨店として知られています。創業以来、旗艦店は日本橋にあるのです。

小伝馬町

　日比谷線に小伝馬町という駅があります。日本橋からもそう遠くないこの街には、江戸時代には牢獄がありました。

　江戸時代には警察機関と司法機関が同じ組織の中にあって、町奉行と呼ばれていました。逮捕された被疑者は、小伝馬町に送られ、奉行所の取り調べを受け、判決を待っていたのです。

Mitsukoshi department store

Having been established in 1673 as a clothing store, and known during the Edo era as "Echigoya," Mitsukoshi in Nihonbashi is the department store with the deepest historical tradition in Japan.

With a branch in the nearby Ginza district, several branches elsewhere across Japan and an international presence with stores in several foreign countries, Mitsukoshi is recognized in Japan as truly representing Nihonbashi, where it originated and still maintains its main store.

Kodenmacho

There is a station on the Hibiya line called Kodenmacho, a neighborhood not too distant from Nihonbashi where a prison had been located during the Edo era.

At that time both the law enforcement agencies and the judicial branch were in the same organization, called the Town Magistrate. People arrested on suspicion of crimes were sent to Kodenmacho where they were investigated by the Magistrate and awaited their verdict.

東京駅とその周辺

東京駅は東京の真ん中、千代田区にあります。

☐ Tokyo Station is located in Chiyoda Ward in central Tokyo.

東京駅は1914年に建てられ、東京の要となる鉄道駅です。

☐ Tokyo Station, built in 1914, is Tokyo's principal train station.

東京駅の元々の本屋は丸の内側に面しています。

☐ The original Tokyo Station building faces the Marunouchi neighborhood.

丸の内は東京の主要なビジネス街のひとつです。

☐ Marunouchi is one of Tokyo's main business districts.

東京駅の裏側は現代的な超高層ビルで、八重洲地区に面しています。

☐ The back of Tokyo Station, which is a modern skyscraper, faces the Yaesu neighborhood.

毎日3000本以上の列車が東京駅を通過しています。

☐ More than 3,000 trains pass through Tokyo Station every day.

東京駅は新幹線の終着駅です。

☐ Tokyo Station is the terminus for the Shinkansen.

Tokyo in Single Sentences

東京駅の地下街にはたくさんの店やレストランがあります。

- [ ] There are many shops and restaurants in the basement of Tokyo Station.

東京駅の周りにはたくさんのオフィスビルやホテルがあります。

- [ ] There are many office buildings and hotels around Tokyo Station.

東京駅は皇居の真東に位置しています。

- [ ] Tokyo Station is located just east of the Imperial Palace.

19世紀の終わりに、丸の内には西洋風の建物がたくさん建てられ、「ロンドンタウン」の異名をとるほどでした。

- [ ] In the late nineteenth century many Western-style buildings were built in Marunouchi, which earned it the nickname "Londontown."

丸ビルや新丸ビルといった丸の内のオフィスビルの多くには、レストランや小売店が入っています。

- [ ] Many of Maruouchi's office buildings, such as the *Maru Biru* and the *Shin-Maru Biru*, also contain restaurants and shops.

大手町・日本橋とその周辺

東京駅とその周辺

近年、無数のレストランや小売店が加わったことにより、丸の内はよりおしゃれな地域へ変わってきています。

☐ With the addition of numerous restaurants and shops in recent years, Marunouchi has become a more fashionable neighborhood.

大手町・日本橋とその周辺

大手町は千代田区にある地域です。

☐ Otemachi is a neighborhood in Chiyoda Ward.

大手町は皇居の近くに位置しています。

☐ Otemachi is located near the Imperial Palace.

大手町には、千代田線、半蔵門線、丸ノ内線、東西線、三田線の5路線の地下鉄が通っています。

☐ Five subway lines pass through Otemachi's subway station: the Chiyoda, Hanzomon, Marunouchi, Tozai and Mita lines.

Tokyo in Single Sentences

大手町には日本の大企業の本社がいくつも置かれており、金融の中心となる重要な地域です。

☐ Otemachi is a key financial center, and many of Japan's biggest companies have their headquarters in Otemachi.

日本橋は中央区にある地域です。

☐ Nihonbashi is a neighborhood in Chuo Ward.

日本橋は銀座の北、大手町の東に位置しています。

☐ Nihonbashi is located north of Ginza and east of Otemachi.

日本橋には地下鉄銀座線、東西線、都営浅草線が停まります。

☐ Nihonbashi is a stop on the Ginza, Tozai and Toei-Asakusa subway lines.

日本橋とは、「日本の橋」という意味で、地域内に同名の橋があります。

☐ Nihonbashi means "Japan Bridge," and there is a bridge of the same name in the neighborhood.

▶▶▶ ワンセンテンスで説明する東京

その橋は日本橋川に架かっており、17世紀初頭から存続しています。

- [ ] The bridge crosses the Nihonbashi River and has existed since the beginning of the seventeenth century.

その橋は元来、東京の中心と考えられ、すべての距離はここから測定されています。

- [ ] The bridge is traditionally considered to be the center point of Tokyo, and all distances are measured from it.

現在架かっている橋は1911年に建造されたもので、石造りです。

- [ ] The current bridge, built in 1911, is made of stone.

現在は上を高速道路が走っているために、橋はあまり目立ちません。

- [ ] The bridge is easy to miss, because an expressway now runs above it.

江戸時代の日本橋は、町人が住む活気にあふれた商業地区でした。

- [ ] During the Edo era Nihonbashi was a lively business district for the townspeople.

17世紀、もとは呉服店であった三越が日本最初のデパートを日本橋にオープンしました。

- [ ] The dry-goods shop that would become Japan's first department store, Mitsukoshi, opened in Nihonbashi in the seventeenth century.

東京の魚市場はもとは日本橋にあり、川岸では日本橋川を上ってくる漁船が魚の荷揚げをしていました。

- [ ] Tokyo's fish market was originally located in Nihonbashi, and fishing boats would come up the Nihonbashi River to deposit their goods on the banks.

日本橋には、昔の魚河岸から続く伝統食品を商う老舗がたくさんあります。

- [ ] There are many old shops in Nihonbashi selling traditional foodstuffs that date back to the days of the old fish market.

銀座とその周辺

銀座

　銀座は世界的に知られた東京のショッピング街であることは言うまでもありません。中央通りに沿って、世界的に名の知れたブランドショップ、ブティック、百貨店が並んでいます。少しそれて小さな路地にはいると、派手な看板を出した、数え切れない数のレストランやナイトクラブ、さらには娯楽スポットが軒を連ねています。

　銀座という名前は、江戸時代この一帯に銀の貨幣を鋳造する場所があったことに由来しています。

　今日、銀座の中心となる銀座4丁目交差点付近は、日本でも最も地価の高い場所として知られています。17世紀初頭まで、この地域は現在の東京湾に面した砂浜でした。1612年頃から、この辺り一帯がどんどん埋め立てられ、もはや銀座は海岸からは遠くなってしまいました。明治時代になると、銀座は赤レンガが並ぶ西欧風の通りとして整備され、東京の商業活動の中心地として発展したのです。

Around Ginza

Ginza

It goes without saying that Ginza is known the world over as Tokyo's premier shopping district. Globally recognized brand shops, boutiques and department stores line the main Chuo-dori street, while the alleys and side streets are lined with the bright signs of countless restaurants, nightclubs and other entertainment spots.

Ginza takes its name from the fact that during the Edo era this was the part of town where silver-smithing was concentrated ("*gin*" is the Japanese word for silver), including the minting of silver coins.

Nowadays, the area surrounding the central Ginza 4-chome intersection is known for having the highest property costs in all of Japan. Back then, the Ginza area was where the town of Edo met the waters of Edo Bay, before landfill efforts beginning in 1612 gradually extended the city farther into the Bay, now quite a distance from Ginza. It was during the Meiji era that Ginza began to be transformed into Japan's center of commercial activity, when its main street was lined with red-brick Western-style buildings.

和光ビル

　銀座4丁目の交差点角には、和光のビルがあります。和光ビルは、人や車の雑踏を見下ろす時計台のビルとして知られています。もともとはセイコーの名前で知られる服部時計店の小売店があった場所で、このビルは1881年に建てられ、1932年に現在のビルに建て替えられました。

　第二次世界大戦の東京大空襲の被害も免れ、戦後になると日本を占領したGHQのPX（米軍の売店）にもなりました。現在和光は銀座を象徴する時計店、宝飾店として知られています。

銀座すずらん通り

　銀座すずらん通りは、中央通りと平行して南北に走る銀座の通りの一つです。夜になってこの有名な銀座の通りを歩けば、細いビルの上の階まで無数のネオンサインがあることに気がつきます。

　このネオンサインはすべて日本語でスナックと呼ばれるメンバー制クラブの看板なのです。スナックは、ビジネスマンがお客の接待に使う典型的な場所です。ほかにも仲間とカラオケを楽しむために集まる場所で、「ノミニケーション」を大切にする日本のビジネス文化の一面を象徴する場所といえましょう。

Wako Building

Located at the central intersection of Ginza 4-chome is the Wako Building, well known for the clock tower on its roof overlooking the bustle of people and traffic below. Originally known by the name Seiko, this was the location of the Hattori Watch Shop, built in 1881 and rebuilt in 1932 in its present shape as the Wako Building.

Escaping damage in the bombing of Tokyo during World War II, the building even served as the PX (Post Exchange) for GHQ. Today, the Wako Building is clearly a landmark of Ginza, and houses a famous time-piece and jewelry shop on its prime premises.

Ginza Suzuran Street

A street that runs north-south in Ginza parallel to the main Chuo-dori is called Ginza Suzuran Street. When you walk down this rather well-known Ginza side street at night, what catches your eye is the sight of the many neon-lit signs, climbing the narrow buildings to their top floors.

All these signs are advertising "members-only clubs" known in Japanese as "snacks," where businessmen typically invite their guests for drinks or a relaxed evening of *karaoke*. We might call this area of clubs a good example of Japanese business culture, where casual communication

歌舞伎座

　銀座のすぐ東側、東銀座には、日本の伝統芸能として知られる歌舞伎を上演する歌舞伎座があります。

　独特な節回しや所作に従って繰り広げられる歌舞伎は、江戸時代以降、大阪や京都から伝わり、そして江戸で流行しました。

　当時、歌舞伎は猥雑だということで、幕府は女性が歌舞伎役者になることを禁じていました。そのため、今でも、女性の役であっても、舞台に立つのはすべて男性だけなのです。女性の役を演じる男性の役者は女形と呼ばれています。

　和風のオペラとして知られる歌舞伎を楽しんでもらおうと、歌舞伎座では一幕だけを立ち見できる場所も設けられています。また、歌舞伎の英訳を聞けるオーディオセットも用意されています。歌舞伎は歌舞伎座の他に、皇居の西側にある国立劇場でも楽しむことができます。

takes place over drinks, which has led to a new bilingual term, "nomunication" (in which the prefix "*nomu*" means "to drink," and is combined with "communication").

Kabukiza Theater

In a section of town just east of Ginza, appropriately called "Higashi (East) Ginza," you will find the Kabukiza, a theater in which Japan's traditional theatrical art known as kabuki is performed.

With its distinctive rhythm, voice intonations, and theatrical postures (*shosa* or *kata*) that capture the audience's enthusiastic attention, kabuki originated in the Osaka and Kyoto area during the Edo era, and then spread to Edo.

As kabuki was considered scandalous at the time, the Tokugawa Bakufu prohibited women from acting in kabuki plays, so to this day all the actors on stage, even in women's roles, are male. The men who play the part of women are called *onnagata* (*onna* is one of the words in Japanese meaning "woman").

Considered a Japanese-styled opera, kabuki can be enjoyed in the Kabukiza for even a single act in the standing section, and an audio headphone permits audiences to understand the play in English. In addition to shows at the Kabukiza, kabuki can also be seen in the National Theater located on the western side of the Imperial Palace grounds.

築地

世界最大の魚市場をはじめとした食品市場といえば、まっさきに築地魚市場を思い浮かべることでしょう。残念ながら、海外の観光客にも人気のあった築地の魚市場も、2016年11月には豊洲に移転します。

ただ、築地市場の周辺には、寿司屋をはじめとした、さまざまな和食を楽しめる店やレストランがあり、今後もグルメを楽しむ人々で賑わい続けるかもしれません。

築地に魚市場が移動してきたのは、1923年に関東大震災がおきた後のことでした。元は日本橋にあった魚河岸なのですが、地震と火事によって、壊滅的な被害を受けてしまったのです。

新橋

新橋は東京駅から山手線で南へ2つ目の駅に位置し、もう1つ都心として重要なことを付け加えるとすれば、それは新橋は今やサラリーマンの街という評判を得ていることです。

駅から伸びる路地沿いには、数えきれないほどの居酒屋や飲食店が立ち並び――また、そのどれもが安いのです――帰宅途中のサラ

Tsukiji

Imagine the world's largest seafood market, also selling a wide range of other foods, and you think immediately of the famous Tsukiji Fish Market. To the dismay of many tourists from around the world, in November 2016 the market will be moving to a new location in Toyosu.

In the neighborhood around the market are countless sushi shops and restaurants famous for Japanese cuisine, so it is possible that this area will likely still bustle with those seeking out great gourmet spots to eat.

The fish market's move to Tsukiji in the first place took place after the 1923 Great Kanto Earthquake, as the earlier and famous Nihonbashi Fish Market was damaged beyond repair in that major earthquake and fire.

Shinbashi

Located just two short stops south of Tokyo Station on the Yamanote line, and at one point more important as a city-center, Shinbashi now has the reputation of being a salaried workers' part of town.

In the alleys spreading out from the station are countless *izakaya* drinking spots and restaurants — many of them quite modestly priced — catering to businessmen stopping off with clients, with colleagues, or alone on the way home

リーマンたちが取引先や同僚と一緒に、あるいは一人で立ち寄って、仕事終わりの杯を傾け、つまみに舌鼓を打つのです。

新橋には複数の地下鉄や高架線ゆりかもめが、南北を結ぶJRの路線とともに乗り入れているので、電車の乗り換えを利用して、ちょっと一杯引っかけるにはもってこいの場所なのです。

有楽町

銀座の西側、山手線をはさんで向こう側に有楽町の街が広がっています。

高級な銀座のクラブやレストランとは対照的に、ガード下にはカジュアルで安い居酒屋、飲食店などが並んでいます。

北に向かって歩くと、有楽町と東京駅の間は、丸の内という一画になります。そこには、東京の堂々たる戦後の経済復興を象徴するようなビルがそびえ立っています。しかし、近年この地区も変貌を遂げようとしています。有楽町の「仲通り」や脇道には、多数の高級ブティックや小売店、レストランが立ち並び、皇居や日比谷公園を見下ろすペニンシュラ・ホテルのような高級物件が現れました。

from the office, eager to share a few drinks or a snack at the end of the workday.

It helps that several subway lines and the elevated Yurikamome train line, along with the JR north-south train lines, crisscross Shinbashi, making it a convenient place to stop off for a sip while changing trains.

Yurakucho

To the west of Ginza and on the other side of the JR Yamanote line tracks you will find the Yurakucho district.

In some contrast to the upscale Ginza clubs and restaurants, nestled under the tracks near Yurakucho Station are an assortment of very casual and economical *izakaya*-style pubs and eateries.

Walking north, in the area between Yurakucho and Tokyo Station called Marunouchi you will notice buildings that made this district truly representative of Tokyo's stately postwar business atmosphere. The area has been transformed in recent years, though, with numerous high-end boutiques, shops and restaurants now lining Yurakucho's "Naka-dori" and side streets, and with upscale properties such as the Peninsula Hotel, which overlooks the Imperial Palace and Hibiya Park.

三菱一号館ミュージアム

　モダンなオフィスビルが新しく立ち並んだ有楽町一帯から、北に向かって東京駅の丸ノ内側方面に歩くと、丸ノ内ブリックスクエアと呼ばれるモダンな中庭のある古風な建物が目をひきます。その建物の後ろ側はオフィスタワーですが、その南東の角に三菱一号館美術館があります。

　この建物はイギリスの建築家ジョシア・コンダーによって設計され、1894年にこの地に建てられた旧館の青写真と材料を使って、忠実に復元されたものです。美術館では西欧と日本のアートを交替で展示しています。威厳のある高い天井の「カフェ1984」は、三菱銀行の最初の支店となった場所を使用していますが、通りからも入れます。美術館のツアーを申し分ないものにしてくれます。

Mitsubishi Ichigokan Museum

Among the stylishly rebuilt buildings in the Yurakucho area stretching north to the Marunouchi side of Tokyo Station, one that has retained an impressive historic look while creating a modern urban garden in its courtyard is the Marunouchi Brick Square, with an office tower overlooking the Mitsubishi Ichigokan Museum located on its southeast corner.

A faithful recreation — using the blueprints and materials from the original Mitsubishi Ichigokan, designed by the British architect Josiah Conder and built here in 1894 — the museum rotates exhibits of Western and Japanese art. "Cafe 1894," with its stately, soaring ceiling, is housed in the restored first branch of the Mitsubishi Bank, and though accessible from the street as well, complements a tour of the museum nicely.

伝統芸術

浮世絵など広く知られる伝統芸術は、江戸時代に始まりました。

- [ ] Woodblock prints, called ukiyo-e, are a well-known traditional art that originated in the Edo era.

歌舞伎は江戸時代に発展した舞台芸術です。

- [ ] Kabuki is a form of performing art that developed during the Edo era.

歌舞伎では、女性の役柄も含め、全て男性が演じます。

- [ ] In kabuki performances men play all the roles, even the female ones.

浄瑠璃は、人形劇として江戸時代に江戸や大阪で流行しました。

- [ ] *Joruri* was a form of puppet theater popular in Edo and Osaka during the Edo era.

歌舞伎や浄瑠璃の上演に合わせ、それを支える三味線や鼓などの音楽芸術も流行しました。

- [ ] Musical arts were spread through kabuki and *joruri*, both of which used *shamisen* and drums.

三味線は、バチで弦をならして弾く、日本の伝統的な弦楽器です。

- [ ] The *shamisen*, the strings of which are plucked with a plectrum, is a traditional Japanese instrument.

Tokyo in Single Sentences

江戸時代には、舞台芸術の隆盛とともに、戯曲や小説が数多く出版されました。

☐ The performing arts flourished during the Edo era, and numerous plays and novels were published as well.

銀座とその周辺

Track 43

銀座は中央区にあります。

☐ Ginza is a neighborhood in Chuo Ward.

銀座には銀座線、日比谷線、丸ノ内線などの地下鉄が停まります。

☐ Ginza is a stop on the Ginza, Hibiya, and Marunouchi subway lines.

銀座の隣りには新橋というビジネス街があります。

☐ Ginza neighbors the business district of Shinbashi.

銀座はショッピングや娯楽の街です。

☐ Ginza is a shopping and entertainment district.

KEY WORD ✓

☐ performing arts　　　舞台芸術
☐ puppet theater　　　人形劇

▶▶▶ ワンセンテンスで説明する東京

銀座は東京でも最も地価の高いところです。

☐ Ginza has some of the most expensive real estate in Tokyo.

銀座には三越などいくつかの百貨店があり、シャネルのようなブランドショップもあります。

☐ Ginza has department stores such as Mitsukoshi, and designer boutiques for brands like Chanel.

銀座は東京でも最も高価なレストランやバーのある街です。

☐ Ginza has some of the most expensive restaurants and bars in the city.

銀座には、一人前で数百ドルもする寿司屋があります。

☐ In Ginza, a sushi dinner for one person can cost several hundred dollars.

中央通りは、銀座のメインストリートです。

☐ Chuo Street is the main street in Ginza.

週末の午後、中央通りは車の通行を禁じ、歩行者天国になります。

☐ Chuo Street is closed to cars on weekend afternoons, turning it into a so-called "pedestrian heaven."

銀座にはおしゃれをしてぶらぶら歩いている人がたくさんいます。

☐ You can see many fashionably dressed people strolling around Ginza.

Tokyo in Single Sentences

明治時代、銀座には洋風のレンガ建築が並んでいました。

☐ During the Meiji period many Western-style brick buildings were built in Ginza.

西欧から新たに入ってくるファッションや食は、銀座から東京中に広がりました。

☐ Many new Western-style fashions and foods were introduced to Tokyo for the first time in Ginza.

新橋と有楽町、そして日比谷

Track 44

新橋と有楽町は山手線の隣同士の駅です。

☐ Shinbashi and Yurakucho are neighboring stops on the Yamanote Line.

新橋と有楽町は東京の都心にあります。

☐ Shinbashi and Yurakucho are located in central Tokyo.

新橋も有楽町も共にビジネス街です。

☐ Shinbashi and Yurakucho are both business districts.

KEY WORD

☐ pedestrian heaven　　歩行者天国
☐ stroll around　　ぶらぶら歩く

▶▶▶ ワンセンテンスで説明する東京

1872年、日本初の鉄道が横浜と新橋間で開通しました。

☐ In 1872, Japan's first railway connected Yokohama with Shinbashi.

新橋駅は1914年に東京駅ができるまで、東京の基幹駅でした。

☐ Shinbashi Station was the city's principal train station until Tokyo Station opened in 1914.

新橋と有楽町には「サラリーマン」というホワイトカラーの人が大勢います。

☐ You can see many white-collar workers, called "salarymen," in Shinbashi and Yurakucho.

有楽町は仕事帰りのサラリーマンが集まる人気のスポットです。

☐ Yurakucho is a popular hangout for salarymen after work.

有楽町の山手線の高架下には焼き鳥屋や居酒屋が立ち並んでいます。

☐ There are many *yakitori* restaurants and Japanese-style pubs under the Yamanote Line train tracks in Yurakucho.

日比谷は千代田区にある地区です。

☐ Hibiya is a neighborhood in Chiyoda Ward.

日比谷は銀座と霞が関の間にあります。

☐ Hibiya is located between Ginza and Kasumigaseki.

日比谷には地下鉄日比谷線、千代田線、三田線が停まります。

☐ Hibiya is a stop on the Hibiya, Chiyoda and Mita subway lines.

Tokyo in Single Sentences

東京初の西洋風ホテルである帝国ホテルは、1890年に日比谷で開業しました。

☐ Tokyo's first Western-style hotel, the Imperial Hotel, opened in Hibiya in 1890.

1903年にオープンした日比谷公園は、東京で最も古い公園の一つです。

☐ Hibiya Park, which opened in 1903, is one of Tokyo's oldest public parks.

銀座とその周辺

新橋と有楽町、そして日比谷

KEY WORD ✓

☐ Japanese-style pub　　居酒屋

179

2-04 浅草とその周辺

浅草

　浅草は、下町を代表する古い趣のある街で、東京で最も人気のある観光地の一つです。江戸時代から、芝居小屋や遊興施設が狭い路地に軒を連ねた歓楽街として知られ、浅草寺の門前町としても栄えました。赤い提灯が下がる有名な門から境内へつづく参道は、人々で埋まり、食べ物や手工芸品を売る露店が軒を連ねています。

　今では、浅草寺の周辺を中心に、外国人観光客も多く訪れ、比較的手頃な値段でお土産を買うことのできる場所としても人気があるのです。一方で、料理屋、遊園地、民芸品などの店が集まり、混雑する露店では昔ながらの雰囲気を楽しむことができ、浅草は古風な趣のある歓楽街として、観光客をひきつけるのです。

浅草寺

　浅草の象徴ともいわれる浅草寺は、東京で最も古い寺で、645年に建立されました。観音菩薩を祀って

Around Asakusa

Asakusa

One of the most popular tourist destinations in Tokyo today is the old neighborhood of Asakusa. It was well known from the Edo era as an entertainment district, with playhouses and pleasure-quarter facilities lining its narrow alleys. It also prospered from its proximity to the Senso-ji Temple, with its famous gate, hanging red lantern, and crowded street lined with stalls selling food and handicrafts.

Today, the area surrounding Senso-ji is a popular destination for countless visitors from overseas, who are attracted in part by the chance to buy souvenirs from Japan at reasonable prices while reveling in the historic atmosphere of a bustling street-stall market, with its restaurants, folk-craft shops, and the feel of a quaint entertainment district.

Sensoji Temple

The symbol of the Asakusa area is Senso-ji, the oldest Buddhist temple in Tokyo, dating back to 645 A.D. The

います。言い伝えによると、菩薩は628年に漁師によって隅田川で発見されたことになっています。観音様は、情け深さの象徴であり、人間が悟りを開くように啓蒙してくれるのです。

　浅草寺には、内外を問わず、膨大な数の観光客が訪れますが、本尊は秘仏とされ、一般には公開されていません。浅草寺は浅草の中心に位置し、10世紀には寺院としての伽藍が整えられたといわれています。表参道の入り口にある雷門から本堂や五重塔まで、参拝者が往来し、壁に沿って林立する「仲見世」という小売店では土産物や特産物を扱い、門前町を成しています。

　本堂や五重の塔は第二次世界大戦で焼失したため、戦後に再建されたものですが、東京を訪れた時には見逃すことないよう！

合羽橋商店街

　浅草のそばにある合羽橋商店街は、調理道具やレストラン用品を扱う店がずらりとならぶ場所として知られています。和食が世界的にブームとなり認知

temple houses a statue of the Bodhisattva Kannon, which according to legend was discovered by fishermen in the nearby Sumida River in 628 A.D., Kannon being symbolic of a compassionate, enlightened one devoted to helping all humans reach their own enlightenment.

Senso-ji has an enormous number of visitors from both Japan and abroad, but as a treasured Buddhist relic, the main Kannon statue itself is not open for public view. Senso-ji is located in the center of Asakusa, and it is said that the full array of its temple buildings, including a monastery, was in place by the tenth century. From the main Kaminari-mon entrance of the compound to the temple and its stunning five-storied pagoda, pilgrims traverse a bustling street lined wall-to-wall with *nakamise* shops selling souvenirs and local food in the *Monzen-machi* — a small town unto itself within the precincts of the temple.

Although the temple and pagoda, together with this bustling neighborhood, were destroyed during WWII bombings, they were rebuilt shortly after that, and are not to be missed when you visit Tokyo today.

Kappabashi shopping street

Very close to Asakusa is a shopping street called Kappabashi, famous for its many shops selling cooking utensils and goods used in the restaurant business. With the global boom

されるようになり、今やユネスコの無形文化遺産に指定されたことにより、国内や海外から多くの人がこの場所を訪れ、和包丁など、和食用の調理道具を買い求めます。

日本のレストランなどで注文できるものを通行人にリアルに見せるために、ショーケースに飾られたプラスチックで作った食品サンプルなども合羽橋で人気の商品です。

東京スカイツリー

浅草からもそう遠くない押上地区にある東京スカイツリーは、634メートルの高さを誇る世界で最も高い電波塔です。2012年に周辺のショッピングモールと共に完成しました。展望台からは東京のみならず、関東を一望できます。

and the recognition of Japanese cuisine, now on UNESCO's Intangible Cultural Heritage list, many Japanese shoppers and those from abroad visit the Kappabashi district to search for utensils unique to making Japanese food, including distinctive Japanese kitchen knives.

Another popular item available in Kappabashi is the plastic food models you may have seen in restaurant display windows, giving passersby a very real visual feel for what can be ordered inside.

Tokyo Skytree

Not far from the Asakusa area, in a neighborhood called Oshiage, is the world's tallest free-standing communications tower, Tokyo Skytree, rising to an impressive 634 meters (2,080 feet). Completed in 2012 and opened together with a shopping mall at its base, Skytree offers an unparalleled view from its observation decks not only of the whole of metropolitan Tokyo, but of the entire Kanto Plain as well.

▶▶▶ ワンセンテンスで説明する東京

浅草

浅草は、東京の北東部にある地区です。
- [ ] Asakusa is a neighborhood on the northeast side of Tokyo.

浅草は、台東区にある地区です。
- [ ] Asakusa is a neighborhood in Taito Ward.

浅草は、隅田川の西側にあります。
- [ ] Asakusa is located on the west bank of the Sumida River.

隅田川は東京でもっともよく知られた川です。
- [ ] The Sumida River is Tokyo's most famous river.

浅草から、隅田川からボートで、浜離宮やお台場に行くことができます。
- [ ] From Asakusa you can take a boat down the Sumida River to Hama Rikyu or Odaiba.

浅草は地下鉄銀座線の終着駅です。
- [ ] Asakusa is the terminal of the Ginza subway line.

浅草は、東京の中でもっとも有名な地区の一つです。
- [ ] Asakusa is one of Tokyo's most famous neighborhoods.

浅草には、東京で最も有名な浅草寺という寺があります。
- [ ] Asakusa is the home of Senso-ji, Tokyo's most famous temple.

Tokyo in Single Sentences

浅草寺があることで浅草は旅行者にとって、人気のスポットになっています。

☐ Thanks to the temple Senso-ji, Asakusa is a popular destination for tourists.

東京で最大の伝統的な祭り、三社祭りは浅草で行われます。

☐ Tokyo's biggest traditional festival, the Sanja Matsuri, takes place in Asakusa.

上野や日本橋と同じく、浅草も江戸時代までその起源を遡ることができます。

☐ Like Ueno and Nihonbashi, Asakusa is a neighborhood that has its roots in the Edo era.

浅草は、東京の中でも昔ながらの情緒の残る地区の一つです。

☐ Asakusa is one of the neighborhoods in Tokyo that has maintained an old-fashioned atmosphere.

20世紀初め頃、浅草は映画館やカフェ、そしてキャバレーの並ぶ歓楽街でした。

☐ In the early twentieth century Asakusa was an entertainment district filled with cinemas, cafés, and cabarets.

20世紀初め頃、浅草は東京のモンマルトルと言われていました。

☐ In the early twentieth century Asakusa was known as the Montmartre of Tokyo.

▶▶▶ ワンセンテンスで説明する東京

ノーベル文学賞を受賞した川端康成が、1930年代に『浅草紅団』という浅草についての小説を執筆しています。

☐ Yasunari Kawabata, the Nobel Prize—winning author, wrote a book about Asakusa in the 1930s called *The Scarlet Gang of Asakusa*.

花やしきは、浅草にあって日本で最も古い遊園地です。

☐ Japan's oldest amusement park, Hanayashiki, is located in Asakusa.

浅草では昔ながらの人力車に乗ることができます。

☐ You can ride in a traditional rickshaw in Asakusa.

浅草は昔から職人たちが住む地区です。

☐ Asakusa was traditionally a neighborhood where craftsmen lived.

浅草には、伝統工芸品を売る店があります。

☐ In Asakusa you can find stores selling traditional crafts.

浅草には江戸時代から営業を続ける料理屋があります。

☐ There are restaurants in Asakusa that have been in business since the Edo era.

浅草の近くの合羽橋という通りには、プラスチック製の料理サンプルなど、料理店向けの道具を売る店が並んでいます。

☐ Near Asakusa there is a street called Kappabashi that sells supplies for restaurants, including plastic food models.

浅草寺

浅草寺は仏教の寺です。

☐ Senso-ji is a Buddhist temple.

浅草寺は隅田川のそば、浅草にあります。

☐ Senso-ji is located in Asakusa, next to the Sumida River.

浅草寺は、東京都内で最古の寺であり、誰もが知っています。

☐ Senso-ji is Tokyo's oldest and most recognizable temple.

伝承によると、浅草寺は7世紀に創建されました。

☐ According to legend, Senso-ji was founded in the seventh century.

伝承によると、二人の兄弟が隅田川で仏像を見つけ、それを祀るために寺を建てたといわれています。

☐ According to legend, two brothers found a Buddhist statue in the Sumida River and built a temple to house the statue.

浅草とその周辺

浅草●浅草寺

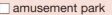

☐ amusement park　　遊園地
☐ traditional craft　　伝統工芸品

▶▶▶ ワンセンテンスで説明する東京

浅草寺への入り口には、雷門という大きな赤い門があります。

☐ At the entrance to Senso-ji there is a big red gate called Kaminarimon, which means "Thunder Gate."

門と本堂との間には、仲見世通りという土産物屋が並ぶ通りがあります。

☐ A street called Nakamise Street, lined with souvenir shops, runs from the gate to the main temple.

浅草寺にお参りをする人は、香の煙を体にかける習慣があります。

☐ It is a popular custom for visitors to Senso-ji to wave incense over their bodies.

浅草寺の参拝客がおみくじという紙の占いを買うのは、よく見かける光景です。

☐ It is a popular custom for visitors to Senso-ji to get a paper fortune, called an "*omikuji*."

毎年、3000万人の人が浅草寺を訪れます。

☐ Around 30 million people visit Senso-ji every year.

浅草寺は東京の最大の観光地で、いつも人でいっぱいです。

☐ Since Senso-ji is one of Tokyo's biggest tourist attractions, it can get very crowded.

浅草寺は入場無料です。

☐ Senso-ji is free to enter.

Tokyo in Single Sentences

東京スカイツリー

東京スカイツリーは高さ634メートルの放送用の電波塔です。

☐ Tokyo Skytree is a 634-meter-tall broadcasting tower.

東京スカイツリーは、世界でも最も高い自立式タワーです。

☐ Tokyo Skytree is the world's tallest freestanding tower.

東京スカイツリーは2012年に完成しました。

☐ Tokyo Skytree was completed in 2012.

東京スカイツリーは東京の東側にあり名所となっています。

☐ Tokyo Skytree is a landmark on the east side of Tokyo.

東京スカイツリーは、墨田区押上にあります。

☐ Tokyo Skytree is located in Oshiage, in Sumida Ward.

東京スカイツリーは浅草から隅田川をわたって東岸にあります。

☐ Tokyo Skytree is located on the east bank of the Sumida River, across from Asakusa.

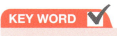

☐ main temple	本堂

浅草とその周辺

浅草寺 ● 東京スカイツリー

▶▶▶ ワンセンテンスで説明する東京

東武スカイツリーラインには、「東京スカイツリー」という駅があります。

☐ Tokyo Skytree has its own train station, "Tokyo Skytree Station," on the Tobu Skytree Line.

東京スカイツリーには、高さ 350 メートルと 450 メートルの場所に、二つの展望台があります。

☐ Tokyo Skytree has two observation decks, one at 350 meters and one at 450 meters.

東京スカイツリーには 4 基の高速エレベーターがあって、最初の展望台まで 50 秒で到達します。

☐ Tokyo Skytree has four high-speed elevators, which can reach the first observation deck in 50 seconds.

東京スカイツリーの展望台からは、関東平野が見渡せます。

☐ From the Tokyo Skytree observation decks you can see across the whole Kanto Plain.

東京スカイツリーの名前は公募で決まりました。

☐ The name "Tokyo Skytree" was chosen by the people of Japan.

夜になると、東京スカイツリーは青や紫のイルミネーションが灯されます。

☐ Tokyo Skytree is illuminated at night with either blue or purple lights.

東京スカイツリーは、震度 8 の地震に耐えるように設計されています。

☐ Tokyo Skytree was built to withstand a magnitude 8 earthquake.

Tokyo in Single Sentences

東京スカイツリーは日本の伝統建築を参考にデザインされました。

☐ The design of Tokyo Skytree is based on traditional Japanese architecture.

東京スカイツリー周辺は、東京スカイツリータウンといって、多くの商店やレストランがあります。

☐ The area around Tokyo Skytree is called Tokyo Skytree Town, and it has many shops and restaurants.

浅草とその周辺

東京スカイツリー

KEY WORD ✓

☐ Kanto Plain　　　　　　関東平野

2-05 新宿とその周辺

新宿

新宿は東京という大都会を代表する都心のひとつです。江戸時代は内藤新宿という宿場町でした。江戸を往来する人たちに一夜の宿を提供していたのです。

現在の新宿は大きく2つに分かれます。山手線を挟んで、新宿の西半分は都庁をはじめ、オフィスビルやホテルなどが並ぶ高層ビル街で、副都心と呼ばれています。新宿の東側は、歓楽街、ショッピング街として知られています。とくに新宿駅の東口近くに広がる歌舞伎町は、ちょうどニューヨークのタイムズスクエアのような地域で、日本最大の夜の歓楽街として知られています。

新宿駅は毎日330万人以上の人が利用する巨大駅です。どれだけたくさんの通勤客で常にごったがえしているかお分かりになるでしょう。この新宿駅の利用者数は、世界一だといわれています。無数の電車、バス、地下鉄が交差するのを見れば納得ですね。

Around Shinjuku

Shinjuku

Shinjuku is one of the key urban centers that typifies Tokyo as a whole. During the Edo era it was an overnight lodging area for travelers approaching or leaving the capital, and was known as Naito-Shinjuku.

Today Shinjuku is split in two by the Yamanote train line, with its western side — known as *Fukutoshin* ("the second core of the city") — housing Tokyo's City Hall and many high-rise hotels and office buildings. The eastern side of Shinjuku is largely an entertainment and shopping district. In particular, the Kabukicho district close to the eastern exits of Shinjuku Station is known as Japan's largest nightlife entertainment area, somewhat symbolic as the equivalent of Times Square in New York City.

A phenomenal 3.3 million people pass through Shinjuku Station on a daily basis, so you can imagine how crowded it appears (and feels!). It is said that Shinjuku has the largest number of people in the world utilizing a station — easy to understand as a crossroads of numerous train, bus, and subway lines.

新宿でのショッピング

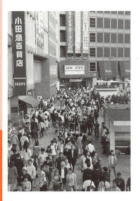

　銀座、渋谷などと並んで、新宿は東京を代表するショッピング街のひとつです。伊勢丹や高島屋などの大型の百貨店をはじめ、数えきれない衣料品店やアクセサリー店などが並んでいます。

　また、新宿はナイトライフ、エンターテインメントの街でもあり、和食はもとより、世界中の多様な食文化が楽しめます。

新宿ゴールデン街

　ゴールデン街は、新宿の歌舞伎町の東端にあり、小さなバーや飲食店がひしめき合っています。まるで1950年代から1970年代にかけての昭和の時代にタイムスリップしたような感覚にとらわれます。

　戦後の闇市からはじまった一角で、この一風変わった地区は、仕事帰りに一杯ひっかけるサラリーマンだけでなく、芸術家、作家など多くの文化人にも愛されてきました。狭い路地に小さいながらも特徴のある飲食店がひしめき合い、1950年代の面影が地元の人たちをひきつけるだけでなく、今では観光名所ともなっています。

Shinjuku shopping area

Along with other areas such as Ginza and Shibuya, Shinjuku is one of the key shopping districts in Tokyo. In addition to a number of major department stores, including Isetan and Takashimaya, there are thousands of other shops, many of them selling clothing and accessories.

As a major nightlife and entertainment area as well, it is a perfect place to explore a vast range of cuisines, starting with Japanese food, of course, but with the world's culinary diversity ready to experience.

Shinjuku Golden-gai

The area known as *Golden-gai* in Shinjuku, on the eastern edge of the Kabukicho, is packed with tiny bars and restaurants that give a nostalgic, time-warp feel of being stuck in the latter Showa era of the 1950's through the 1970's.

With its origins in the post-WWII black-market era, this funky neighborhood has been popular not only with salaried workers stopping in for a drink on the way home, but also with artists, authors, and other cultured intellectuals. The way each of the small but distinctive bars is squeezed into a narrow space has made this area not only attractive as a remnant of the 1950's for locals, but as a must-see for many visiting tourists as well.

新宿西口商店街

　新宿駅の西口近くには狭い路地にひしめき合うように、昔ながらの懐かしさを感じるような飲食店が立ち並びます。焼き鳥屋、ラーメン屋などが狭い路地にひしめき合っていて、1950年代の世界に迷いこんだようなレトロな一角であることから、別名「思い出横丁」ともいわれています。

新大久保

　新宿から山手線を池袋方面に1駅行けば、新大久保という駅につきます。駅の周辺は東京で最大の韓国人街となっていて、韓国系の食品雑貨、そして韓国料理のレストランがひしめき合っています。韓国料理のレストランの他、中国やインドなど、アジア系の食も堪能できる地域です。

新宿御苑

　新宿御苑は、明治時代に農業試験場として整備され、戦後に公園として一般に公開された庭園です。広大な敷地には日本庭園をはじめフランス、イギリス風の庭園などがあり、ピクニックや散歩など、市

Shinjuku West Exit shopping area

Squeezed into an alley close to the west-side exit of Shinjuku Station is a "blast from the past" assortment of bars and restaurants. Shops featuring such fare as *yakitori* chicken skewers and ramen noodles are nestled into tiny spaces next to each other. This alleyway gives the distinct feel of having never emerged from the 1950's, so it is no wonder that its affectionate alternative name is "Nostalgic Alley."

Shin-Okubo

One station north on the Yamanote loop-line from Shinjuku — in the direction of Ikebukuro — is Shin-Okubo. Situated around Shin-Okubo station is Tokyo's largest concentration of Korean shops selling food and a full range of goods, and in addition to the many Korean restaurants there are Chinese, Indian, and numerous other Asian spots where you can enjoy a full range of Asian culinary delights.

Shinjuku Gyoen

With its origins during the Meiji era, the Shinjuku Imperial Gardens (*Gyoen*) began as an agricultural / horticultural testing center, but it was opened as a public park after World War II. In addition to stunning Japanese gardens, Shinjuku

民の憩いの場所になっています。

とくに、春に桜が満開になり、秋に錦秋に包まれると、御苑では多くの人が集まり、青空の下でシートを広げ、祭り気分で飲んだり、食べたりしながら、自然の美しさを堪能するのです。

バスタ新宿

新宿駅南口には、「バスタ新宿」という高速バスターミナルがあります。ここは羽田や成田空港、さらには全国に向けて高速バスが発着します。バスタ新宿の到着ロビーには外国人向けの東京観光情報センターもあります。

Gyoen also contains separate French- and British-style gardens, and as it has spacious grounds it is a favorite place for the public to enjoy picnics and relaxing strolls.

In the spring and autumn, particularly, when the cherry blossoms are in full bloom and when the leaves have turned a full range of bright colors, crowds throng the Gardens, spreading out mats in the open air to take in nature's beauty, while sharing drinks and snacks in a festive mood.

Shinjuku Expressway Bus Terminal

Near the south exit of Shinjuku Station there is an expressway bus terminal called *Busta Shinjuku*. Here you can catch buses bound for Haneda and Narita airports as well as expressway buses going to various parts of the country. There is also a Tokyo Tourist Information Center for foreign visitors in the Busta Shinjuku arrival lobby.

新宿とその周辺

東京に居住している外国人は、登録しているだけで44万人ですが、おそらくもっと多くの外国人がいるでしょう。

- [ ] There are 440,000 registered foreign residents in Tokyo, although there are probably more in addition to that number.

1000万人ほどの外国人が毎年東京を訪れます。

- [ ] Tokyo sees around 10 million visitors from overseas every year.

東京都に登録して居住する外国人のうち、約34万人がアジア系の人で、中国人、韓国人だけで26万人を占めています。

- [ ] Among the registered foreign residents in Tokyo, 340,000 are from Asian countries, with 260,000 foreign residents just from China and Korea alone.

東京都に登録して居住している外国人のうち、アメリカ人は約1万7000人、ヨーロッパ系の人々は約2万3000人です。

- [ ] There are 17,000 Americans and 23,000 Europeans among the registered foreign residents in Tokyo.

Tokyo in Single Sentences

東京には、いくつかの外国人コミュニティがあります。新大久保には韓国人、江戸川区にはインド人、高田馬場にはミャンマー人、東京都に隣接する埼玉県蕨市にはクルド人などが集まっています。

☐ There are several foreign communities in Tokyo, including the Korean community in Shin-Okubo, the Indian community in Edogawa Ward, the Myanmar community in Takadanobaba, and the Kurdish community in Warabi City in neighboring Saitama Prefecture.

東京都とその周辺には６万人以上の留学生が生活しています。

☐ There are more than 60,000 foreign exchange students in and around Tokyo.

神楽坂界隈では、フランス人をよくみかけます。近くに日仏会館があるからです。

☐ It is common to see French people in Kagurazaka neighborhood, and the French Cultural Center is located nearby.

欧米出身の居住者は、多くが港区に住んでいます。

☐ Many foreign residents from the U.S. and Europe live in Minato Ward.

六本木、麻布から渋谷にかけては、欧米から来た人々が多く居住しています。

☐ Many foreign residents from the U.S. and Europe live in the area that stretches from Roppongi and Azabu to Shibuya.

▶▶▶ ワンセンテンスで説明する東京

多国籍企業は、東京に支社を置き、活動拠点にしています。

☐ Many multinational companies have branch offices and have established their base of operations in Tokyo.

東京とその周辺には2600社以上の外資系企業があり、日本全国で活動する外資系企業の8割以上を占めています。

☐ There are more than 2,600 foreign corporations in and around Tokyo, and they make up 80 percent of all foreign corporations active in Japan.

東京は、ニューヨーク、パリ、北京、モスクワ、ソウルなど、世界の主要な11都市と姉妹都市になってっています。

☐ Tokyo has eleven sister cities among the world's leading cities, including New York, Paris, Beijing, Moscow and Seoul.

新宿御苑

Track 49

新宿御苑は、新宿にある公園です。

☐ Shinjuku Gyoen is a public garden in Shinjuku.

新宿御苑に行くには、丸ノ内線の新宿御苑駅があります。

☐ Shinjuku Gyoen has its own subway station on the Marunouchi line, Shinjuku Gyoen-mae.

Tokyo in Single Sentences

新宿御苑には、フランス、イギリス、そして日本風の３つの異なる庭園があります。

☐ Shinjuku Gyoen has three different styles of garden: English, French and Japanese.

新宿御苑は、19世紀につくられました。

☐ Shinjuku Gyoen was built in the nineteenth century.

新宿御苑は、もともと皇室の庭園として使用されていましたが、1949年に公苑になりました。

☐ Shinjuku Gyoen used to belong to the Imperial Family, but it became a public park in 1949.

新宿御苑には、桜の木をはじめ２万本ほどの木が植えられています。

☐ There are around 20,000 trees in Shinjuku Gyoen, including many cherry trees.

特に春の桜が咲く頃に新宿御苑を訪ねるのがお勧めです。

☐ The best time to visit Shinjuku Gyoen is in the spring, when the cherry trees bloom.

新宿御苑には熱帯の植物が植えられている温室があります。

☐ A greenhouse with tropical plants is located inside Shinjuku Gyoen.

東京にある他の庭と異なり、新宿御苑には大きな芝生の敷地があります。

☐ Unlike many of Tokyo's gardens, Shinjuku Gyoen has a large grassy lawn.

新宿とその周辺

新宿とその周辺 ● 新宿御苑

大きな芝生の広場があるので、新宿御苑はピクニックに向いています。

☐ With its large grassy lawn, Shinjuku Gyoen is a nice place for a picnic.

新宿

新宿は東京の中心地の一つです。

☐ Shinjuku is one of Tokyo's major hubs.

新宿は東京の西側に位置しています。

☐ Shinjuku is located on the west side of Tokyo.

神楽坂や高田馬場も新宿区にあります。

☐ Shinjuku Ward includes Kagurazaka and Takadanobaba.

超高層ビルや歓楽街を見たいなら新宿がおすすめです。

☐ If you want to see skyscrapers and bright lights, you should go to Shinjuku.

今の東京を感じたければ、新宿がおすすめです。

☐ If you want to get a feel for modern Tokyo, you should go to Shinjuku.

江戸時代の頃の新宿は、市街地のはずれにありました。

☐ During the Edo era, Shinjuku lay outside the city borders.

Tokyo in Single Sentences

新宿という地名は「新しい宿」という意味です。

☐ Shinjuku means "New Lodge."

江戸時代、新宿が中央から山梨県へ向かう街道の最初の宿場でした。

☐ In the Edo era, Shinjuku became the first stop on the road from the capital to Yamanashi Prefecture.

1920年に新宿は東京都に組み込まれ、1947年に区となりました。

☐ Shinjuku was incorporated into Tokyo in 1920 and became a ward in 1947.

新宿地区の大部分は20世紀の間に発展しました。

☐ Much of Shinjuku was developed during the twentieth century.

新宿は20世紀の東京を象徴する地域です。

☐ Shinjuku serves as a symbol of twentieth-century Tokyo.

新宿駅は山手線のメイン駅のひとつです。

☐ Shinjuku Station is one of the principal stations on the Yamanote Line.

新宿駅は世界でもっとも混雑した鉄道駅だと言われています。

☐ Shinjuku Station is said to be the world's busiest train station.

毎日300万人以上の乗客が新宿駅を利用しています。

☐ Over 3 million passengers use Shinjuku Station every day.

新宿とその周辺

新宿御苑 ● 新宿

▶▶▶ ワンセンテンスで説明する東京

新宿駅には小売店や飲食店がたくさんあり、駅自体が一つの町のようです。

☐ Shinjuku Station is like a town in itself, with many shops and restaurants.

新宿駅から郊外や西部の山へ向かう通勤電車が出ています。

☐ Commuter trains depart from Shinjuku Station for the suburbs and mountains to the west.

新宿駅の西側は西新宿と呼ばれています。

☐ The area to the west of Shinjuku Station is called Nishi-Shinjuku.

西新宿には東京都庁ビルを含め、たくさんの超高層ビルが立っています。

☐ Nishi-Shinjuku has many skyscrapers, including the Tokyo Metropolitan Government Building.

東京都庁は1991年に有楽町から西新宿へ移転しました。

☐ The Tokyo Metropolitan Government moved to Nishi-Shinjuku from Yurakucho in 1991.

東京都庁ビルは日本の建築家、丹下健三が設計しました。

☐ The Tokyo Metropolitan Government Building was designed by the Japanese architect Kenzo Tange.

東京都庁ビルの45階は一般に公開された無料の展望台になっています。

☐ The Tokyo Metropolitan Government Building has a free public observatory on the 45th floor.

Tokyo in Single Sentences

晴れた日には東京都庁ビルの展望台から富士山が見えます。

☐ From the observatory in the Tokyo Metropolitan Government Building you can see Mt. Fuji on a clear day.

西新宿にはたくさんのオフィスビルがあり、会社員もたくさんいます。

☐ There are many office buildings in Nishi-Shinjuku, and you can see many office workers there.

西新宿にはホテルがたくさんあり、パークハイアットもそのうちのひとつです。

☐ There are many hotels in Nishi-Shinjuku, including the Park Hyatt.

パークハイアットホテルは、映画『ロスト・イン・トランスレーション』に出てきました。

☐ The Park Hyatt Hotel appears in the movie *Lost in Translation*.

西新宿にはロバート・インディアナ氏の彫刻『LOVE』など、芸術作品がいくつか置かれています。

☐ There are a number of public artworks in Nishi-Shinjuku, including Robert Indiana's "Love" sculpture.

新宿とその周辺

新宿

KEY WORD ✓

☐ Tokyo Metropolitan Government Building
　　　　　　　　　　東京都庁ビル

▶▶▶ ワンセンテンスで説明する東京

新宿駅の東側は、西側とはまったく様子が異なっています。

☐ The east side of Shinjuku Station is very different from the west side.

新宿駅の東側は活気に溢れた歓楽街です。

☐ The east side of Shinjuku Station is an entertainment district with a lively atmosphere.

夜になると、新宿の東側にはたくさんのネオンと巨大なスクリーンが現れます。

☐ At night you can see many neon lights and giant video screens on the east side of Shinjuku.

超高層ビル、ネオンと巨大なスクリーンがある新宿の景色は、映画『ブレード・ランナー』のワンシーンのようです。

☐ With its skyscrapers, neon lights, and giant video screens, Shinjuku looks like a scene from the movie *Blade Runner*.

歌舞伎町は新宿駅の東側にある地区で、東京最大の歓楽街です。

☐ Kabukicho, a district to the east of Shinjuku Station, is Tokyo's largest entertainment district.

4000を超えるレストラン、バー、クラブがある歌舞伎町は、アジア最大の歓楽街です。

☐ With more than 4,000 restaurants, bars and clubs, Kabukicho is the largest entertainment district in Asia.

Tokyo in Single Sentences

新宿には、日本最大のゲイタウンである新宿二丁目があります。

☐ Shinjuku is home to Japan's largest gay neighborhood, Shinjuku Ni-chome.

新宿は現代的な地域ですが、懐かしい雰囲気の場所も多少残っています。

☐ Even though Shinjuku is a modern district, there are still some places with an old-fashioned atmosphere.

新宿には、思い出横丁とゴールデン街という、昔の東京を感じさせてくれる２つのスポットがあります。

☐ Two places in Shinjuku that feel like old Tokyo are Omoide-yokocho and Golden Gai.

新宿にはたくさんデパートや家電販売店があって買い物に便利です。

☐ Shinjuku is convenient for shopping, with numerous department stores and electronics stores.

必要なものはなんでも新宿で手に入ります。

☐ You can get everything you need in Shinjuku.

新宿と その周辺

新宿

KEY WORD ✓

☐ lively atmosphere   活気に溢れた

▶▶▶ ワンセンテンスで説明する東京

新宿は交通の中心なので、人々は仕事帰りに立ち寄って買い物をしたり、食事をしたり、一杯やったりしています。

- [ ] Because Shinjuku is a transit hub, people stop there on their way home from work for shopping, eating and drinking.

新宿には、新宿御苑と新宿中央公園という二つの公園があります。

- [ ] Shinjuku has two parks, Shinjuku Gyoen and Shinjuku Chuo-koen.

新大久保

新大久保は、山手線で新宿から北へ1駅のところにあります。

- [ ] Shin-Okubo is a train station one stop north of Shinjuku on the Yamanote Line.

新大久保駅は新宿区に位置しています。

- [ ] Shin-Okubo Station is located in Shinjuku Ward.

新大久保駅の周辺は、東京のコリアン・タウンとして知られています。

- [ ] The area around Shin-Okubo Station is known as Tokyo's Korean Town.

新大久保駅周辺には、本格的な韓国料理レストランや韓国製品を売る店がたくさんあります。

- [ ] There are many authentic Korean restaurants and shops selling Korean goods around Shin-Okubo Station.

Tokyo in Single Sentences

新大久保駅周辺には、韓国語の看板がたくさん出ています。

☐ Around Shin-Okubo Station you can see many signs written in Korean.

新大久保は韓流の俳優やポップ歌手を愛好する女性たちに人気があります。

☐ Shin-Okubo is a popular destination for women who are fans of Korean actors and pop singers.

高田馬場

Track 52

高田馬場は山手線で新宿から北へ2駅のところにあります。

☐ Takadanobaba is two stops north of Shinjuku on the Yamanote Line.

高田馬場は新宿区内の地域です。

☐ Takadanobaba is a neighborhood in Shinjuku Ward.

高田馬場のニックネームは「ババ」です。

☐ Takadanobaba is nicknamed "Baba."

高田馬場の近くには早稲田大学があり、たくさんの学生がこの地域で生活しています。

☐ Takadanobaba is near Waseda University, so many students live in the neighborhood.

新宿と その周辺

新宿 ● 新大久保 ● 高田馬場

▶▶▶ ワンセンテンスで説明する東京

学生がとても多いので、高田馬場には安い食事処や酒場があります。

☐ Because so many students live in Takadanobaba, there are many inexpensive restaurants and bars.

高田馬場は漫画のキャラクター、鉄腕アトムが生まれた街です。

☐ Takadanobaba is the birthplace of the cartoon character "Astro Boy."

東京で楽しむ世界の料理

Track 53

東京は日本で最も国際色豊かな料理を楽しむことができる場所です。

☐ Tokyo has the most cosmopolitan dining scene in Japan.

世界中の食べ物が東京で手に入ります。

☐ In Tokyo you can get food from anywhere in the world.

新大久保にはたくさんの韓国料理店があります。

☐ There are many Korean restaurants in Shin-Okubo.

神楽坂には何軒かフランス料理店があります。

☐ There are some French restaurants in Kagurazaka.

高田馬場にはミャンマー料理の店があります。

☐ There are a number of Burmese restaurants in Takadanobaba.

Tokyo in Single Sentences

池袋には中華やインド料理の店が多くあります。

☐ There are many Chinese and Indian restaurants in Ikebukuro.

原宿にはアメリカっぽいレストランやカフェが集まっています。

☐ There are many American restaurants and cafés in Harajuku.

アメリカにおけるカリフォルニア巻きのように、日本も多彩な西洋料理を創り出してきました。

☐ Like California Rolls in America, Japan has created many variations of Western foods.

東京には本格的なナポリ風ピザもあれば、海苔やイカ、半熟卵をのせたピザもあります。

☐ You can find authentic Neapolitan-style pizza in Tokyo, and you can also find pizza topped with seaweed, squid and soft-boiled eggs.

新宿とその周辺

高田馬場 ● 東京で楽しむ世界の料理

中野

中野は新宿の西にある地区です。

☐ Nakano is a neighborhood to the west of Shinjuku.

中野は中央線で新宿から西にひと駅のところにあります。

☐ Nakano is one stop west of Shinjuku on the Chuo Line.

中央線沿いはだいたいそうなのですが、中野も大部分は住宅街です。

☐ Like many neighborhoods on the Chuo Line, Nakano is largely a residential neighborhood.

中央線沿いの他の地域と同じく、中野は1960年代に開発が進みました。

☐ Like many neighborhoods on the Chuo Line, Nakano was developed in the 1960s.

中野ブロードウェイは1960年代のレトロな雰囲気の商店街です。

☐ Nakano Broadway is an old shopping mall with a retro 1960s feel.

秋葉原と同じく、中野は漫画、アニメのファンが集う場所です。

☐ Like Akihabara, Nakano is a gathering place for fans of comic books and anime.

高円寺

高円寺は新宿の西、杉並区にある地区です。
- [ ] Koenji is a neighborhood west of Shinjuku in Suginami Ward.

高円寺は中野の隣にあり、新宿からは中央線で2駅です。
- [ ] Koenji is next to Nakano, two stops from Shinjuku on the Chuo Line.

高円寺は自由な雰囲気の街で、ミュージシャンが大勢集まっています。
- [ ] Koenji is a bohemian neighborhood where many musicians gather.

高円寺には小さなクラブやバーがあり、ライブ演奏を聴くことができます。
- [ ] There are many small clubs and bars in Koenji where you can hear live music.

夏には、高円寺阿波踊りと呼ばれるお祭りが行われ、人々が通りで踊ります。

☐ Koenji holds a summer festival called the *Koenji Awa Odori* where people dance in the street.

吉祥寺

吉祥寺は新宿の西、武蔵野市にあります。

☐ Kichijoji is a neighborhood west of Shinjuku in Musashino City.

吉祥寺は中央線で新宿から15分ほどのところにあります。

☐ Kichijoji is a stop on the Chuo Line, 15 minutes from Shinjuku.

吉祥寺は、最も住みたい街としてよく名前をあげられる地域です。

☐ Kichijoji is often voted as the neighborhood where people would most like to live.

Tokyo in Single Sentences

吉祥寺は新宿から近く、それでいて東京の繁華街よりも静かで、便利な街です。

☐ Kichijoji is convenient, because it is near Shinjuku, but it feels more peaceful than downtown Tokyo.

吉祥寺は、多くの大学へのアクセスが良く、学生に人気があります。

☐ Kichijoji is popular with students because it has easy access to many universities.

吉祥寺には井の頭公園という大きな公園があり、週末は人で賑わいます。

☐ There is a big park in Kichijoji, called Inokashira Park, which is popular on weekends.

新宿とその周辺

高円寺 ● 吉祥寺

渋谷・六本木とその周辺

渋谷

渋谷として知られる東京のこの地域は、11世紀終わりから12世紀初めにかけてこの辺りに住んでいた豪族渋谷氏の名前がその起源です。その後、江戸時代(17世紀から19世紀半ば)には、渋谷付近は幕府のある江戸の中心からも近かったことから、往来する人向けの宿場がありました。渋谷は谷の底にあり、昔はそこに渋谷川が流れていましたが、今は暗渠になっていて、見ることはできません。

現在の渋谷は、他のどこよりも若者を魅了する街となり、若い活気に満ち、評判になっています。また、商業の中心地として発展し、東京の文化活動の発信地としても知られています。地下鉄や私鉄、そしてJRなどの交差する交通の拠点でもあり、いつも多くの人が訪れる東京を代表する街の一つとなっています。

渋谷駅の北西にあるスクランブル交差点は、国内はもとより海外にも知れ渡っており、信号が変わる

Around Shibuya and Roppongi

Shibuya

The area of Tokyo known as Shibuya takes its name from an aristocratic family named Shibuya who lived here in the late eleventh / early twelfth centuries. Later, during the Edo era that lasted from the seventeenth to the middle of the nineteenth centuries, there were inns to accommodate travelers, as this was on the outskirts of the capital city of Edo. In olden times the Shibuya River ran through the neighborhood, which is situated in a valley, but the river has been channeled underground in modern times and is hard to find.

Shibuya today is a town that predominantly attracts young people, giving it a youthful feel and reputation. It has also evolved into a commercial center, known as Tokyo's hot spot for emerging cultural developments. With a number of subway and train lines crisscrossing the station that is also served by Japan Rail, Shibuya is one of Tokyo's best-known neighborhoods, with a constant flow of people.

The intersection at the northwest side of the station is known not only in Japan but abroad, famous for its traffic

と膨大な数の人たちが近くにある歓楽街、ショッピング街を目指して行き来することで有名です。

　もう一つの名物は、ハチ公という犬の銅像で、このスクランブル交差点と同じ出口側にあり、友だちとの待ち合わせ場所として利用されています。

ハチ公

　渋谷駅にハチ公口という改札口があります。その前にある犬の銅像から名前をとったのです。ハチ公は、2009年にリチャード・ギアが主演した『HACHI 約束の犬』という映画のモデルにもなったハチ公という犬の実話を記念して製作されたものです。

　ハチ（公は犬を呼ぶときの日本語の愛称です）は、1925年に急死した飼い主の大学教授のことが忘れられず、その後9年間も主人が帰宅するのではと、主人を出迎えに駅に通い続けたといわれている犬で、日本では「忠犬ハチ公」の名前で知られています。

lights geared to accommodate the enormous crowds crossing to and from the entertainment and shopping districts nearby.

The bronze statue of a dog named Hachiko at the station exit on this side is also famous, as it serves as a convenient (if often crowded) meeting spot for friends to find each other.

Hachiko

One of the station exits at Shibuya is called *Hachiko*, named after the bronze statue of a dog nearby. The 2009 film starring Richard Gere called *Hachi: A Dog's Tale* took its name and inspiration from the real-life story of the dog memorialized by the statue.

Ever-faithful to its owner, Hachi would greet the university professor each day on his commute home to Shibuya Station. In 1925, when the professor unexpectedly passed away and didn't return, Hachiko patiently waited nonetheless — coming to the station every day for a full nine years! He earned the name "Faithful Hachiko" and is loved to this day in Japan. (The dog's name was simply "Hachi," but "*ko*" is an affectionate suffix added to a pet's name in the Japanese language.)

六本木

六本木は、東京の中でも特に世界各地のおしゃれなレストランやバーなどが並び、外国人の居住者や観光客も多く活動する地域です。

六本木は地下鉄大江戸線と日比谷線とが交差するところにあって、大変便利なことから、六本木交差点周辺には外資系のオフィスや外国の大使館も多くあります。

江戸時代の六本木周辺は、多くの武家の屋敷や大名の屋敷が並ぶ地域でした。その後、第二次世界大戦が始まる前までは、軍事関連の施設がここにベースをおき、つい最近までは防衛庁(現在の防衛省)の本部もこの地域にありました。しかし、現在はそうした施設は一掃され、東京を代表する国際的な街として、昼も夜も人で賑わっています。

六本木ヒルズ

六本木ヒルズは、大規模な都市開発によって生まれ変わった地域にあります。もともとは、ディスコやナイトクラブ、レストラン、さらには旧大名屋敷

Roppongi

If you imagine a district in Tokyo well known for its many bars and unique restaurants with cuisine from around the world, frequented by many foreign residents and tourists, Roppongi is the place.

As the crossing point for both the Oedo and the Hibiya subway lines this is an area convenient to access, and you can find a number of international firms and foreign embassies within easy reach of Roppongi Intersection.

In olden days going back to the Edo era this was an area where many *daimyo* maintained their residences in Tokyo, as did others in the *samurai* class. Later, in the years preceding World War II the district was home to a number of military bases and facilities, and until recently the nation's Defense Agency (now known as the Defense Ministry) maintained its headquarters there as well. Those traces have now disappeared entirely, however in their place you will find a truly international flavor, bustling with activity both day and night.

Roppongi Hills

In a part of town that used to thrive with discos, nightclubs and restaurants, and more quietly with the gardens of estates that used to house the feudal *daimyo* residences, Roppongi

の庭園跡があった場所でした。

　再開発により、周辺地域は高級ショッピング、企業のオフィス、高級アパート街となりました。数多くの外資系企業や、テレビ朝日などのメディア関連会社がここ六本木ヒルズで活動しています。2003年に完成して以来、六本木ヒルズは六本木地域の中心となり、日本国内だけでなく、海外からの観光客も多く引き寄せています。

東京ミッドタウン

　六本木ヒルズと並ぶ、六本木の顔となるもう一つのビジネスセンターが、東京ミッドタウンです。

　ここは元々防衛庁の施設があった場所で、施設が移転したあとに再開発をして、2007年に完成しました。多くのレストランや小売店などの施設の他に、サントリー美術館もここに移転しました。サントリー美術館は、とりわけ日本の伝統工芸作品などを展示する美術館として知られています。

　六本木交差点へつながる便利な地下通路や地下鉄網で結ばれ、東京ミッドタウンは大東京圏の主要な中間地区として、その名に恥じない発展を遂げています。

Hills is a large-scale revitalization of the urban landscape.

The neighborhood now thrives with high-end shopping, corporate offices, and high-rise apartments. With a number of foreign-capitalized firms locating their offices here as key tenants, this is also the home of major media outlets, including TV Asahi. Completed in 2003, Roppongi Hills has since become the central attraction of the Roppongi district, attracting visitors from across Japan and from abroad.

Tokyo Midtown

As a close rival to the Roppongi Hills in providing a business-oriented core and a glamorous face to the Roppongi landscape is the Tokyo Midtown complex.

Occupying a large area that formerly housed the Defense Agency, Tokyo Midtown, opened in 2007, represents a revitalization of the neighborhood. Not only are many restaurants and shops now located here, but the Suntory Museum also relocated to the attractive and upscale Tokyo Midtown development. The Suntory Museum is widely known for its strong collection of, among other genres, traditional Japanese arts and craft-work.

Connected by a convenient underground set of tunnels to the Roppongi Intersection and subway lines, Tokyo Midtown makes a great effort to live up to its name as a midtown hub in the broader Tokyo metropolis.

麻布十番

六本木の東側には、麻布十番という気軽にショッピングや飲食を楽しめる街があります。このあたりはもともと、江戸時代に有力な大名として知られた仙台藩の大名屋敷のあったところです。

今では、目と鼻の先にある六本木の雑踏とは対照的に、麻布十番には、こじんまりとした商店や気の利いたレストランが並び、散歩を楽しむ家族やカップルで賑わっています。

8月に東京にいたら見逃せないのが、麻布十番祭りというイベントです。生演奏あり、昔ながらの子ども向けの遊興施設あり、数百に及ぶ食べ物の屋台も立ち並び、そこを埋め尽くすような群集が、2日間に渡って、朝から夜まで飲めや歌えのお祭り騒ぎを楽しんでいます。

恵比寿・広尾

山手線の恵比寿駅周辺と、そこから日比谷線で一駅の広尾、さらに恵比寿から広尾の反対側にあたり、渋谷に近い代官山は、国際企業に勤める外

Azabu-Juban

Azabu-Juban is a casual shopping and dining neighborhood to the east of Roppongi. Historically, this is where the *daimyo* of the Sendai feudal domain maintained their residence in the Edo era.

These days one finds the streets of Azabu-Juban filled with families and couples out for a stroll, shopping in small shops and dining in small, distinctive restaurants that provide a contrast to the bustling atmosphere in Roppongi just a short ten-minute walk away.

A notable event — not to be missed if you are in Tokyo in August — is the Azabu-Juban street fair, with live music, traditional kids' amusements, hundreds of food stalls, and wall-to-wall people enjoying the festive revelry from morning to night over a two-day period.

Ebisu, Hiroo

The area around Ebisu Station on the Yamanote line, and the two neighborhoods close by — Hiroo on the Hibiya line just one stop away, and Daikanyama in the opposite direction closer to Shibuya — are where many foreigners working for global firms in Japan live. You will find this part of town even more international than others, with many

国人駐在員などが多く住む地域です。付近にはレストランやカフェなども多く、どこよりも国際的な雰囲気です。外資系企業のオフィスなども多く、恵比寿とその周辺は東京の中でも特におしゃれな場所として、知られています。

restaurants and cafés that give the area a cosmopolitan flavor. The offices of many foreign-capitalized companies are concentrated in this part of town, so the combination of offices and eateries has led to an image of Ebisu and its surroundings as a particularly stylish part of Tokyo.

渋谷

渋谷は東京の南西に位置しています。
- Shibuya is located in the southwest of central Tokyo.

渋谷は、原宿や恵比寿と同じく、渋谷区にあります。
- Shibuya is a neighborhood in Shibuya Ward, which also includes Harajuku and Ebisu.

新宿と同様、渋谷は山手線の主要駅の1つです。
- Like Shinjuku, Shibuya is a major hub on the Yamanote Line.

渋谷からは、南部の郊外への通勤電車が出ています。
- Commuter trains leave from Shibuya for the suburbs south of the city center.

渋谷はショッピングと娯楽の街です。
- Shibuya is a shopping and entertainment district.

渋谷にはたくさんの店、ファーストフード店、カラオケ店、ナイトクラブがあります。
- There are many shops, fast food restaurants, *karaoke* parlors and nightclubs in Shibuya.

渋谷は十代の若者が繰り出す、活気にあふれた街です。
- Shibuya is a popular hangout for teenagers, and it has a lively atmosphere.

Tokyo in Single Sentences

東京の若者文化を見たいのであれば、渋谷をおすすめします。

☐ If you want to see Tokyo's youth culture, you should go to Shibuya.

渋谷にも新宿のように、巨大なスクリーンや歓楽街があります。

☐ Like Shinjuku, Shibuya has giant video screens and bright lights.

渋谷にくる十代の若者は、最新ファッションに身を包んでいます。

☐ You can see teenagers dressed in the latest fashions in Shibuya.

渋谷の通りは常に人が絶えません。

☐ In Shibuya, you can see people on the street at all hours.

渋谷駅の前には忠犬ハチ公の像があります。

☐ There is a statue of Hachiko the dog in front of Shibuya Station.

犬のハチ公は毎夕、飼い主を駅まで迎えに行き、飼い主が亡くなった後も通い続けたのです。

☐ Hachiko was a dog who came to Shibuya Station to meet his master every evening, even after the master passed away.

KEY WORD ✓

☐ bright lights　　　歓楽街

▶▶▶ ワンセンテンスで説明する東京

ハチ公の主人への忠実さに人々は胸を打たれ、彼を称える像を建てました。

☐ People were so impressed by Hachiko's loyalty that they put up a statue in his honor.

渋谷で待ち合わせをするとき、ハチ公の前を指定されることがきっとあるでしょう。

☐ If you are meeting someone in Shibuya, there is a good chance that they will ask you to meet them in front of the Hachiko statue.

なぜなら、ハチ公は待ち合わせ場所としてよく知られていて、その辺りはいつも人でごった返しているのです。

☐ Because the Hachiko statue is a popular meeting place, there is always a crowd of people around it.

渋谷駅の前には渋谷交差点という、いつも大変混雑する交差点があります。

☐ There is a very busy intersection called Shibuya Crossing in front of Shibuya Station.

渋谷交差点は世界一混雑する交差点だと言われています。

☐ Shibuya Crossing is said to be the world's busiest intersection.

渋谷交差点はスクランブル方式で、あらゆる方向から一斉に人々が道を渡るのです。

☐ Shibuya Crossing is a so-called scramble crossing, where everyone crosses at once from different directions.

Tokyo in Single Sentences

渋谷交差点の様子は東京のワンシーンとして有名で、テレビや映画にもよく登場します。

☐ Shibuya Crossing is one of Tokyo's most famous locations, and it often appears in films and on TV.

渋谷の中心はセンター街と呼ばれる通りで、たくさんの小売店や飲食店があります。

☐ The heart of Shibuya is a street called "Center Gai," which has many shops and restaurants.

道玄坂は渋谷のナイトクラブやラブホテルが多いエリアです。

☐ Dogenzaka is an area in Shibuya with many nightclubs and love hotels.

六本木

Track 58

六本木は港区にあります。

☐ Roppongi is a neighborhood in Minato Ward.

六本木には地下鉄の日比谷線と大江戸線が停まります。

☐ Roppongi is a stop on the Hibiya and Oedo subway lines.

六本木は外国からきた人が大勢集まるところで、東京でもっとも国際的な地域です。

☐ Roppongi is Tokyo's most cosmopolitan neighborhood, where many people from foreign countries gather.

▶▶▶ ワンセンテンスで説明する東京

六本木には国際色豊かなレストランや、洋風のバー、ナイトクラブなどがたくさんあります。

☐ There are many international restaurants and Western-style bars and nightclubs in Roppongi.

六本木はどんな時間でも出歩いている人がいます。

☐ You can see people out at all hours in Roppongi.

六本木には外資系企業の本社がたくさん置かれています。

☐ The headquarters of many foreign companies are in Roppongi.

六本木ヒルズは巨大複合施設で、映画館、森美術館、展望台、たくさんの小売店や飲食店、バーなどを備えています。

☐ Roppongi Hills is a large complex with a movie theater, the Mori Art Museum, an observatory, and many shops, restaurants and bars.

魅力的な施設がたくさんあるので、六本木ヒルズは人気のデートスポットです。

☐ With so many attractions, Roppongi Hills is a popular date spot.

東京ミッドタウンもまた巨大複合施設で、たくさんの小売店と飲食店、サントリー美術館と 21_21 DESIGN SIGHT という二つのミュージアムを備えています。

☐ Tokyo Midtown is another large complex with shops, restaurants and two museums, the Suntory Museum of Art and 21_21 Design Sight.

Tokyo in Single Sentences

森美術館、サントリー美術館、国立新美術館の3館が作る三角地帯は「六本木アート・トライアングル」と呼ばれています。

☐ Together, the Mori Art Museum, Suntory Museum of Art and the National Art Center Tokyo make up what is called "Art Triangle Roppongi."

かつて六本木はいかがわしいイメージがありましたが、この十年でイメージを一新し、アートとデザインの中心地になりました。

☐ Roppongi used to have a sleazy image but in the last decade it has rebranded itself as a center for art and design.

年に一度、六本木では六本木アートナイトという夜通しの芸術の祭典が開催されます。

☐ Once a year, Roppongi holds an all-night art festival called Roppongi Art Night.

恵比寿

Track 59

恵比寿は東京の南西部に位置しています。

☐ Ebisu is located in the southwest of central Tokyo.

恵比寿は渋谷区内の地域です。

☐ Ebisu is a neighborhood in Shibuya Ward.

KEY WORD ✓

☐ large complex　　巨大複合施設

恵比寿は渋谷から山手線で南に１駅のところにあります。

☐ Ebisu is one stop south of Shibuya on the Yamanote Line.

恵比寿の地名は、かつてこの地にあったヱビスビールの醸造所に由来するものです。

☐ Ebisu is named for the Yebisu beer brewery, which used to be located here.

Ebisu（えびす）は、Yebisu（ゑびす）とも綴り、これは七福神の一人、福の神の名前です。

☐ Ebisu, also spelled *Yebisu*, is one of the seven gods of good fortune.

恵比寿には屋外型ショッピングセンターの恵比寿ガーデンプレイスがあります。

☐ There is an open-air shopping center in Ebisu called Yebisu Garden Place.

恵比寿ガーデンプレイスはおしゃれなショッピングセンターで、東京都写真美術館とヱビスビール記念館もここにあります。

☐ Yebisu Garden Place is a fashionable shopping center with two museums: the Tokyo Metropolitan Photography Museum and the Beer Museum Yebisu.

恵比寿は新宿や渋谷ほどの混雑や活気はありませんが、レストランやバーがたくさんあります。

☐ Even though Ebisu isn't as crowded or as lively as Shinjuku or Shibuya, there are many restaurants and bars.

広尾

広尾は渋谷区にあり、六本木と隣り合っています。

☐ Hiroo is a neighborhood in Shibuya Ward, next to Roppongi.

広尾には地下鉄日比谷線が停まり、駅は恵比寿駅と六本木駅の間にあります。

☐ Hiroo is a stop on the Hibiya subway line, between Ebisu and Roppongi.

広尾にはたくさんの外国人世帯が暮らしています。

☐ Many foreign families live in Hiroo.

広尾にはインターナショナル・スクールや輸入品を揃えたスーパーがあります。

☐ There are international schools and international supermarkets in Hiroo.

広尾で見かけるのは、日本人ではない人の方が多いかもしれません。

☐ You may see more non-Japanese people than Japanese people in Hiroo.

広尾では日本語を一切話さずに生活することができます。

☐ In Hiroo, you can get by without speaking any Japanese.

2-07 原宿・表参道・青山とその周辺

原宿

　原宿の独創的なところが世界に知れ渡ったことで、今や原宿には世界中からの人が集まるようになりました。所狭しと並ぶ店やブティックが目当てです。

　山手線の原宿駅の東側にある竹下通りとその一角がそうした地域で、安く、そして創作力に富んだ衣料やアクセサリーを売る店が並んでいます。オタク文化、アニメ文化、コスプレなどといった言葉が世界で流行しましたが、原宿と秋葉原がそうした文化の発信地としてライバル関係になったのは、90年代になってからでした。

　原宿は渋谷からも歩いていけ、別方向には明治神宮という有名な大きな神社もあります。

明治神宮

　原宿駅のすぐ西側に広がる森の奥まったところに、明治神宮があります。明治神宮は、日本古来の宗教

Around Harajuku, Omotesando, Aoyama

Harajuku

Recognized globally for its creative characteristics, Harajuku is now a mecca of people gathering from around the world to visit and shop in its countless boutiques.

In the neighborhood surrounding Takeshita-dori in particular, close to the eastern exit of Harajuku Station, shops are gathered selling creative, fashion-setting clothing and accessories, all at very reasonable prices. It was in the 1990's that Harajuku — and across town, Akihabara — gave birth to some trends that have gone viral, known around the world and popular as "*otaku* culture," anime, and cosplay, among others.

All of this is within a short walk from another youthful part of town, Shibuya. In the other direction there is a large and famous Shinto shrine, Meiji Jingu Shrine.

Meiji Jingu Shrine

Meiji Jingu Shrine is located deep in a wooded area that stretches from the western side of Harajuku Station.

原宿・表参道・青山とその周辺

241

である神道の神社ですが、明治神宮自体の歴史は浅いのです。

　この神社は、19世紀後半に日本が飛躍的に近代化を遂げた時代の天皇であった明治天皇とそのお妃の昭憲皇太后を祀る神社として、代々木から原宿に至る広大な土地を整備して1920年に完成したものです。神社に至る森や、その外苑は昔のままの姿で残され、都民の憩いの場となっています。

　ただし、付け加えておかなければならないのは、正月には膨大な人々が参拝に訪れるということです。来る年がやりがいのある、いい一年になるように祈願するのです。

表参道

　表参道として知られるケヤキ並木の大通りが、青山通りからまっすぐ明治神宮前まで荘厳に伸びています。「表参道」とは、「参拝する場所へ導く本道」という意味で、正月に明治神宮にお参りするための正式な参拝路となっています。まさにぴったりのネーミングですね。

　今では、道の両側には、魅力的な高級店が店舗を構え、そしてそこから伸びる無数の路地にはおしゃれなお店やレストランが並んでいます。このような

Although it is a shrine symbolic of Japan's ancient Shinto religion, Meiji Jingu Shrine itself is actually quite new by historical standards.

Built in 1920 to memorialize the Empress and Emperor Meiji, who had ruled in the latter half of the nineteenth century as Japan underwent rapid and dramatic industrial modernization, Meiji Jingu Shrine was allocated a vast stretch of forested land between Yoyogi and Harajuku. Today, the shrine's surrounding forest and gardens are valued by the public as an unspoiled, refreshing place to spend relaxed leisure time.

It might be added, though, that enormous crowds visit the shrine in a pilgrimage at New Year's, an important time of prayers for a rewarding and successful year.

Omotesando

The wide, tree-lined boulevard stretching rather majestically from Aoyama-dori to the entrance of Meiji Jingu Shrine is known as Omotesando. The word "Omotesando" means "a main road leading to a place of worship," and as this is the formal route used by crowds visiting the Meiji Jingu Shrine in their pilgrimage at New Year's, the name is quite fitting.

Nowadays, both sides of the boulevard are lined with attractive, upscale storefronts, and numerous side streets leading off the main avenue are home to stylish shops,

環境に包まれた特別感が表参道の評判を高め、東京人がゆったりとした精錬された「シティ文化」を楽しめる場所になっているのです。

さらに原宿から扇状に広がる路地は、「裏原(うらはら)」の愛称で呼ばれ——文字通り、「原宿の裏通り」のこと——表参道付近は、若者文化の発信地でもあるのです。

根津美術館

青山にある根津美術館は、鉄道ビジネスで財を成した根津嘉一朗が収集した印象的な作品を展示するために、1941年に創設されました。1945年の東京大空襲の難を逃れる幸運にめぐまれ、常設展では商や周の時代の中国の珍しい青銅の作品を見ることができます。

西洋や東洋の数多くの芸術作品の中でも、尾形光琳による江戸時代の一双屏風「燕子花図(かきつばた)」(国宝)は、本館に収蔵されています。

本館は隈研吾によって設計され、2009年に建て替えが完成しました。館内にある居心地のいいカフェからは、手入れの行き届いた根津邸の伝統的な日本庭園を眺めることができます。こ

boutiques and restaurants. The distinctive feel and ambience of the neighborhood has led to Omotesando's well-earned reputation as a place where Tokyo residents can enjoy an unhurried and refined "city culture."

In addition, the network of alleys fanning out from Harajuku has gained the affectionate nickname "Urahara" — literally the "back-street side of Harajuku" — as this Omotesando area is seen as a creative spawning ground of youth-oriented culture.

Nezu Museum

The Nezu Museum in Aoyama was established in 1941 to display the impressive art collected by Nezu Kaichiro (1860 –1940), who amassed a fortune in the railroad business. Fortunate to avoid destruction during the bombing of Tokyo in 1945, the permanent exhibit includes a rare collection of Chinese bronzes from the Shang and Zhou dynasties.

From among many works of art from both the West and East, a pair of Edo-era folding screens of irises by Ogata Korin — registered as National Treasures — is housed in the main museum building.

The building was designed by architect Kengo Kuma and rebuilt and completed in 2009. A pleasant café in the grounds overlooks the well-preserved traditional Japanese gardens of the Nezu estate. The museum, café and gardens

の美術館とカフェと庭園は、都心の雑踏の中で一服の清涼を醸し出してくれます。

太田記念美術館

多くの日本美術の信奉者には、浮世絵の説明は必要ないでしょうが、原宿にある太田美術館に所蔵された、浮世絵のコレクションは一見の価値があります。

浮世絵に傾倒し、生涯で1万2000作品を蒐集した五代目、太田清蔵(1893～1977)を記念して創設された美術館——数少ない浮世絵専門の美術館——は、1980年にオープンしました。

江戸情緒を極彩色に彩った浮世絵は19世紀の終盤に欧米にも伝えられ、当時の印象派などに大きな影響を与えました。ある意味で、当時のグラフィックアートともいわれる浮世絵は、絵図面を描く絵師、版画を作る彫り師、複雑な色合いを重ねて印刷する刷り師などの分業によって作成される工房芸術でもあり、江戸時代の生活をいきいきと描いています。太田美術館には、そうした浮世絵の傑作が数多く展示されています。

provide an enjoyable, quiet solace in the heart of the bustling city.

Ota Museum

Many admirers of Japanese art will need no introduction to ukiyo-e, woodblock print "images of the floating world" from the Edo era, but they should not miss the remarkable collection of ukiyo-e housed in the Ota Museum in Harajuku.

Memorializing the devotion to ukiyo-e of Ota Seizo V (1893–1977), who collected nearly 12,000 prints during his lifetime, the museum — one of only a handful devoted exclusively to ukiyo-e — opened in 1980. An art form with astonishing colors that uniquely captures the atmosphere of the Edo era, ukiyo-e was well received overseas and can be seen to have had a great influence on the European Impressionists of the late nineteenth century.

Ukiyo-e represents a unique division of labor to have produced what might be called the graphic art form of its era, combining the separate skills of design illustrators, those carving the wood block itself, and those mixing the complex colors to create such stunning depictions of life in the Edo era. The Ota Museum is a great space in which to appreciate such jewels of the ukiyo-e tradition.

赤坂見附

　赤坂見附というビジネス街には、地下鉄が何本か乗り入れており、渋谷、新宿、日本橋、大手町などへも、アクセスがしやすくなっています。

　活気あふれる六本木にも近く、高級ホテルや飲食店、高級料亭などが集中する場所としても知られています。

　赤坂見附の「見附」とは、江戸時代に交通の要所などにおかれた見張所のことで、江戸城にも近いこの地域には当時いくつもの有力な大名の屋敷があったことで知られています。

Akasaka-Mitsuke

The business area of town called Akasaka-Mitsuke is located where several subway lines converge, conveniently linking this neighborhood with Shibuya, Shinjuku, Nihonbashi and Otemachi.

It is also known for its concentration of high-end hotels, restaurants and *ryotei* — highly exclusive restaurants specializing in traditional Japanese cuisine — and it is also close to the vibrant Roppongi entertainment district.

The term *mitsuke* in the Akasaka-Mitsuke place name derives from the sentry posts checking people's identities during the Edo era, as this area is also close to where Edo Castle was, and is known as the location of the official residences of powerful *daimyo* during that era.

原宿・表参道

原宿は東京都心の西部に位置しています。
- [ ] Harajuku is located on the west side of Tokyo.

原宿は、恵比寿や広尾もある渋谷区に位置しています。
- [ ] Harajuku is a neighborhood in Shibuya Ward, which also includes Ebisu and Hiroo.

原宿は山手線で新宿から南へ2駅のところにあります。
- [ ] Harajuku is two stops south of Shinjuku on the Yamanote Line.

買い物をしたいなら、原宿に行くといいでしょう。
- [ ] If you want to go shopping, you should go to Harajuku.

原宿にはおしゃれな店やカフェがたくさんあります。
- [ ] There are many fashionable shops and cafés in Harajuku.

原宿はファッションに興味がある若者たちの聖地です。
- [ ] Harajuku is a popular hangout for young people who are interested in fashion.

原宿はストリートファッションの街として有名です。
- [ ] Harajuku is famous for its street fashion.

Tokyo in Single Sentences

原宿発のファッショントレンドがたくさんあります。

☐ Many fashion trends start in Harajuku.

原宿には独創的なファッション、かっこいいファッション、奇抜なファッションの人々がいます。

☐ In Harajuku, you can see people dressed in creative, cool, and sometimes crazy outfits.

週末は特に、日本中から、さらには海外から訪れる人々で、原宿は大変な混雑となります。

☐ Especially on the weekends, Harajuku can get very crowded with people visiting from all over Japan and overseas.

原宿の竹下通りは歩行者専用で、活気にあふれたストリートです。

☐ Takeshita Street is a pedestrian-only street in Harajuku with a lively atmosphere.

竹下通りは特に十代の若者から愛されており、安価で流行の服を売る店がたくさんあります。

☐ Teenagers especially love Takeshita Street, which has many shops selling inexpensive and trendy clothes.

表参道は、原宿駅と表参道駅を結ぶ並木道の大通りです。

☐ Omotesando is a large boulevard that runs between Harajuku Station and Omotesando Station.

原宿・表参道・青山とその周辺　原宿・表参道

251

▶▶▶ ワンセンテンスで説明する東京

表参道にはルイヴィトンやグッチといった高級ブティックが多数出店しています。

☐ There are many expensive boutiques on Omotesando, such as Louis Vuitton and Gucci.

表参道は「東京のシャンゼリゼ」と言われています。

☐ Omotesando is nicknamed the "Champs-Élysées of Tokyo."

表参道と垂直に交わるキャットストリートには、小さなブティックがたくさん並んでいます。

☐ Cat Street runs perpendicular to Omotesando and has many small boutiques.

原宿では、流行の飲食店が次々にオープンしています。

☐ Fashionable new restaurants are always opening in Harajuku.

原宿で行列を見かけたら、それはきっと新たにオープンした飲食店に並ぶ列でしょう。

☐ If you see a line of people in Harajuku, they are probably waiting for a table at a new restaurant.

原宿には代々木公園という大きな公園があり、週末は人々で賑わいます。

☐ There is a big park in Harajuku, called Yoyogi Park, which is a popular place to hang out on weekends.

青山

青山は港区にあります。

☐ Aoyama is a neighborhood in Minato Ward.

表参道、外苑前、青山一丁目などの駅があり、青山へは地下鉄が便利です。

☐ Convenient subway stops for Aoyama include Omotesando, Gaienmae and Aoyama-Itchome.

青山はブティックやカフェ、レストランのあるおしゃれな地域です。

☐ Aoyama is a fashionable neighborhood, with boutiques, cafés and restaurants.

青山には高級住宅地があります。

☐ Aoyama has some wealthy residential quarters.

江戸時代、青山には有力な武士の屋敷がありました。

☐ During the Edo era, important samurai families had villas in Aoyama.

青山霊園には著名な政治家や文化人たちが埋葬されています。

☐ There are some famous politicians and intellectuals buried in Aoyama Cemetery.

▶▶▶ ワンセンテンスで説明する東京

春になると青山霊園には桜が咲きます。

☐ In the spring, the cherry blossoms bloom in Aoyama Cemetery.

赤坂

Track 63

赤坂は港区にあります。

☐ Akasaka is a neighborhood in Minato Ward.

赤坂は永田町と六本木の間にあります。

☐ Akasaka is located between Nagatacho and Roppongi.

赤坂には地下鉄千代田線が停まります。

☐ Akasaka is a stop on the Chiyoda subway line.

日系、外資系を問わず、赤坂にはたくさんの会社があります。

☐ Many companies, both domestic and international, are based in Akasaka.

アメリカ大使館やカナダ大使館など、赤坂にはたくさんの大使館があります。

☐ There are many embassies in or near Akasaka, including the American and Canadian embassies.

赤坂迎賓館は海外の要人、高官のための公式の宿泊施設です。

☐ The Akasaka Palace is the official state guesthouse for visiting foreign dignitaries.

Tokyo in Single Sentences

赤坂迎賓館の前身は東宮御所で、皇太子の住居でした。

☐ Previously, the Akasaka Palace was the residence of the Crown Prince.

赤坂には、そこで働く重役たちのための高級レストランやバーがたくさんあります。

☐ Akasaka has many expensive restaurants and bars for executives who work in the area.

原宿・表参道・青山とその周辺 　青山●赤坂

KEY WORD ✓

☐ official state guesthouse　　公式の宿泊施設

255

神田・秋葉原とその周辺

神田

神田は新橋によく似たサラリーマンの街です。海外から来た人には、夜の散策をおすすめします。

山手線の高架線の下に並ぶ居酒屋、寿司屋、そしてラーメン屋といった場所に、人々が集まって同僚や友人とお酒と食事、そして会話を楽しむ東京ならではの風景にであえます。

もちろん、そうした人々の中にまじって、お酒や焼き鳥など、東京の下町グルメを楽しむのも一案です。

神田明神

江戸時代よりはるか昔、神田一帯がまだ原野だった8世紀までさかのぼることができる東京の神社、それが神田明神です。神田明神は神田から東京の中

Around Kanda, Akihabara

Kanda

Similar to the neighborhood of Shinbashi, Kanda is a salaried worker's kind of town, recommended for an evening stroll for visitors from abroad.

In the area where the JR Yamanote train line runs overhead through Kanda, you will get a feel and atmosphere unique to Tokyo, with affordable *izakaya* bars, sushi restaurants, and ramen shops where people gravitate after work for a drink, a light meal, and conversations with colleagues and friends.

As one way to mingle with the ordinary working people in Tokyo, we recommend that you stop by, have a sip and order some *yakitori* chicken skewers, and experience a relaxed part of this city.

Kanda Myojin

Imagine finding a Shinto shrine in Tokyo that dates back not just to the Edo era, but to the eighth century when Kanda was a rural village, not yet part of a thriving city. The Kanda

心、日本橋にかけての一帯を守護する神社として知られています。

神田古本屋街

神田の駿河台下交差点から靖国通りに行けば、そこは古本屋さんがずらりと並んでいます。和綴じ（と）と呼ばれる日本古来の製本による日本の古書や、時にはヨーロッパやアメリカの希少な古書に出遭うこともできます。

周辺には、出版社なども多く、そうした人々が著者との次作の打ち合わせに使う喫茶店やレストランも並んでいます。

秋葉原

神田から北へ少し歩けば、世界最大の電気街として、大小の家電量販店や電化製品の小売店が並ぶ秋葉原にたどり着きます。秋葉原には、まだ他にもあります。

「アキバ」の略称で知られ、アニメ、ゲーム、そし

Myojin Shrine is said to watch over and provide divine protection to the area stretching from Kanda all the way to Nihonbashi, the historical heart of Tokyo.

Kanda used bookstores

If you stroll from the intersection at Surugadai-shita towards Yasukuni-dori, you will find countless used-book stores in the part of town known as Kanda. Along the way, depending on which shop you stop into, you might run across rare and old books bound in the *watoji* style of Japanese bookbinding, or perhaps hard-to-find European and American works waiting to be rediscovered.

As there are a number of publishing houses located in the area, you will find quite a few coffee shops and restaurants as well, where you might see publishers in animated discussion with authors on their next project together.

Akihabara

If you stroll north from Kanda for a few minutes, your feet will lead you to Akihabara, the world's largest electronics neighborhood, where the streets are lined with retail stores large and small, selling general household appliances and electronic goods. Akihabara, though, is much more.

Known as "Akiba" for short, this is also the headquarters

てコスプレなどのサブカルチャーの発信地として世界中で有名なのです。この地域に行けば、こうした文化に興味を持つ日本人や海外からの訪問客にも多数出会います。家電量販店やコンピュータショップのはいるビルの合間には、コスプレをした少女が集うメイドカフェなどの人気のスポットがあります。路上パフォーマンスに引き寄せられる若者が内外からもやってくることもあります。

秋葉原は、東京を東西に貫く総武線と山手線とが交差する交通の拠点でもあるのです。アキバにまだ行ったことがないのなら、行かないとね！

湯島聖堂

神田明神のすぐそばにある聖廟は、湯島聖堂と呼ばれ、1690年に当時の将軍徳川綱吉によって学問所として造られました。江戸幕府が奨励した儒教教育を行う大学として設立されました。

湯島聖堂の中心は孔子を祀る大正殿と呼ばれる建物です。この施設は日本の高等教育の中心として機能し、後の東京大学や御茶ノ水大学など、日本を代表する教育施設の前身となりました。

for a number of Japanese subcultures known around the world, including *anime, manga*, and *cosplay*. When you get there you will see that it is a mecca for Japanese young people and visitors from around the world seeking out shops serving these subcultural interests. In the spaces and alleys between the large appliance stores and computer shops you can find maid cafés and other popular spots where young women are decked out in cosplay outfits. Occasionally live performances attract young visitors from all over Japan and around the world.

Akihabara is located right at the crossing-point of the Yamanote loop line and Japan Rail's Sobu train line, which traverses Tokyo from east to west. If you haven't been to Akihabara yet, don't miss it!

Yushima Seido

The Yushima Seido is a mausoleum located next to the Kanda Myojin Shrine, constructed in 1690 during the rule of Shogun Tokugawa Tsunayoshi as a place of study. This was a university established in order to promote Confucian education, which had been adopted by the Edo Bakufu.

At the center of the Yushima Seido is a main hall called the Dai Seiden to memorialize Confucius. This institution served as the heart of Japan's higher learning at the time, and it may be seen as a forerunner of notable schools that came

浅草橋（人形問屋街）

　その昔江戸城の支配がつづいていたころ、浅草橋と呼ばれる橋が堀にかけられていました。その橋の名に因んで、現在浅草橋と呼ばれるようになりました。今はJRの総武線浅草橋駅がありますが、この駅の東口一帯は、日本の伝統的な人形を商う問屋や小売店が並んでいます。

　特に日本では３月３日のひな祭りと、５月５日の端午の節句はそれぞれ女の子と男の子を祝う伝統的な行事があり、その行事に合わせて昔の貴人や武士の人形を飾ります。この地域にはそうした人形を扱う店が多く並んでいるのです。

　また、浅草橋のそばで大江戸通りと交差する蔵前橋通り周辺は、昔からの問屋街で、散歩をしながら蔵前通りを西に歩けば、「越おかず横丁」と呼ばれる昭和の情緒たっぷりの古い商店街に至ります。

later, such as Tokyo University and nearby Ochanomizu University.

Asakusabashi (Ningyo tonya-gai)

In the olden days of Edo Castle's dominance, a bridge across the moat called Asakusa-bashi gave its name to the present-day Asakusa-bashi. There is a station by this name on the Sobu JR line, and if you exit the eastern side of the station you can find small-scale shops and wholesalers dealing with Japan's traditional dolls (*ningyo*) lining the streets of the neighborhood.

In particular on March 3 and May 5 — celebrated as Girl's Day and Boy's Day in the traditional calendar — dolls elaborately dressed as noblemen, court ladies, and samurai are displayed in conjunction with these festivals. In the neighborhood there are many shops that carry this type of celebratory doll.

Nearby, in the old merchant neighborhood where Oedo Street crosses Kuramaebashi Street, if you stroll west on Kuramae Street you will come across an old-fashioned, Showa-era shopping street called "Etsu okazu yokocho," which should not be missed.

東京の「麺」

麺類は、昼食や夕食、また夜食としても食べられています。
- People eat noodles for lunch, dinner, or as a late-night snack.

鉄道の駅構内にも麺類のお店が出ているところがあります。
- You can often see noodle shops inside train stations.

麺類は伸びてしまう前に素早く食べるといいでしょう。
- Noodles should be eaten quickly, before they get soggy.

日本では、音を立てて麺をすする習慣があります。
- In Japan, it is customary to slurp noodles.

「立ち食い」と呼ばれるそば屋には座席がありません。
- Some noodle shops, called "*tachigui*," don't have seats.

麺類は安くてすぐに食べられるので、立ち食いはごく一般的です。
- *Tachigui* are very popular because the food is quick and cheap.

本格的に東京を体験したいのであれば、立ち食いで麺をすすりましょう。
- If you want an authentic Tokyo experience, go eat noodles at a *tachigui*.

Tokyo in Single Sentences

東京では、うどんよりそばのほうが人気です。

☐ Soba noodles are more popular in Tokyo than udon noodles.

東京風のラーメンはスープが醤油だしです。

☐ Tokyo-style ramen comes in a soy-sauce broth.

秋葉原

Track 65

秋葉原は東京の真ん中に位置しています。

☐ Akihabara is a neighborhood in central Tokyo.

秋葉原は有楽町と同じく、千代田区にあります。

☐ Akihabara is a neighborhood in Chiyoda Ward, along with Yurakucho.

KEY WORD ✓

☐ late-night snack	夜食
☐ slurp noodles	麺をすする
☐ soy-sauce broth	醤油だし

神田・秋葉原とその周辺　東京の「麺」　●　秋葉原

▶▶▶ ワンセンテンスで説明する東京

秋葉原は東京駅から山手線で北に２駅のところにあります。

☐ Akihabara is two stops north of Tokyo Station on the Yamanote Line.

秋葉原は「アキバ」のニックネームで呼ばれています。

☐ Akihabara is nicknamed "Akiba."

秋葉原は電器店がたくさんあることで有名です。

☐ Akihabara is famous for its electronics stores.

最新の電子機器を買いたい人には、秋葉原がおすすめです。

☐ If you want to shop for the latest electronics, you should go to Akihabara.

秋葉原には「電気街」と呼ばれる一角があり、「Electric（電気の）Town（街）」という意味です。

☐ There is a district in Akihabara called "Denki-gai," which means "Electric Town."

秋葉原は漫画やアニメを愛好する人々の聖地です。

☐ Akihabara is a hangout for people who love comic books and anime.

秋葉原には漫画専門店がたくさんあります。

☐ In Akihabara there are many stores selling comic books.

秋葉原には、お気に入りの漫画キャラクターの格好をする（コスプレ）人向けにコスチュームを売る店があります。

☐ In Akihabara there are stores that sell costumes for people to dress up as their favorite comic-book characters.

秋葉原には、メイドの格好をしたウェイトレスがいるメイドカフェがあります。

☐ In Akihabara, you can visit maid cafés where the waitresses dress like French maids.

ウェイトレスが来ているメイド服は、人気マンガに着想を得たものです。

☐ The maid costumes worn by waitresses in maid cafés were inspired by a popular comic book.

秋葉原は日本の大人気女性アイドルグループ、AKB48の本拠地です。

☐ Akihabara is the home of Japan's most popular all-girl singing group, AKB48.

秋葉原には、缶入りのラーメンやパンの自動販売機があります。

☐ In Akihabara, there are vending machines selling cans of noodles and bread.

神保町

神保町は千代田区にあります。
- [ ] Jinbocho is a neighborhood in Chiyoda Ward.

神保町は秋葉原の西に位置しています。
- [ ] Jinbocho is located to the west of Akihabara.

神保町には200店ちかくの古書店があります。
- [ ] Jinbocho is home to nearly 200 used bookstores.

神保町は本好きの街として知られています。
- [ ] Jinbocho is known as the book-lovers' neighborhood.

店で売られている本のほとんどは日本語ですが、英語やその他の言語の本もあります。
- [ ] Most of the stores sell books in Japanese, but you can also find books in English and other languages.

神保町には学術書や、江戸時代の本、ヴィンテージものの漫画などが売られています。
- [ ] In Jinbocho there are stores that sell serious academic books, books from the Edo era, and vintage manga.

神保町には大きな出版社がたくさんあります。
- [ ] Many big publishing companies are located in Jinbocho.

Tokyo in Single Sentences

神保町の近くには明治大学や日本大学など、いくつか大学があります。

☐ Meiji University and Nihon University are two major universities located near Jinbocho.

当然ながら、本好きの集まる街にはたくさんのカフェがあります。

☐ Of course, a neighborhood for book lovers has many cafés.

神保町にはカレー屋がたくさんあります。

☐ Jinbocho has many curry restaurants.

カレーは片手で食べられるので、本を読みながら食べるのに最も適した料理だと言われています。

☐ It is said that curry is the perfect food to eat while reading a book, because you can eat it with one hand.

神田・秋葉原とその周辺

神保町

KEY WORD ✓

☐ academic book　　学術書

漫画喫茶

漫画喫茶では、漫画を読んだりインターネットをしたり、DVD鑑賞ができます。

- [ ] A manga café is a place where you can read manga, surf the internet or watch DVDs.

漫画喫茶では、コンピューターかテレビのある個室を1時間単位で借りることができます。

- [ ] At manga cafés you can rent private cubicles with computers or TV sets by the hour.

漫画喫茶はメールチェックをするのに便利な場所です。

- [ ] Manga cafés are useful if you need to check your email.

漫画喫茶の個室はそれなりに快適で、中には寝ている人もいます。

- [ ] The cubicles in manga cafés are fairly comfortable, so sometimes people sleep in them.

漫画喫茶で夜を過ごすのは、ホテルに泊まるよりずっと割安です。

- [ ] A night in a manga café is much cheaper than a night in a hotel.

終電を逃してしまったときは、漫画喫茶かカラオケ店で夜を過ごすことができます。

- [ ] If you miss your last train, you can stay the night in a manga café or a *karaoke* parlor.

KEY WORD

- [ ] surf the internet　　　インターネットをする
- [ ] cubicle　　　　　　　小さな個室

2-09 上野・谷中とその周辺

上野

　上野は、都心の北部にある街で、そこにある上野駅は元々北から東京にはいる長距離列車のターミナルでした。今でも上野駅は重要な乗り換え駅として、北部からの通勤客などが使用しています。

　上野の名前は、江戸時代初期に、藤堂高虎(とうどうたかとら)という大名の屋敷がそのあたりにあって、彼の領地が紀伊半島の伊賀上野にあったことに由来するといわれています。その後、徳川将軍の菩提寺として寛永寺がこの地に建てられたことにより、東京の現代史における上野の重要性が高まったのです。

Around Ueno, Yanaka

Ueno

Located in the northern sector of Tokyo, the neighborhood of Ueno, and particularly Ueno train station, became important as the terminal for many of the long-distance trains linking the capital with destinations in the north of Japan. Even today it remains important as a transit point for countless commuters coming to the city from the northern suburbs of Tokyo.

The name "Ueno" is said to come from one of the feudal lords who maintained his Edo-era residence nearby. The domain ruled by Todo Takatora, a *daimyo* from the Kii Peninsula, had an area known as Iga-Ueno, and this led to his part of old Edo taking on the place name Ueno. Later, the Tokugawa Shogun commissioned his family's main Buddhist temple, Kanei-ji — which is important in Japanese culture as having the graves of the family's lineage on the temple grounds — to be built in the Ueno area, increasing the importance of this district in Tokyo's modern history.

寛永寺

　寛永寺は上野にあるお寺で、徳川将軍の菩提寺として1625年に建てられました。元々は、現在の上野公園を中心に沢山の施設や僧院のある巨大な寺で、歴代の将軍のうち、5人がここに埋葬されていました。

　しかし、1868年の明治維新の余波を受け、徳川家に忠誠を誓った人々が寛永寺の周辺で新政府軍と戦争をしたため、そのほとんどが焼け落ちました。この内戦は上野戦争と呼ばれています。その後寛永寺の中心部分は上野公園として整備され、寛永寺の面影も今なお散見することができます。

　残念なことに、残された多くの歴史的な建造物も、第二次世界大戦での空襲でさらに破壊され、今では上野公園の北側にいくつかの伽藍が残っているだけになりました。

上野公園

　上野駅の西側一帯の丘、通称上野の山にある公園

Kanei-ji Temple

Located in the Ueno area, Kanei-ji was commissioned to be built by the Tokugawa Shogun in 1625 to serve as his family's main Buddhist temple. Originally this was an enormous temple compound with numerous halls and a monastery in the center of what is now Ueno Park, and five of Tokugawa Shogun's graves are memorialized within the Kanei-ji Temple's grounds.

However, much of the temple was burned down in the aftermath of the 1868 Meiji Restoration, when battles took place in the Ueno vicinity between supporters of the Tokugawa Shogunate and the newly established government's forces. This came to be known as the Battle of Ueno. In the aftermath, what had been the main Kanei-ji Temple grounds were transformed into Ueno Park, and some of the remnants of the temple could still be found in this area.

Unfortunately, most of the historical temple structures that had been preserved from that time were destroyed in the heavy bombing of Tokyo during World War II, and what remains today are some temples to the north of Ueno Park.

Ueno Park

On the hilltop area to the west of Ueno Station are the large

で、国立科学博物館、国立西洋美術館、東京国立博物館などの施設がある文京公園です。

ここは春の桜のシーズンはお花見の場所として知られています。園内には上野動物園や、蓮の花で有名な不忍池などがあります。不忍池はもともと寛永寺の庭として江戸時代初期(17世紀)に整備されたものです。

東京国立博物館

日本には、東京国立博物館の他に京都、奈良、そして九州の太宰府に国立博物館があり、日本と東洋の歴史的遺物や美術品を収集展示しています。東京国立博物館は上野公園にあって、そんな4つの博物館の中でも特に規模がおおきく、多彩な美術品を展示していること知られた博物館です。明治維新から4年後の1872年に完成した博物館には、11万点を超える収蔵品があり、国宝が87点、重要文化財が634点含まれています。

grounds of Ueno Park, with an impressive array of cultural establishments including the National Museum of Nature and Science, the National Museum of Western Art, and the Tokyo National Museum.

The park grounds are particularly well known for outdoor flower-viewing parties under the trees during cherry-blossom season. Elsewhere in the park is the very popular Ueno Zoo with its famous panda bears, and Shinobazu-no-ike Pond, known for its beautiful lotus plants, particularly when these are in bloom. Shinobazu Pond was originally constructed in the early seventeenth century as part of the traditional Japanese gardens of the Kanei-ji Temple.

Tokyo National Museum

In addition to the National Museum in Tokyo, there are branches of the National Museum located in Kyoto, Nara, and in a town called Dazaifu in Kyushu, each with a collection of historic remains and works of art from Japan, Asia, and around the world. The Tokyo National Museum is in Ueno Park, and among the four museums around Japan it has the largest collection. Established in 1872, just four years after the Meiji Restoration, the museum's collection of 110,000 pieces includes 87 Japanese National Treasures and 634 of Japan's registered Important Cultural Properties.

アメヤ横丁

　上野駅の南側にある「アメ横」の名前で親しまれている地域は、第二次世界大戦で空襲を受けた後にひしめいたバラックの闇市が起源の市場街です。

　最近までは日本食の食材などを売る店がぎっしりと並んでいましたが、今ではアジア各地の雑貨や食材を売る店も混ざった活気ある界隈に変貌しています。

谷中・根津

　山手線の日暮里駅から西へ道を歩けば、そこは谷中と呼ばれる地域です。道の両側や近くの路地に昔ながらの畳屋さんや骨董屋、さらには「和食のタパス」ともいえる小料理屋さんなどが並んでいます。

Ameya Yokocho

South of Ueno Station is a shopping area fondly known as *Ameyoko*. In the aftermath of the destruction of the city from bombing during World War II, a black-market shopping street crowded with stalls peddling hard-to-get commodities and daily goods sprang up, giving rise to a bustling shopping street still popular by this name today.

Until not long ago the street was lined with countless shops selling ingredients for Japanese cuisine, but in recent years there has been a transformation, as many shops now cater to customers looking for goods and foodstuffs from other Asian countries, and the neighborhood is now an even more diverse, fun, and thriving marketplace.

Yanaka, Nezu

If you get off of the Yamanote JR line at Nippori Station and walk along the boulevard heading west, the district you will find is called Yanaka. Here, on both sides of the street and in the nearby side alleys, you will find traditional tatami mat--making shops, antique shops, and, not to be missed, small restaurants specializing in what has been called Japanese tapas — many varieties of folksy food served in small dishes.

「谷中銀座」のレトロな一角は、古き良き時代の東京の風情が残っていて、散歩にはもってこいです。

谷中を南に行けば根津という地域に至ります。谷中から根津にかけては、古くからお寺も多く、落ち着いた界隈になっています。根津からさらに南へ行けば、緑に覆われ、素晴らしい博物館のある上野公園まで散策できます。谷中から根津を経て上野に至るこの地域は、下町情緒を堪能できる隠れた観光スポットなのです。

谷中霊園

日暮里駅のすぐ近く、谷中にある大きな墓地は、谷中霊園といって桜の名所としても知られています。霊園の中央の通りを抜けて、言問通りまで歩けば、その一帯が寺町として知られ、料理屋や古くからの小売店の並ぶ根津の中心となります。

This is a neighborhood that is well worth an exploratory, leisurely stroll, as the "Yanaka Ginza" has retained an old-fashioned, retro-type feel of "the good old days" of traditional Tokyo.

Walking a bit to the south of Yanaka is a neighborhood known as Nezu. Here, many Buddhist temples from olden days can be found in the short stroll from Yanaka, providing a tranquil, serene atmosphere far from the bustle of the big city. Strolling even farther south from Nezu, you come to Ueno Park, with all of its greenery and notable museums. In this area, from Yanaka through Nezu and on down to Ueno, you will find a hidden gem, a quiet and friendly neighborhood that has kept the atmosphere of traditional, small-town Tokyo.

上野・谷中とその周辺

Yanaka Reien

A short walk from Nippori Station is a large cemetery in the Yanaka neighborhood — the Yanaka Reien — which is known as one of the best places in Tokyo to view cherry blossoms in the spring. If you walk along the path through the middle of the cemetery and then down Kototoi-dori Street, the whole area you've covered is known as Teramachi, and is at the heart of the Nezu district, its streets lined with restaurants and small-scale shops.

上野

上野は東京の北東部、台東区に位置しています。

☐ Ueno is located in the northeast of central Tokyo, in Taito Ward.

新宿や品川と同じく、上野も交通の要所です。

☐ Like Shinjuku and Shinagawa, Ueno is a major hub.

上野は山手線で東京駅から北へ4駅のところにあります。

☐ Ueno is four stops north of Tokyo Station on the Yamanote Line.

上野から、北と東の郊外に向かう通勤電車が出ています。

☐ Commuter trains leave from Ueno for the suburbs to the north and to the east.

新宿や池袋と同じく、上野にもデパート、電器店、飲食店、バーなどがあります。

☐ Like Shinjuku and Ikebukuro, Ueno has department stores, electronics stores, restaurants and bars.

新宿や池袋に比べると、上野の歴史は古いです。

☐ Compared to Shinjuku and Ikebukuro, Ueno is a much older neighborhood.

Tokyo in Single Sentences

新宿や池袋といった新しい街とは違い、上野は江戸時代から続く歴史があります。

☐ Unlike newer neighborhoods such as Shinjuku and Ikebukuro, Ueno has a history going back to the Edo era.

上野には多くのミュージアムがあり、東京国立博物館もそのひとつです。

☐ Ueno has many museums, including the Tokyo National Museum.

広大な上野公園には、ミュージアムが数館あります。

☐ Ueno has a big park, Ueno Park, where several museums are located.

ミュージアムが好きな人には、上野をおすすめします。

☐ If you like museums, you should go to Ueno.

上野公園は、東京一の花見の名所です。

☐ Ueno Park is the most famous cherry blossom viewing spot in Tokyo.

KEY WORD ✓

☐ cherry blossom viewing spot　　花見の名所

▶▶▶ ワンセンテンスで説明する東京

上野には昔ながらの商店街、アメヤ横丁があります。

☐ Ueno has an old-fashioned open-air market, called Ameya-yokocho.

上野公園は1873年に、日本初の公園に指定されました。

☐ Ueno Park was designated in 1873 as the first public park in Japan.

上野公園は300エーカーの広さがあります。

☐ Ueno Park covers 300 acres.

ミュージアムも多くあることから、上野公園は東京の文化的中心といえます。

☐ With its many museums, Ueno Park is one of Tokyo's principal cultural centers.

上野公園には、東京国立博物館、国立科学博物館、国立西洋美術館などのミュージアムがあります。

☐ Ueno Park has several museums, including the Tokyo National Museum, the National Science Museum, and the National Museum for Western Art.

上野公園には、寛永寺、清水観音堂、弁天堂という3つの寺と、東照宮という神社があります。

☐ Ueno Park has three temples, Kanei-ji, Kiyomizu Kannon-do, and Benten-do, and one shrine, Toshogu.

Tokyo in Single Sentences

上野公園には不忍池という池があり、睡蓮がたくさん生育しています。

☐ Ueno Park has a pond, Shinobazu Pond, with many water lilies.

上野公園には、上野動物園という、日本で一番古い動物園があります。

☐ Ueno Zoo, located in Ueno Park, is Japan's oldest zoo.

上野公園には桜の木が1000本以上あります。

☐ Ueno Park has over 1,000 cherry trees.

上野公園は東京の昔ながらのお花見スポットです。

☐ Ueno Park is Tokyo's classic cherry blossom viewing spot.

週末の上野公園には、アーティストたちが集まってパフォーマンスを披露しています。

☐ On the weekends, performance artists perform in Ueno Park.

谷中・根津・千駄木(谷根千)

Track 69

谷中、根津、千駄木の3つの地区はそれぞれ隣接しています。

☐ Yanaka, Nezu and Sendagi are three neighborhoods that border each other.

谷中、根津、千駄木はまとめて「谷根千」として知られています。

☐ Together, the neighborhoods of Yanaka, Nezu and Sendagi are known as Yanesen.

谷中は台東区にありますが、根津と千駄木は文京区にあります。

- [ ] Yanaka is in Taito Ward while Nezu and Sendagi are in Bunkyo Ward.

根津と千駄木には地下鉄千代田線が停まります。

- [ ] Nezu and Sendagi are stops on the Chiyoda subway line.

谷根千は上野の西側にあります。

- [ ] Yanesen is located to the west of Ueno.

谷根千には20世紀初頭に建てられた木造建築がたくさん残っています。

- [ ] The neighborhoods of Yanesen have many wooden buildings that date back to the early twentieth century.

谷根千には古い建物がたくさん残っていて、昔懐かしい雰囲気があります。

- [ ] Because Yanesen has many old buildings, it has an old-fashioned atmosphere.

人々は「昔の東京」を求めて谷根千を訪れます。

- [ ] People come to Yanesen to experience "old Tokyo."

谷根千には坂道や路地がたくさんあり、散策するのが楽しい地域です。

- [ ] There are many hills and alleyways, which makes Yanesen a fun neighborhood to explore on foot.

谷中にはいたるところに寺があります。

- [ ] There are dozens of temples in Yanaka.

Tokyo in Single Sentences

谷中には谷中霊園という墓地があり、最後の徳川将軍がここに眠っています。

☐ There is a cemetery in Yanaka, Yanaka Reien, where the last Tokugawa shogun is buried.

谷中銀座は谷中にある商店街で、50年前の東京を感じさせてくれます。

☐ Yanaka Ginza is a street in Yanaka that's filled with shops, with an atmosphere that feels like Tokyo fifty years ago.

近くに芸術大学があるため、谷中にはたくさんの芸術家が暮らしています。

☐ Yanaka is near an art university, so many artists live in the neighborhood.

谷根千には、朝倉彫塑館のような、地元の芸術家を記念した小さな美術館がいくつもあります。

☐ Yanesen has many small museums dedicated to local artists, such as the Asakura Choso Museum.

上野・谷中とその周辺　谷中・根津・千駄木（谷根千）

KEY WORD ✓

☐ explore on foot　　　散策する

銭湯体験

昔、東京のアパートには風呂がなかったので、人々は銭湯へ通っていました。

☐ In the past, Tokyo apartments didn't have baths, so people went to public bathhouses.

公共浴場のことを銭湯といいます。

☐ A public bathhouse is called a *sento*.

昔はどこの地域にも銭湯がありました。

☐ In the past, every neighborhood had a *sento*.

東京にはかつて1000を超える銭湯がありましたが、現在も残っているのは数百軒ほどです。

☐ There used to be over a thousand *sento* in Tokyo, but now there are only a few hundred left.

銭湯は近隣住民が顔を合わせ、たわいのない会話をする場でした。

☐ The bathhouse was a place where neighbors met and gossiped.

現在ではほとんどの家庭に風呂があり、地元の銭湯に行く人はほんのわずかです。

☐ Now that most homes have baths, few people visit the local bathhouses.

Tokyo in Single Sentences

公共浴場は男湯と女湯が分かれています。

☐ At public bathhouses there are separate baths for men and women.

新規顧客を獲得するために、サウナやジェットバスを備えた銭湯もあります。

☐ Some public bathhouses have saunas or baths with jets to attract new customers.

銭湯へ行けば、手っ取り早く昔の東京文化を体験することができます。

☐ A trip to a public bathhouse is a good way to experience old Tokyo culture.

上野・谷中とその周辺

銭湯体験

KEY WORD ✓

☐ public bathhouse　　　銭湯

2-10 月島・深川とその周辺

下町

　東京は17世紀にはいって、徳川家康がここに幕府を開いて以来、大きく発展しました。その当時、江戸城の周辺には大名や身分の高い武士の屋敷がならんでいました。大名は江戸に居を構えることを求められ、幕府によって、その忠誠心を試されたのです。

　それに対して庶民の多くは、東京湾に近い江戸の東側で生活をしていました。この庶民の住む地域を下町といい、今でもあちこちに江戸時代の町人文化の名残が散見できます。ちなみに、下町に対して、明治時代以降発展した東京の西側のことを山手と呼んでいます。

Around Tsukishima, Fukagawa

Shitamachi

Tokyo has evolved dramatically in the centuries since Tokugawa Ieyasu established his military government (*Bakufu*) here in the early days of the seventeenth century. At that time, neighborhoods surrounding Edo Castle were lined with the residences of the feudal lords (*daimyo*) and samurai of high status — the *daimyo* were required to maintain an Edo residence as a means by which the *Bakufu* could monitor and ensure their loyalty.

In contrast to the *daimyo* and samurai, the common people lived east of the castle closer to Edo (today, Tokyo) Bay. That area came to be known as "*Shitamachi*" (literally, "downtown" or "lower town"), and there are many remnants of Edo-era common-folk traditions in the *Shitamachi* part of Tokyo even today. We should note that the western part of Tokyo that was developed from the time of the Meiji period, beginning in 1868, was referred to as "*Yamanote*" (the name of the JR above-ground loop line), which also has the meaning, from "*yama*" (mountain) of being on higher ground.

隅田川

　浅草と向島との間を流れる隅田川は、荒川の分流として東京の古い地域をぬって東京湾に注ぐ川で、東京の下町を縦断する水路として江戸時代から人々に利用されてきた、東京の下町を代表する川として親しまれています。

　古くから小説や浮世絵などに描かれてきた川でもあります。川辺には散策路があり、浅草から両国にかけて、下町を散策しながら川辺の風景を楽しむことができます。また、水上バスに乗って、例えば浜離宮から浅草までを遡ったりして、川から東京の風景を楽しむこともできます。

　その途上で、ボートは隅田川にかかり、両岸をつなぐ形状や色合いがどれも個性的な12本もの橋をくぐり抜けるのです。

月島（もんじゃ焼き）

　月島は、明治時代になって埋め立てられてできた街です。ここは東京の庶民的なグルメとしてしられるもんじゃ焼きの店が数多く並んでいることで知られています。

Sumidagawa River

Flowing between Asakusa and Mukojima, the Sumida River — a branch of the Arakawa River — empties into Tokyo Bay after gracefully visiting the banks of the older areas of Tokyo. Used by its neighboring residents for a variety of purposes since the Edo era, the river both symbolizes the city and has earned its affection for centuries.

What's more, it has found its way into many a novel, and is depicted in ukiyo-e woodblock prints and other forms of art. The path overlooking the river is a perfect place for a leisurely stroll, while taking in the sights of the old city between Asakusa and Ryogoku, and you can enjoy the view by riding the "Water Bus" as well, for instance from the Hama-Rikyu detached gardens upriver to Asakusa.

Along the way, your ferry will go under a dozen bridges, each unique in its construction, shape and color, spanning the Sumida and nicely connecting its neighborhoods.

Tsukishima (monjayaki)

Tsukishima is a neighborhood created by landfill during the Meiji era. Today it is known as an area with countless shops serving up a dish known as "*monjayaki*," which was originally created to cater to the tastes of commoners, but which is now quite popular as a form of local cuisine.

もんじゃ焼きは、スープ状にした小麦粉を鉄板で調理して食べる料理で、目の前で多彩な材料を加えて、鉄板の上で平らにしながら、自分の好みの味付けにします。

　同じように鉄板を使った料理にお好み焼きがあります小麦粉の生地を使うのは一緒ですが、もっとねっとりとさせたもので、それにいろいろな材料を煉り込みます。もんじゃ焼きもお好み焼きも日本人のB級グルメの代表として親しまれています。B級グルメは、世界中で評価されている高級な和牛ほど知られてはいませんが、試してみる価値はあります。

門前仲町・富岡八幡宮

　門前仲町は、富岡八幡宮の門前町として江戸時代に発展した地域です。富岡八幡宮は、江戸時代初期に建立された神社です。今でも八幡宮界隈には神社や寺とともに発展した町によく見られるような歴史を感じさせる独特の雰囲気が残っています。参道沿いには、食材や日常生活に使う小物を販売する店がならび、昔ながらの門前町の雰囲気をだしています。

It is made from flour mixed into a soupy batter and poured onto a metal grill, cooked in front of you with a variety of ingredients added to taste as you flatten it out on the built-in *teppan* grill tabletop.

Together with another tabletop meal known as *okonomiyaki* — similarly made from flour-based batter, but thicker and incorporating a variety of ingredients that you choose when you prepare it — *monjayaki* is a good example of the so-called B-class gourmet foods once popular with commoners. While these are not as well known as the higher-end Japanese cuisines that are appreciated around the world, they are popular dishes that are worth trying.

Monzen-Nakacho

Monzen-Nakacho emerged as a flourishing part of the city during the Edo era, know for its location near the front gates of the Tomioka Hachiman Shrine. The shrine, in turn, was established early in the Edo era, and to this day the neighborhood has retained many of the historic qualities and characteristics typical of a town that developed around a shrine or temple. The streets are lined with shops selling foodstuffs and a variety of small items useful in daily life, giving the area its unique atmosphere as a continuing reminder of the traditional downtown of the Edo era.

江戸東京博物館

両国にある江戸東京博物館は、江戸時代から現在までの東京の歴史を振り返ることのできるユニークで面白い博物館です。江戸時代の街の様子、人々の暮らしなどが立体的に楽しめます。

また、明治時代以降、江戸が東京となったあと、現在に至るまでの人々の暮らしの移り変わり、戦争中の苦難をどうやって耐えてきたのかがわかる展示も豊富です。東京の歴史を生活に結びつけて展示しているので、楽しみながら理解ができ、この躍動感あふれる都市に対する洞察力が深まる博物館です。

国技館

国技館は、江戸東京博物館のすぐそば、両国駅の前にあります。国技館は日本の国技といわれる格闘技、相撲の聖地です。文科省管轄の日本相撲協会による主催で、1月、5月、9月にそれぞれ15日間大相撲が開催されます。他の都市でも、年に数回、大相撲が開催されます。

Edo-Tokyo Museum

Located in the part of town known as Ryogoku, the Edo Tokyo Museum is a unique and entertaining space in which to experience and look back on the city, from its historical origins as Edo to its present existence as modern Tokyo. Many of its exhibits are 3-D reproductions of life as it was lived in olden times, depicting scenes around town from when it was known as Edo.

Proceeding to modern times, we can see the transition in the Meiji era to its new identity as Tokyo, getting a feel for the transformation of people's lives and how they survived the hardships of World War II, for instance. The museum offers unparalleled insights into this dynamic city, based on exhibits that bring its historical roots to life in an entertaining and understandable manner.

Kokugikan

Situated next to the Edo Tokyo Museum in front of the Ryogoku train station on the Sobu Line is the Kokugikan, home to Japan's national sport, a martial art form known as sumo. The Japan Sumo Association, acting under the purview of the nation's Ministry of Education, Culture, Sports, Science and Technology (MEXT), oversees three 15-day sumo tournaments a year in the Kokugikan, held each

相撲は日本文化をかいま見ることのできる窓口でもあり、日本人だけでなく海外からの見物客も楽しんでいます。売り切れになることもよくあるようです。

深川

深川は、江戸時代から庶民の街として栄えた場所です。もともと東京湾に近かったので、そこで採れるアサリやハマグリなどをしょうゆ味で、お米と炊き込んだ深川めしは、この地域を代表する庶民の料理として、今でも親しまれています。

深川には歓楽街としての顔もありました。飲食の店だけでなく、男性客に売春婦を無許可で斡旋していたのです。なお、深川にある深川江戸資料館は、江戸時代に深川に住んでいた人々の暮らしぶりが再現されている興味深い博物館です。

January, May, and September, with other tournaments held elsewhere in Japan at other times of the year.

Sumo is a fascinating window into Japan's culture, and is enjoyed by foreign residents and visitors as well as many Japanese, in often sold-out bouts.

Fukagawa

Fukagawa is a commoner's part of town that prospered during the Edo era. As it was originally close to the bay (before more and more area was created through landfill extensions of the city), it came to be known for its *Fukagawa-meshi*, which is a rice dish that has been cooked with fresh shellfish such as clams and mussels, giving it a special aroma and making it popular as a cuisine unique to this neighborhood.

Fukagawa also served as an entertainment district, not only with restaurants and drinking establishments but with unlicensed bordellos catering to a male clientele. A unique space known as the Fukagawa Archival Museum has recreated the life of Edo-era townsfolk in the Fukagawa neighborhood, and is an interesting place to visit.

亀戸

総武線に沿って秋葉原から東に4駅離れたところに位置する亀戸周辺は、比較的静かな地域です。元来、お江戸の「下町」の一部として、活気溢れる街でしたが、いまでも往時の面影が残っています。その一方で、現代的な商店街が主要駅から南へ伸びており、周辺の住宅地を活気づかせています。

他の古い街並みと同様に、この地域にもひっそりとした路地裏、商店、趣のある古い建物などがありますが、この地区の多くの神社仏閣の中でも亀戸天神が最も有名であり、東京の他の地域をはじめ、日本全国や海外からも多くの参拝客を惹きつけています。

亀戸天神

1662年に建立された亀戸天神は、東京滞在中に訪れる価値のある名所です。その伝統的な日本庭園は見どころが多く、池には有名な太鼓橋がかかり、種々さまざまな植物が植えられていますが、亀戸天神は特に次の2つの理由で有名です。

1つは、4月から5月にかけての藤まつりです。100株以上の花盛りの藤——美しい紫色の花が、木や竹で組まれた藤棚に咲き誇っています——満開時には数千人もの参拝客が訪れ、神社の庭中が芳香に包まれます。

Kameido

Located along the JR Sobu train line four stops east of Akihabara is the relatively quiet neighborhood of Kameido. Originally an active part of Edo's downtown *Shitamachi*, it retains an atmosphere reminiscent of olden times, while a modern shopping street running south of the main train station enlivens the residential surroundings.

As with other older parts of town, there are quiet back streets, shops, and quaint, aging buildings. Among the many temples and shrines in this area, the Kameido Tenjin Shrine is best known, attracting large numbers of visitors from elsewhere in Tokyo, from around Japan and from overseas.

Kameido Tenjin Shirine

Founded in 1662, the Kameido Tenjin Shrine is a destination landmark worth visiting when you are in Tokyo. With a traditional Japanese garden replete with ponds, the notable Drum Bridges, and many kinds of plants, the shrine is famous for two reasons in particular.

One is the Wisteria Festival held in April and May, in which over 100 flowering wisteria — their beautiful purple-colored blossoms held up by wooden and bamboo trellises — draw thousands of visitors when in full bloom, when their aromas waft through the shrine's gardens.

2つ目の理由は、日本人の学者としては初期のころに活躍した菅原道真を祀って、神社や庭園が350年以上前（実際に道真が生きていたのは1000年以上前のことであるにもかかわらず）に造られたということです。文学や学問に対する道真の献身を崇めて、学生たちは受験前に道真という学問の神様の恩恵に与りたいという熱意から、必ず神社を訪れるのです。

清澄庭園

　深川にある清澄庭園は、東京を代表する日本庭園で、三菱財閥を築いた岩崎弥太郎が江戸時代に有名な商人が所有していたこの地を買い上げました。彼は戦国大名が好んだであろうような庭園に造りかえ、大切な客人をもてなしたり、社員が楽しめる場所として使ったのです。大きな池の周りを周遊しながら庭を楽しめる回遊式庭園です。

　三菱グループは、この地を1932年に東京に寄贈し、1979年に東京都指定名勝となりました。

The second reason is the early Japanese scholar Sugawara no Michizane, in whose honor the shrine and its gardens were constructed over 350 years ago, although he lived more than 1,000 years ago. Revered for his dedication to literature and to learning, he has made the shrine a popular destination for students eager to be blessed with his educator's good fortune before they take their exams.

Kiyosumi Garden

Located in the Fukagawa neighborhood is the Kiyosumi Teien Gardens, noteworthy as a good example of a traditional Japanese garden. Iwasaki Yataro, founder of the Mitsubishi Group of companies, bought this property, which was formerly owned by a famous merchant in the Edo era. He had it landscaped into a garden in a style similar to something that would have been maintained by a feudal *daimyo*, and used it to entertain important guests and as a place for employees of the Mitsubishi firm to enjoy a pleasant outing. This "*kaiyu*" style of garden has a large pond, and visitors are able to enjoy strolling through the gardens around the pond.

The Mitsubishi Group donated the property to Tokyo City in 1932, and it was later officially designated as a Place of Scenic Beauty in 1979.

柴又

江戸川には、今でも江戸時代にあった渡し舟があり、「和船」と呼ばれる船底が平たい日本独特の小舟にのって観光客が川を横断しています。

この渡し舟を「矢切の渡し」といい、400年以上につづいています。

矢切の渡しの東側は柴又という町で、その中心には帝釈天と呼ばれる1609年に創建した仏教寺院があります。この帝釈天から伸びる門前町は、昔からかわらない伝統的な商店街の風情が残っています。

この地域は日本人にとって国民的映画ともいわれた、旅から旅を繰り返す「テキ屋」稼業を営む寅さんが主人公となった映画『男はつらいよ』という喜劇映画で取り上げられたことで知られています。この映画は48作もつくられたメガヒット映画シリーズとなったのです。

Shibamata

The Edo River also has some unique characteristics. From early in the Edo era to this day, you can see ferries called *wasen* — fairly small boats with a unique flat-bottomed design that came to be known as a "Japanese-style" boat.

These boats carry passengers across the river, including tourists who cherish the views and the memory. Called *yagiri-no-watashi* this type of boat has been ferrying people across the Edo River for over 400 years.

On the eastern side of the river is the Shibamata neighborhood, at the center of which is a Buddhist temple called Taishakuten, constructed in 1609. Stretching from Taishakuten is the Monzencho neighborhood, which has a shopping street that has kept its distinctive atmosphere from olden times.

Set in this neighborhood was a film series called "*Otoko wa tsurai yo*" ("It's tough being a man") which became a phenomenal success, a mega-hit that spanned 48 films. It was a comedy centered on a main character named "Tora" (Tiger), something of a lovable huckster who travels constantly, running an open-air street stall at shrine fairs and festivals, and who became a lasting figure in modern Japanese culture.

深川とその周辺

深川は東京の東部にある街です。
- Fukagawa is a neighborhood on the east side of Tokyo.

深川は、隅田川の東岸にあります。
- Fukagawa is located on the east bank of the Sumida River.

深川は江東区に位置しています。
- Fukagawa is located in Koto Ward.

深川へ地下鉄でいくには半蔵門線と大江戸線の清澄白川駅、大江戸線と都営新宿線の森下駅があります。
- The subway stops for Fukagawa are Kiyosumi-Shirakawa, on the Hanzomon and Oedo subway lines, and Morishita, on the Oedo and Toei-Shinjuku subway lines.

浅草や日本橋と同じく、深川はその起源を江戸時代まで遡ることができます。
- Like Asakusa and Nihonbashi, Fukagawa has its roots in the Edo era.

深川の静かで飾り気のない街並みは、東京の中心街とは異なった趣があります。
- Fukagawa is a quiet, unpretentious neighborhood that feels different from central Tokyo.

Tokyo in Single Sentences

江戸時代の深川は、職人と商人の街でした。

☐ During the Edo era Fukagawa was a neighborhood for artisans and merchants.

深川江戸資料館で、深川の昔の様子を知ることができます。

☐ You can see a recreation of old Fukagawa at the Fukagawa Edo Museum.

俳人として有名な松尾芭蕉は深川に住んでいたことがあります。

☐ The famous haiku poet Matsuo Basho lived for a time in Fukagawa.

江戸時代、深川にある富岡八幡宮で最初に相撲の取り組みが行われました。

☐ During the Edo era the first sumo tournaments took place at Tomioka Hachiman, a shrine in Fukagawa.

下町の食

Track 72

東京のローカルフードにもんじゃ焼きがあります。

☐ One Tokyo local food you should try is *monjayaki*.

もんじゃ焼きは、自分の席で自ら調理するパンケーキのようなものです。

☐ *Monjayaki* is a pancake that you cook yourself on a grill at your table.

▶▶▶ ワンセンテンスで説明する東京

もんじゃ焼きの生地は、キャベツや豚肉などさまざまな素材を混ぜ合わせてつくります。

☐ *Monjayaki* batter comes mixed with many different kinds of fillings, such as cabbage and pork.

もんじゃ焼きは見た目はいまいちですが、とても美味しいです。

☐ *Monjayaki* doesn't look very good, but it tastes great!

東京の月島一帯は、もんじゃ焼き屋が集まるところで有名です。

☐ Tokyo's Tsukishima neighborhood is famous for its many *monjayaki* restaurants.

東京では、江戸時代に起源を持つような料理を楽しむことができます。

☐ In Tokyo you can sample dishes that have been around since the Edo era.

江戸時代に遡る料理の一つにアサリと米で作る「深川めし」というものがあります。

☐ One example of an Edo-period dish is *Fukagawa-meshi*, a dish made with rice and clams.

「深川めし」という昔ながらの料理は、お米にアサリを炊き込んだものです。

☐ A traditional dish named *Fukagawa-meshi* is rice cooked with littleneck clams.

Tokyo in Single Sentences

月島・深川と
その周辺

下町の食

池袋・巣鴨とその周辺

池袋

　池袋は、都心に向かう通勤客にとって重要な乗換駅であり、西武池袋線と東武東上線がこの繁華街に乗り入れています。

　池袋駅の東口には西武百貨店があり、西口には東武百貨店があり、東京有数のショッピングセンターとしても知られています。渋谷と新宿、そして池袋は都心を循環する山手線で繋がっていて、それぞれ都心の西側を代表する街となっています。

巣鴨

　江戸時代は静かな村であったこの地域ですが、今では都心を周回する山手線の最北部に位置し、にぎやかな街へと発展しました。
　とくに、駅の北西側に伸びる商店街にある高岩寺は、針を飲み込んだ女性がこのお寺のお札を飲むと

Around Ikebukuro, Sugamo

Ikebukuro

Ikebukuro is an important transit point for many people commuting to central Tokyo, as both the Seibu Ikebukuro Line and the Tobu Tojo Line connect people through this thriving sub-center of the city.

With the Seibu Department Store on the east side of the station and the Tobu Department Store on the west side, Ikebukuro has one of Tokyo's major concentrations of shopping opportunities. Together with the other popular core areas of Shibuya and Shinjuku, also on the western side of central Tokyo, Ikebukuro is a distinctive part of the city, linked closely to the others by the Yamanote loop line.

Sugamo

A quiet village during the Edo era, Sugamo has evolved into the vibrant neighborhood it is today, located at the top of the Yamanote loop line which circles central Tokyo.

One of Sugamo's famous landmarks is a Buddhist statue in the Kogan-ji Temple located northwest of the train station.

無事に針を吐き出して治癒したという伝説から、病気の治癒にご利益があるとされる「とげぬき地蔵」で有名です。

そしてこの高岩寺周辺の地蔵通りは、「おばあちゃんの原宿」と呼ばれ、年配者向けのファッションや、昔ながらのお菓子屋、小物やが並ぶ商店街として知られています。

もうひとつ巣鴨を有名にしたのが、巣鴨プリズンです。日本が敗戦した後、東京裁判の被告人が収容されていました。

染井町

巣鴨のそばにある染井町は、その昔染井村と呼ばれ、そこに育った桜がソメイヨシノとして品種改良を加えられました。ソメイヨシノはその美しさが、世界中に知られており、ワシントンDCにあるジェファーソン記念館やタイダルベイスンの春を彩る桜も、100年以上前に日本から贈られたソメイヨシノなのです。

The statue memorializes a woman said to have swallowed a needle, but who then also swallowed a fortune-telling slip from the temple, after which she was able to dislodge the needle from her throat and recover completely. Ever since, people suffering from health issues have come to pray at this temple, hoping to be healed as she was.

A shopping street has grown up in the vicinity of the temple selling old-fashioned goods, Japanese sweets, and fashionable clothing geared to the elderly, giving this part of town the nickname "Granny's Harajuku."

Another historical site that has made Sugamo famous is the prison that housed the defendants in the Tokyo War Crimes Trial following Japan's defeat in World War II.

Someicho

Located next to Sugamo is a neighborhood called Someicho, which takes its name from a historic village of the same name. It was in this village that the *Somei-Yoshino* cherry tree was developed as a recognized new species. Known for their beauty the world over, *Somei-Yoshino* trees were the trees donated to Washington, DC, more than a century ago, gracing the Jefferson Memorial and Tidal Basin area with stunning blossoms each spring.

六義園

六義園は、1695年に徳川幕府の5代目の将軍にあたる徳川綱吉の側用人を務めた柳沢吉保が自らの下屋敷として造営した庭として知られています。

それ以来、幸運にも戦災も受けることなく、驚くことに現在でも当時の庭の様子を見ることができます。『古今和歌集』の中にある和歌に描かれた紀州（和歌山県）の風景を再現しようとして造園されたといわれています。

1938年に東京に寄贈され、その後1953年に特別名勝に指定されて以来、六義園は、四季の変化を楽しみながら、高低差のある「築山泉水」という日本古来の庭園を回遊できる都民の憩いの場所となっています。

Rikugien

The Rikugien Gardens were created in 1695 by Tokugawa Tsunayoshi, the fifth ruler in line in the Tokugawa Shogunate, for the residence of Yanagisawa Yoshiyasu, a strong supporter to whom the Shogun wanted to show his appreciation.

Despite the passage of time, the gardens as we see them today are amazingly close to their original design, as they avoided damage during wartime. It is said that the gardens were designed so that viewers could imagine the special scenery of Kishu in present-day Wakayama Prefecture, which had been described in a Japanese *Waka* poem that appears in a famous anthology of historical *Waka* poetry (known as the *Kokin Wakashu*).

Since the time the gardens were donated to the City of Tokyo in 1938, and were later designated as an Important Cultural Asset in 1953, the Rikugien Gardens have been a special place for the public to relax while enjoying not only Japan's four seasons, but the unique high and low aspects of the "mountain and pond" style of traditional Japanese gardens.

旧古河庭園

　一段高くなったところにある洋風庭園とその下に広がる日本庭園で有名なこの旧古河庭園は、明治時代(1868–1912)に古河男爵の邸宅として造られました。

　1956年に一般に公開され、男爵邸となった洋館と庭園は見事に一体化し、洋風のバラ園と京都で数々の作庭を手がけた小川治兵衛による素晴らしい日本庭園も調和して並んでいる。西欧の文化が日本の古典的な文化に融合した、明治時代から大正時代にかけての造園を代表する場所であるといえましょう。

Kyu-Furukawa Garden

The Kyu-Furukawa Gardens — notable for a combination of Western-style gardens in the elevated portion and a classical Japanese garden in the lower area — were created during the Meiji era (1868–1912) at one of the residences of the noted Furukawa family.

Opened to the public in 1956, the gardens complement a Western-style mansion built for the aristocratic family, and they harmoniously juxtapose a Western rose garden and a remarkable Japanese garden designed by Ogawa Jihei, famous for his Kyoto-style gardens. The house and gardens perfectly represent the late-Meiji and early-Taisho period cross-influences in Japan of Western, "modernizing" cultures, while retaining many of the elements of traditional Japanese culture.

六義園

六義園は風景式の日本庭園です。
- [ ] Rikugien is a Japanese-style landscape garden.

六義園は東京の北部、文京区にあります。
- [ ] Rikugien is located in the north of Tokyo, in Bunkyo Ward.

六義園は、山手線の駒込駅の近くにあります。
- [ ] Rikugien is located near Komagome Station, a stop on the Yamanote Line.

六義園は1700年頃に造営されました。
- [ ] Rikugien was built around the year 1700.

六義園には、「6つの和歌の庭園」という意味があります。
- [ ] Rikugien means "six-poem garden."

六義園には、有名な和歌の風景に似せた、88ヵ所の景勝地があります。
- [ ] In Rikugien there are 88 scenes from famous poems.

六義園の中央には池があります。
- [ ] There is a pond in the center of Rikugien.

六義園には茶室があり、お茶を飲んで休憩することができます。
- [ ] There is a teahouse in Rikugien where you can stop for tea.

Tokyo in Single Sentences

紅葉が色づく秋が、六義園のもっとも美しい季節です。

☐ The best time to visit Rikugien is in the fall, when the maple leaves change color.

池袋

Track 74

池袋は東京の北西部に位置しています。

☐ Ikebukuro is located in the northwest of central Tokyo.

新宿と同じく、池袋も東京の交通の要所です。

☐ Like Shinjuku, Ikebukuro is one of Tokyo's major hubs.

池袋は豊島区にあります。

☐ Ikebukuro is a neighborhood in Toshima Ward.

池袋は山手線で新宿から北へ4駅のところにあります。

☐ Ikebukuro is four stops north of Shinjuku on the Yamanote Line.

池袋駅から北部の郊外へ向かう通勤電車が出てます。

☐ Commuter trains depart from Ikebukuro Station for the northern suburbs.

池袋には、デパート、電化製品店、レストラン、バーがあります。

☐ Ikebukuro has department stores, electronics stores, restaurants and bars.

▶▶▶ ワンセンテンスで説明する東京

池袋駅の西側、西池袋は繁華街です。

☐ There is an entertainment district in Nishi-Ikebukuro, on the west side of Ikebukuro Station.

新宿と同じように、池袋も仕事帰りに食事をしたりお酒を飲んだりするのにいい場所です。

☐ Like Shinjuku, Ikebukuro is a place to meet for dinner and drinks after work.

池袋には、サンシャインシティという大きな複合施設があります。

☐ There is a big shopping plaza in Ikebukuro called Sunshine City.

サンシャインシティにはプラネタリウム、映画館、展望台、テーマパークのナンジャタウンなどがあります。

☐ Sunshine City has a planetarium, a theater, an observatory, and a theme park called Namja Town.

池袋にある乙女ロードは、漫画好きの女性たちに人気のあるエリアです。

☐ In Ikebukuro, Otome Road is a popular destination for comic-book fangirls.

巣鴨

巣鴨は東京の北部に位置し、池袋から山手線で2駅のところにあります。

☐ Sugamo is located in the north of Tokyo, two stops past Ikebukuro on the Yamanote Line.

Tokyo in Single Sentences

池袋と同じく、巣鴨は豊島区にあります。

☐ Sugamo is a neighborhood in Toshima Ward, like Ikebukuro.

巣鴨はお年寄りに人気の地域で、「おばあちゃんの原宿」とも呼ばれています。

☐ Because Sugamo is a popular hangout for elderly people, it is nicknamed "Granny's Harajuku."

巣鴨にあるお寺は、体の痛みをやわらげてくれると信じられています。

☐ There is a temple in Sugamo that is believed to relieve aches and pains.

当然、このお寺はお年寄りに人気があります。

☐ Naturally, this temple is popular with elderly people.

巣鴨地蔵通り沿いには、伝統的な生薬や食品、その他お年寄りに人気のある商品を売るお店が並んでいます。

☐ Along Sugamo's Jizo Street there are shops selling traditional medicines and food and other products that are popular with elderly people.

巣鴨で赤い下着が売られているのを見かけるはずです。赤い下着は体力、気力を増幅させるといわれています。

☐ In Sugamo you can see stores selling red underwear, which is said to increase one's energy and vigor.

品川・海浜とその周辺

品川

　品川は、江戸時代には、当時の京都、京都に向かうときの最初の宿場でした。当時、ほとんどの人が江戸から京都まで、東海道を徒歩で、2週間以上かけて、寝泊まりしながら旅したのです。東海道には53の宿場があり、いつ、どこで休むかは天候やその日の進み具合によって決まりました。

　現在、品川は山手線南端のビジネスセンターとして賑わっていて、東海道新幹線も発着します。2027年には、品川を起点として名古屋へ向かって最高時速570キロで走るリニアモーターカーも走り出します。

Around Shinagawa, Kaihin

Shinagawa

In the olden days of Edo (the name of the capital city Tokyo during the 250-year-long Tokugawa Period), Shinagawa was the first overnight stopping point in the journey to the ancient capital, Kyoto. Most travelers along the Tokaido route connecting Edo and Kyoto made the journey on foot, stopping along the way for the two weeks or more that the trip used to take.

As there were 53 way-stations offering meals and lodgings, there was flexibility on when and where to stop, depending on the weather and how much progress could be made each day. These days Shinagawa is a bustling business district at the southern end of Yamanote train line circling the city, and it is a stop on the Tokaido Shinkansen. In 2027, moreover, Shinagawa will be the starting point for the Linear Motor Car, initially running to Nagoya, that will travel at the astounding speed of 570 kilometers per hour.

お台場

　新橋から、高架式新交通システムのゆりかもめに乗ると、新しく東京の一部となった、活気あるお台場という地域に簡単に行くことができます。ゴム製のタイヤで、なめらかに滑走するゆりかもめは、眺めのいい吊り橋であるレインボーブリッジを渡り、お台場のある埋立地へと進みます。

　ここは、江戸時代の末期に、徳川幕府に圧力をかけてきた外国船から江戸を守るために、砲台が設置されていた場所であったことからこの名前がついています。今では、臨海副都心と呼ばれ、ショッピングモール、オフィスビル、ホテル、コンベンションセンターなどが並ぶ、活気あふれる新しい都市へと生まれ変わっています。

浜離宮

　築地魚市場からも、スタイリッシュな高層ビルが立ち並ぶ汐留からも、非常にアクセスが良く、浜離宮は都心にある伝統的な庭園として必見です。江戸時代初期の1654年に造園されたとき、浜離宮は要塞のような石造りの築堤が江戸湾に突き出ていましたが、そのために園内の池には自然の循環による潮の干満によって、江戸湾の海水が注がれていました。

Odaiba

From the Shinbashi area it is an easy trip to an exciting new part of Tokyo known as Odaiba, reached by riding the new elevated line called Yurikamome. The rubber-wheeled train (often mistaken for a monorail) glides quietly over the Rainbow Bridge, a picturesque suspension bridge, to the expanding landfill islands where Odaiba is located. The name "Odaiba" reflects a late Edo-era reference to this part of Tokyo Bay, where fortress walls were built to defend against foreign vessels seeking to pressure the Tokugawa regime. Today, the Odaiba area is known as the Seaside City Sub-center of Tokyo, as shopping malls, corporate towers, hotels, and a convention center have gone up, transforming this part of the bay into a thriving new part of metropolitan Tokyo.

Hama Rikyu Detached Palace

Easily accessible from the stylish, high-rise neighborhood of Shiodome, the Hama Rikyu Detached Palace is a must-see traditional garden near the heart of Tokyo. When it was constructed in 1654, early in the Edo era, it jutted into Edo Bay with its fortress-like stone embankment, but its ponds were fed by the bay's tides, rising and falling according to nature's cycles. Two of the ponds were used for duck

池の中の2つは当時日本を治めていた徳川家の鴨場として使用されたりしましたが、浜離宮は明治維新後に宮内省付属の離宮となり、皇室の訪問のために管理されるようになりました。ところが1945年から、このすばらしい歴史の一編を東京が担うことになり、現代都市でありながら江戸時代の庭園を散策できるという珍しい一面を提供できるようになったのです。池の上に架けられた伝統的な高架歩道や日本の正式なお茶や和菓子を体験できる茶屋がある浜離宮は、水上バスの発着場にもなっています。その水上バスは乗客を乗せて、お台場を横切り、12本もの橋を通過しながら隅田川を遡ります。

旧芝離宮恩賜公園

　東京でもっとも美しいとされる公園の1つ、旧芝離宮恩賜公園は、JR山手線の浜松町駅と地下鉄の大門駅からほど近いところにあります。この地域は江戸が都になってまもなくの1655年から1658年にかけて、江戸湾を埋め立てたところで、当時は海沿いに位置した庭園には浜もありました。1678年からはこの敷地は徳川将軍家に仕える武将の公邸となり、およそ200年以上、途中何度か持ち主は変わったものの、典型的な江戸時代の日本庭園の姿をとどめてきました。1875年から1924年にかけては宮内庁の所有となり、洋風の迎賓館が建てられ、皇室一家の離宮とし

hunting by the Tokugawa family that ruled Japan, and after the Meiji Restoration the gardens became a Detached Palace as part of the Imperial Household Agency, overseen for visits by the Imperial Family. Since 1945, however, this impressive piece of history has been administered by the City of Tokyo, and it offers a rare place to see the modern city while walking through Edo-era gardens. With a traditional elevated walkway over the ponds and a teahouse to experience Japan's ceremonial tea and sweets, the Hama Rikyu is also a stopping-point for the Water Bus passenger ferry that travels across to Odaiba, and up the Sumida River under a dozen different bridges.

Shiba Imperial Villa

One of Tokyo's most beautiful public gardens is the former Shiba Imperial Villa, located a short distance from Hamamatsucho Station on the JR Yamanote loop-line and Daimon subway station. Not long after Edo became the capital, from 1655 to 1658 this area was reclaimed from Edo Bay, and the gardens originally had a beach along the shore. From 1678 the property included the official residence of a retainer to the ruling Tokugawa family, and over the next two hundred years, although it changed ownership several times, it was maintained as a classical Edo-era Japanese garden. From 1875 to 1924 the Imperial Household Agency

て使用されました。しかし、1923年に東京を襲った関東大震災の後、東京市に下賜され、一般に公開されたのは、1924年に修復された後のことでした。中央に大きな池があり、そこに架かる橋は小島を経由してピクニック場や藤棚へと通じています。光り輝く高層ビルに囲まれたこの庭園はまさにオアシスです。ぜひ足を運んでください。

増上寺・芝公園

　東京タワーもある芝公園内にたつ増上寺には、並々ならぬ歴史があります。本山は京都にあり、浄土宗の教えを関東地方に広めるために1393年に建立されました。徳川家康（1603年に日本を統一し江戸時代を開いた人物）が江戸に領地を移すと、増上寺は1598年に現在の場所に移転しました。特筆すべきことに、日本を1868年まで支配することになる徳川一族の菩提寺になりました。見事な正門は1622年に建造され、1923年の関東大震災も1945年の東京大空襲をも生き抜きました。寺の敷地内には数多くの日本国指定、東京市指定、港区指定の重要文化財が収蔵されています。増上寺の巨大な鐘楼は江戸三大名鐘の一つに数えられ、日に二度鳴らされるのみならず、大晦日には前年の煩悩をはらうため、108回鳴らされます。新年にも、鐘

owned the property and used it — with a European-styled Guest House — as a Detached Palace to be visited by the Imperial Family, but after the Great Kanto Earthquake of 1923 it was given to the City of Tokyo, which opened it to the public after it was restored in 1924. With a large central pond, bridges connecting via an island, a picnic area and a wisteria trellis, these gardens are an oasis surrounded by shining new skyscrapers, not to be missed.

Zojo-ji Temple

Zojo-ji Temple, located in the Shiba Koen park (which is also home to Tokyo Tower), has a remarkable history, having been founded in 1393 to help spread the Pure Land sect (*Jodo-shu*) of Buddhism in the Kanto area from its head temple in Kyoto. The temple was moved to its present site in 1598, after Tokugawa Ieyasu, who ruled Japan from 1603 at the start of the Edo era, located his feudal domain in Edo. Notably, it became the family temple of the Tokugawa clan which went on to rule Japan until 1868. With a stunning Main Gate, built in 1622 and a survivor of both the Great Kanto Earthquake of 1923 and the bombing of Tokyo in 1945, the temple grounds contain numerous Important Cultural Properties designated by the Japanese Government, the City of Tokyo, and Tokyo's Minato Ward. Its giant bell, one of the three largest from the Edo era, is rung twice a day,

を鳴らそうと数千人が増上寺へ集まってきます。

東京タワー

　1958年の完成当時、東京タワーは世界一高い自立式の塔でした。モデルとしたパリのエッフェル塔より13メートル高く建てられました。高さ333メートルの東京タワーは、データ通信の送電塔として建てられ、現在でもその役割を担っていますが、2012年に完成したさらに高い東京スカイツリーが、いくつかの通信機能を引き継ぎました。

　その年、日本ではデジタル放送への切り替えを行うため、遠くまで電波を伝えられるように、東京タワーより高い塔が必要だったのです。

　東京タワーには、150メートル地点と250メートル地点にそれぞれ一般の人々が入れる展望台があり、現在でも日本国内からも海外からも多くの人が訪れる人気スポットです。

　東京タワーは港区の芝公園内にあり、近くには2つの地下鉄駅があります。タワーからは関東平野を一望でき、晴れた日には富士山まで見通すことができます。

and on New Year's Eve is rung 108 times to dispel the past year's evil. Thousands crowd the grounds of Zojo-ji to also ring in the new year.

Tokyo Tower

When it was completed in 1958, Tokyo Tower was the tallest free-standing tower in the world, 13 meters taller than the Eiffel Tower in Paris, on which it was modeled. Standing 333 meters high, Tokyo Tower was built as a telecommunications transmission tower, and it still serves that purpose, although the taller Tokyo Skytree took over some of its transmission functions when it was completed in 2012, as Japan switched to digital broadcasting and needed a higher elevation to reach farther than was possible with Tokyo Tower.

With two observation decks accessible for public viewing — at 150 meters and 250 meters high, respectively — Tokyo Tower remains a very popular tourist destination both from within Japan and for visitors from overseas.

Located in Shiba Koen park in Minato Ward, it is accessible by two nearby subway stations, and provides a panoramic view of the Kanto Plain, all the way to Mt. Fuji on clear days.

目黒

目黒は東京の南西部にあります。
- [ ] Meguro is located in the southwest of central Tokyo.

目黒は、中目黒や自由が丘などもある、目黒区の地域です。
- [ ] Meguro is a neighborhood in Meguro Ward, which also includes Nakameguro and Jiyugaoka.

目黒は渋谷から山手線で南に2駅のところにあります。
- [ ] Meguro is two stops south of Shibuya on the Yamanote Line.

目黒の地名は「黒い目」という意味で、目黒不動尊という寺に立つ目の黒い仏像から来ています。
- [ ] Meguro means "Black Eye," and is named for a statue with black eyes in the Meguro Fudoson temple.

江戸時代、目黒不動尊は江戸の町を守る5つの寺の一つとして建立されました。
- [ ] In the Edo era, Meguro Fudoson was one of five temples established to protect the city.

目黒は『目黒のさんま』という落語に登場する地で、空腹のお殿様が初めてさんまを口にするという物語です。
- [ ] Meguro is the setting for a comic story called *Meguro no Sanma*, about a great lord who eats a humble Pacific saury fish for the first time.

Tokyo in Single Sentences

毎年９月には「目黒さんま祭り」が開催され、多くの人が無料のサンマを求めて行列を作ります。

☐ Every September, Meguro celebrates the "Meguro *Sanma* Festival," and thousands of people line up to get a free Pacific saury.

目黒には家具店が多いことで知られています。

☐ Meguro is known for its furniture stores.

目黒通り沿いには十数店の家具店が軒を連ねています。

☐ There are dozens of furniture stores standing side by side along Meguro Street.

品川

Track 77

品川は東京の南に位置し、東京湾に接しています。

☐ Shinagawa is in the southern part of central Tokyo and borders Tokyo Bay.

品川は、大崎などもある品川区内の地域です。

☐ Shinagawa is a neighborhood in Shinagawa Ward, which also includes Osaki.

KEY WORD ✓

☐ comic story　　　落語

品川は新宿や池袋と同じく、山手線が通る主要駅です。

☐ Shinagawa is one of the major hubs on the Yamanote Line, along with Shinjuku and Ikebukuro.

品川は新幹線の停車駅です。

☐ Shinagawa is a stop for the Shinkansen.

品川から羽田空港への直通電車が出ています。

☐ There is a train that goes directly from Shinagawa to Haneda Airport.

江戸時代、品川は都心から京都へ向かう街道の、最初の宿場でした。

☐ In the Edo era, Shinagawa was the first stop on the road from central Tokyo to Kyoto.

江戸時代から品川は交通の要所なのです。

☐ Shinagawa has been an important transit hub since the Edo era.

交通の便がいいので、品川にはホテルや企業の本社が多く置かれています。

☐ Because of its convenient location, there are many hotels and company headquarters located in Shinagawa.

浜離宮

浜離宮は伝統ある風景式庭園です。

☐ Hama Rikyu is a traditional landscape garden.

Tokyo in Single Sentences

浜離宮は東京の真ん中、中央区内にあります。

☐ Hama Rikyu is located in central Tokyo in Chuo Ward.

浜離宮は隅田川の河口にあります。

☐ Hama Rikyu is located at the mouth of the Sumida River.

浜離宮の最寄りの地下鉄駅は、大江戸線の汐留駅です。

☐ The nearest subway station to Hama Rikyu is Shiodome Station on the Oedo Line.

浅草から船で浜離宮へ行くことができます。

☐ You can reach Hama Rikyu by boat from Asakusa.

江戸時代、浜離宮は将軍家の所有地でした。

☐ During the Edo era, Hama Rikyu belonged to the Shogun.

1946年に浜離宮は公共の公園になりました。

☐ Hama Rikyu became a public park in 1946.

浜離宮は東京の真ん中にある静かな憩いの場です。

☐ Hama Rikyu is a peaceful oasis in the middle of Tokyo.

品川・海浜とその周辺

品川●浜離宮

KEY WORD ✓

| ☐ at the mouth of | 河口に |

▶▶▶ ワンセンテンスで説明する東京

浜離宮の中央には、潮入りの池という池があります。

☐ There is a pond called Shioiri Pond at the center of Hama Rikyu.

池の中央には中島のお茶屋という休憩所があり、お抹茶と伝統的な和菓子を味わえます。

☐ In the middle of the pond is a teahouse, called Nakajima no Ochaya, where you can have green tea and traditional Japanese sweets.

庭園の歴史や象徴的な意義を解説してくれるオーディオガイドがあります。

☐ There is an audio guide that explains the history and the symbolism of the garden.

お台場・東京湾

Track 79

東京湾には、お台場や夢の島など、人工の島がいくつかあります。

☐ There are several man-made islands in Tokyo Bay, including Odaiba and Yumenoshima.

お台場は1853年に徳川幕府によって街の防衛を固めるために造られました。

☐ Odaiba was created in 1853 by the Tokugawa Shogunate as an extra defense for the city.

今日のお台場は娯楽とレジャーの街です。

☐ Today, Odaiba is an entertainment and leisure district.

Tokyo in Single Sentences

お台場は、20世紀の終わり頃に開発プロジェクトが始まった、東京臨海副都心の一部です。

☐ Odaiba is part of the Tokyo Waterfront Secondary City Center, a late twentieth-century development project.

お台場は江東区と港区にまたがっています。

☐ Odaiba includes parts of Koto, Minato and Shinagawa wards.

お台場にはりんかい線とゆりかもめ線で行くことができます。

☐ Odaiba can be reached by the Rinkai and Yurikamome train lines.

お台場には大江戸温泉物語や日本科学未来館など、魅力ある施設があります。

☐ Odaiba's attractions include Oedo Onsen Monogatari and the National Museum of Emerging Science.

レインボーブリッジがお台場と東京をつないでいます。

☐ The Rainbow Bridge connects Odaiba with the mainland.

2020年の東京夏季オリンピックの会場の多くは、東京湾の島々に置かれる予定です。

☐ Major venues for the 2020 Tokyo Summer Olympics will be located on islands in Tokyo Bay.

品川・海浜とその周辺
浜離宮・お台場・東京湾

KEY WORD ✓

☐ Tokyo Waterfront Secondary City Center
東京臨海副都心

▶▶▶ ワンセンテンスで説明する東京

新しい東京都中央卸売市場は、東京湾の埋立地、豊洲に置かれる予定です。

☐ The new Tokyo Central Wholesale Market will be located in Toyosu, a neighborhood on Tokyo Bay made from reclaimed land.

東京タワー

東京タワーは通信のための塔です。

☐ Tokyo Tower is a communication tower.

東京タワーは港区の芝公園にあります。

☐ Tokyo Tower is located in Shiba-koen, in Minato Ward.

東京タワーの最寄りの地下鉄駅は、都営新宿線の赤羽橋駅です。

☐ The closest subway station to Tokyo Tower is Akabanebashi on the Oedo Line.

東京タワーは1958年に完成しました。

☐ Tokyo Tower was completed in 1958.

東京タワーの高さは333メートルです。

☐ Tokyo Tower is 333 meters tall.

東京タワーは、建てられた当時は、世界一高い塔でした。

☐ When Tokyo Tower was built, it was the tallest tower in the world.

Tokyo in Single Sentences

東京タワーには、150メートル地点と250メートル地点の2ヵ所に展望台があります。

☐ Tokyo Tower has two observation decks, one at 150 meters and one at 250 meters.

東京タワーは東京のシンボルの1つです。

☐ Tokyo Tower is one of the symbols of Tokyo.

東京タワーは、東京が20世紀に成し遂げた急速な高度成長のシンボルです。

☐ Tokyo Tower is a symbol of Tokyo's rapid growth in the twentieth century.

東京タワーは日本の映画や漫画によく登場します。

☐ Tokyo Tower often appears in Japanese movies and comic books.

東京タワーはエッフェル塔のデザインと似ています。

☐ Tokyo Tower has a similar design to the Eiffel Tower.

東京タワーは航空交通規制に従い、オレンジと白で塗られています。

☐ Tokyo Tower is painted orange and white to comply with air traffic regulations.

東京タワーは夜になると光り、その色は時期によって変わります。

☐ Tokyo Tower is illuminated at night with different colors at different times of the year.

品川・海浜とその周辺 お台場・東京湾●東京タワー

2-13 後楽園・神楽坂とその周辺

東京ドーム

東京ドームシティ アトラクションズ(旧称「後楽園」)は、東京の中心にある遊園地で、そこには東京のプロ野球チームの巨人(読売ジャイアンツ)のホームグラウンドとして知られる東京ドームもあります。巨人はニューヨークヤンキースのように、伝統あるプロ野球チームとして人気があります。

東京には、その他にヤクルト・スワローズというチームがあり、表参道の近くにある神宮球場を本拠地としています。

家族連れで、野球観戦することもよくあります。東京ドームに隣接した東京ドームシティ アトラクションズには、本格的なローラーコースターなど、多くの乗り物や、スケートリンク、そして美味しそうな飲食店があり、デートや家族で楽しめます。

小石川後楽園

東京ドームシティのすぐそばには、小石川後楽園

Around Korakuen, Kagurazaka

Tokyo Dome City

Located near the heart of Tokyo is an amusement park known as Tokyo Dome City Attractions (formerly called Korakuen), and in the same massive property is Tokyo Dome itself, the home playing field for one of Tokyo's two professional baseball teams, the Giants (officially, the Yomiuri Giants). Along the lines of the Yankees in New York, the Giants are quite popular as a local team with a lot of sporting tradition.

The other major baseball team in Tokyo is the Yakult Swallows, whose home field is Jingu Kyujo, located close to Omotesando.

Family outings to ball games are not uncommon, and in the Tokyo Dome City Attractions amusement park next to Tokyo Dome you can find a serious roller-coaster, many other rides, an ice-skating rink, and tempting pubs and restaurants to help you enjoy your date or family outing.

Koishikawa Korakuen

Situated quite close to Tokyo Dome City is Koishikawa

という江戸時代の大名のために造られた庭園もあります。江戸時代に200年以上にわたって将軍職を受け継いでいた徳川家は、本家の他に水戸と尾張（現在の名古屋）、そして紀州（現在の和歌山）に親戚があり、その3つの家を御三家と呼んでいました。

　将軍に後継がないときは、この御三家から将軍をだすことができたのです。その御三家の一つである水戸の徳川家が1629年に造ったのがこの小石川後楽園なのです。

小石川植物園

　樹木、灌木、顕花植物、薬草といった4000種以上の植物を配した40エーカーもある植物園が都心から遠くない場所にあるなんて思いもよらないでしょうが、それが小石川植物園です。

　1684年に当時の徳川将軍によって、御薬園として設立されたもので、園内の植物園本館には100万点以上の植物標本や数千冊の学術書が所蔵されています。現在は東京大学大学院理学研究科によって運営されていますが、明治維新直後の1877年に東京大学の付属となり、日本の植物学の研究において重要な役割

Korakuen, a Japanese-style garden built for one of the daimyo during the Edo era. A group known as the *Honorable Three Families* was made up of the major strands of the Tokugawa clan, who for over two hundred years carried on the role of Edo Bakufu. These were comprised of the Tokugawa-related families based in Mito and Owari (the latter in present-day Nagoya), as well as in Kishu (present-day Wakayama).

When there was no male offspring to serve the key role of Shogun to lead the nation, the clan was able to select someone to be the next Shogun from among these three related families. It was one of these three families — the one based in Mito — that had these Koishikawa Gardens built in 1629.

Koishikawa Shokubutsu-en

Imagine a botanical garden covering 40 acres located not far from the center of Tokyo, with over 4,000 plant species including trees, bushes, flowering plants and herbs, and you have the Koishikawa Shokubutsu-en.

Established in 1684 as a medicinal herb garden by the then-Shogun, the on-site herbarium contains over a million herbal specimens and thousands of scholarly books. It is no wonder that the gardens are operated by the University of Tokyo's Graduate School of Science, as they became part of the university in 1877, shortly after the Meiji Restoration,

を果たしてきたこともうなずけます。

　植物園はわずかな入園料で公開されており、特に、桜や他の多くの花が咲き誇る春が見ごろです。

矢来能楽堂

　歌舞伎が江戸時代に発展した庶民のための舞台芸術ならば、能はもっと格式の高い芸術形式であり、奥深く、高い評価を得つづけてきたこの舞台芸術の血統は14世紀まで遡ります。

　独特なお面をかぶり、舞台での抑制され、洗練された動作によって能は、武士の間に広く愛好されました。また、この荘厳な舞台芸術とうまくバランスをとり、スローペースの能の幕間に演じられるのが狂言で、コメディとして楽しまれ、不遜で淫らなテーマがよく使われます。千駄ヶ谷の国立能楽堂と神楽坂の矢来能楽堂は、そんな能や狂言を楽しむには最適な劇場です。

神楽坂

　神楽坂は、1920年代はいわゆる花街として知られ

and played an important role in Japan's botanical research.

Open to the public for a modest fee, the gardens are particularly beautiful in the spring, with flowering cherry trees and many other species.

Yarai Noh Theater

If we consider kabuki to be a popular theatrical form developed for public enjoyment in the Edo era, Noh theater is an even more traditional art form, with a deep and highly successful theatrical lineage dating back to the fourteenth century.

With its performers wearing uniquely stylized masks, moving in highly refined, restrained motion on the stage, Noh was a theatrical form dearly loved by the elite samurai class. Balancing this stately form of theater, and performed between the slow-paced Noh plays, was Kyogen, enjoyed as a comic interlude, often irreverent and even bawdy in its theatrical themes. The National Noh Theater located in Sendagaya and Yarai Theater located in Kagurazaka are fitting places to enjoy both Noh and its lighter cousin, Kyogen.

Kagurazaka

Kagurazaka was, in the 1920s, known primarily as a red-

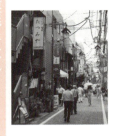

ていた場所でした。今やそんなことは知る由もなく、飯田橋から坂を登れば、その両側にレストランや店が並ぶ散歩道となります。

周辺には、花街の名残もあり、路地へ迷い込んで、そうした昔の雰囲気を楽しむのも一案です。運がよければ、今でも三味線を練習する音が、側道の２階の窓から聞こえてきます。一昔前までは、よくある情景だったのでしょう。

靖國神社

靖國神社は、明治維新の翌年、1869年にできた神社で、ここには1853年のペリー来航以来の戦没者が祀られています。

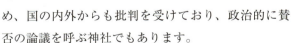

第二次世界大戦の戦犯も他の戦没者と共に祀られていることから、戦時中の侵略で被害を受けた周辺のアジア諸国をはじめ、国の内外からも批判を受けており、政治的に賛否の論議を呼ぶ神社でもあります。

正面の大きな鳥居が印象的です。本殿は1872年に

light entertainment district. You wouldn't know this now, as the Kagurazaka hill you climb on a leisurely walk from Iidabashi Station is lined on both sides of the road with shops and restaurants.

One suggestion is to stroll through the neighborhood, getting a bit lost in the side streets to experience a trace of those olden times, which retain a lingering atmosphere of the pleasure houses that tempted clients to visit. If you're lucky you might even hear someone practicing the stringed *shamisen* instrument from an upstairs window on a side street, the way it would have sounded those many years ago.

Yasukuni Shrine

First built in 1869 following the Meiji Restoration of the previous year, Yasukuni Shrine has enshrined the spirits of those killed in wars ever since Commodore Perry's ships arrived in Japan in 1853.

As the Shinto Shrine has enshrined not only Japan's war dead, however, but also those convicted in the Post-WWII War Crimes Trials as war criminals, the shrine has been at the center of a political debate, being criticized both domestically and from abroad, and particularly by neighboring countries in Asia that suffered at the hands of Japan's wartime aggression.

The inner sanctum of the shrine was constructed in

建てられたものです。なお、靖國神社の中には遊就館という軍事博物館があり、新政府軍と旧幕府勢力の間で起こった戊辰戦争(1868–69)以降の軍事関連の資料が展示されています。この遊就館の展示が日本の過去の戦争行為を肯定するものだという批判にさらされていることもまた事実です。

椿山荘

とても美しい椿山荘の庭園は、文京区にある椿山荘ホテルの施設の一部で、地下鉄の江戸川橋駅から、坂を登ってでも行く価値があります。正式な記録としては1877年に造園されましたが、今日、我々の目を楽しませてくれるこの庭園の豊かな歴史は、1600年代に遡ります。

その後、政治家の山縣有朋が、この土地独特の地形をうまく利用して庭園と、椿山荘という名の邸宅を造り、明治天皇との御前会議にも使っていました。

この庭園のもう一つユニークなところは、千年前に建てられた三重塔や、京都の神社など日本中の文化的重要建築物を園内に移築していることです。それらが、巧妙に手を加えられた自然の風景と見事に調和して、椿山荘を必見の庭たらしめているのです。

1872, and there is an impressively large *torii* gate situated at the entrance of the shrine. Also on the shrine grounds is the Yushukan, a military museum housing artifacts and documents from the wars Japan has been engaged in since the Boshin Civil War between Imperial and Shogunate forces in 1868–1869. It should also be noted that the Yushukan has been heavily criticized for seeking to justify Japan's wartime activities.

Chinzanso

Located in Bunkyo Ward, the stunning Chinzanso Gardens — part of the Hotel Chinzanso property — are well worth the uphill stroll from Edogawabashi subway station. Although formally founded in 1877, the gardens that we enjoy today have a rich history, stretching back to the 1600s.

Later, the unique landscape was used very effectively by the statesman Prince Yamagata Aritomo, both for his mansion — which he named "House of Camellia" — and for stately meetings, including some involving Emperor Meiji himself.

The gardens are unique in another way: important cultural buildings from across Japan have been relocated to this secluded garden, including a 1,000-year-old pagoda and a Shinto shrine from Kyoto, for instance, blending in perfectly with the artfully cultivated natural scenery of the gardens.

後楽園（庭園）

後楽園は伝統的な日本庭園です。
- [ ] Korakuen is a traditional Japanese garden.

後楽園は文京区の小石川にあります。
- [ ] Korakuen is located in Koishikawa in Bunkyo Ward.

後楽園の最寄り地下鉄駅は、丸ノ内線の後楽園駅です。
- [ ] The nearest subway station to Korakuen is Korakuen Station on the Marunouchi Line.

六義園と同様、後楽園も東京でもっとも美しい庭園と認められています。
- [ ] Along with Rikugien, Korakuen is considered to be one of Tokyo's most beautiful gardens.

後楽園の歴史は17世紀にさかのぼります。
- [ ] Korakuen dates from the seventeenth century.

江戸時代、後楽園は大きな権力を持つ水戸家の所有地でした。
- [ ] During the Edo era Korakuen belonged to the powerful Mito family.

他の日本庭園と同じように、後楽園にも中央に池があります。
- [ ] Like many Japanese gardens, Korakuen has a central pond.

Tokyo in Single Sentences

後楽園には、日本と中国の名所をごく小規模に模した景観が造られています。

☐ In Korakuen, there are miniature versions of famous landscapes from Japan and China.

後楽園に行くときは、橋と水面の反射が満月を描く、円月橋をぜひご覧になってください。

☐ When you go to Korakuen don't miss the Full Moon Bridge, which forms a full circle with its reflection.

後楽園を訪れるのに一番いい季節は、紅葉が色づく秋です。

☐ The best time to visit Korakuen is in the fall, when the maple leaves change color.

神楽坂

神楽坂は新宿区にあります。

☐ Kagurazaka is a neighborhood in Shinjuku Ward.

神楽坂には地下鉄東西線が停まります。

☐ Kagurazaka is a stop on the Tozai subway line.

20世紀初頭の神楽坂は、芸者の置屋がある歓楽街でした。

☐ In the early twentieth century, Kagurazaka was an entertainment district with *geisha* houses.

▶▶▶ ワンセンテンスで説明する東京

神楽坂にある、石畳の曲がりくねった通りは、ヨーロッパの雰囲気を感じさせます。

☐ Kagurazaka has winding, cobblestone streets that give it a European atmosphere.

神楽坂にはたくさんのフランス料理店があるので、日本に住むフランス人に人気のエリアです。

☐ Kagurazaka has many French restaurants and is a popular place for French expats to live.

神楽坂にはたくさんの料亭があります。料亭とは伝統的で品のあるレストランのことです。

☐ Kagurazaka has many *ryotei*, which are elegant traditional restaurants.

神楽坂の料亭といえば、企業の重役や政治家たちが重大な会合をもつ場所として知られています。

☐ Executives and politicians are known to use Kagurazaka *ryotei* for important meetings.

Tokyo in Single Sentences

後楽園・神楽坂とその周辺

神楽坂

東京から日帰りできる観光名所

東海道

　日本の木版画、浮世絵を愛好する人の中には、この見出しを見て、江戸時代最高かつ最後の浮世絵師歌川広重による連作「東海道五十三次」を思い起こした人もあるかもしれません。

　東海道は、徳川幕府のある江戸と、古代の首都であり1868年の明治維新まで皇族が住んでいた京都を結ぶ道路でした（ところどころには道路というよりは小道のような箇所もありました）。

　東海道は非常に往来の盛んな道でした。公務で京都と江戸を行き来することが多く、また封建制を維持するための制度として、藩主（大名）たちは封地に戻るときは家族を江戸に残し、公用で江戸に滞在する間は家族を封地に戻すように、江戸幕府に求められていたからです。今日でも人里離れた場所には、かつての東海道が残っていて、当時を偲ぶことができます。箱根の芦ノ湖近くにあった関所も、復元されたものを見ることができます。

Day Trips from Tokyo

Tokaido

Those who have known and enjoy Japan's woodblock prints — ukiyo-e — may recall a series by one of the best and last masters during the Edo era, Utagawa Hiroshige, entitled *The Fifty-three Stations of the Tokaido*.

The Tokaido was the road (and in some places little more than a path) linking the Tokugawa Bakufu capital of Edo, with the ancient capital of Kyoto where the Imperial Family continued to reside until the Meiji Restoration in 1868.

This was a well-traveled road, as official business required frequent visits between Kyoto and Edo, and the system of feudal control utilized by the military government in Edo required the feudal lords — *daimyo* — to leave their families in Edo when visiting their domains, and move their families to their feudal domains while they were residing on official business in Edo. To this day, the Tokaido can still be found "off the beaten track" and a window into traditional times. The closely watched guard posts can also be seen, as with the reconstructed post at Hakone near Lake Ashinoko.

東京ディズニーランド

　認可を受けてアメリカ国外に建造された最初のディズニーのテーマパークが、東京ディズニーランドであり、115エーカー（47ヘクタール）の敷地面積を持ち、絶大な人気を誇り、大成功を収めています。フロリダ州オーランドにある同系列のディズニーワールドとマジック・キングダムの複合リゾートに次いで世界二位となる、年間およそ2000万人の来場者を集めています。

　東京ディズニーランドは30年以上も前、1983年にオープンしました。その後、子供や親子連れだけでなく、若者や一般の大人たちの要求を満たす、対になるテーマパークの東京ディズニーシーを建造し、規模を広げました。正面入口のすぐ隣に舞浜駅があるなど、東京から電車によるアクセスもよく、系列ホテルを持つリゾートとして、日本中、アジア中から観光客を引きよせています。

成田山

　1000年以上の歴史をもつ真言密教のお寺として知られる成田山新勝寺は、成田空港のすぐ近くにあります。飛行機の乗り継ぎなどで、日本の滞在が短い人にとっては、

Tokyo Disneyland

As the first Disney theme park licensed and built outside the United States, the 115-acre (47-hectare) Tokyo Disneyland is very popular and highly successful. With almost 20 million visitors each year, it is the world's second-most visited theme park after its namesake in Orlando, Florida, the Walt Disney World complex of parks.

Tokyo Disneyland opened over thirty years ago, in 1983, and was joined by companion park Tokyo Disney Sea; they are both part of the umbrella organization Tokyo Disney Resort. The parks cater not only to young children and their families, but to young adults and the general public. Easily accessible by train from Tokyo, with its main gate immediately next to Maihama Station, this is a destination resort with several of its own hotels, and a magnet for visitors from all over Japan and Asia.

Naritasan

With a history of over 1,000 years, the Naritasan Shinsho-ji Temple is located fairly close to Narita Airport. A temple of the esoteric Shingon sect of Buddhism, it is accessible even for short-term visitors changing planes at Narita, letting

最も手軽に日本の伝統的な文化を堪能できる本格的な寺院といえましょう。

横浜

横浜は、東京から電車で30分ほどのところにある、370万人の人口を抱える大都市です。江戸時代の末期に外国人の居留区がここにおかれ、港が開かれたことから、横浜は日本を代表す

る港町として早い時期から外国文化がはいった場所でもありました。今でも江戸後期、明治初期の雰囲気を残す場所が多くあります。また、横浜の中華街は、東京とその周辺では最も古く、規模の大きな中国系の人々の居住区として知られています。

鎌倉

鎌倉は東京から電車で1時間ほどのところにある落ち着いた歴史のある町です。鎌倉は1192年から、1333年まで、武士の政権がおかれ、日本を統治した古都で、由緒ある寺や神社を訪ねることができます。歴史のある高級住宅地の裏道を通って、寺巡りをするのも一興です。

them easily experience traditional Japanese culture in an authentic temple setting.

Yokohama

Accessible by train from Tokyo in just thirty minutes, Yokohama is a major city with a population of approximately 3.7 million residents. As foreigners were permitted to reside only in Yokohama from late in the Edo era, and as an open port authorized for international trade, foreign cultural influences entered Japan through Yokohama faster than any other modern city. Even today there are many spots in Yokohama that have retained the old-fashioned atmosphere of those late-Edo, early Meiji times. Yokohama is also known for its Chinatown, as the largest and oldest enclave of Chinese residents in the entire Kanto Plain, which encompasses Tokyo and its surroundings.

Kamakura

Kamakura is a quiet but historical town accessible by train from Tokyo in about an hour. As the seat of national power under the military-dominated samurai rule of the Kamakura Era, from 1192 to 1333, this old capital offers a unique opportunity to visit its venerable Buddhist temples and Shinto shrines. Visitors can stroll from temple to temple

　また、鎌倉の西側に広がる海岸線は湘南海岸といい、夏は海水浴やマリンスポーツをする人で賑わいます。

奥多摩

　奥多摩は、都心から、はるか西にある渓谷ですが、東京都に含まれます。新宿から中央線快速で約1時間でアクセスできます。

　この地域は東京と神奈川県との境を流れる多摩川の上流にあたり、ハイキングや自然の中でもスポーツなどを気軽に楽しめます。都民にとっては、気軽に都会の喧噪を抜け出せる場所として評価されています。

富士五湖

　富士五湖は富士山の東側の麓にある5つの湖のことで、その周辺一帯が東京から日帰りでも訪ねられるリゾート地となっています。もっと長く都会の喧噪を抜け出したければ、快適なロッジが多数あります。湖畔からは富士山の眺めを楽しめ、周辺は深い

through quiet back streets in this upscale residential — but deeply historical — town.

In addition, on the western edge of town is the Shonan coast, offering a chance for many visitors to enjoy swimming and other water sports in the summer months.

Okutama

Okutama is a fairly remote area of forested hills and valleys to the far west of central Tokyo, but within Tokyo's metropolitan boundaries. It is accessible from Shinjuku on the frequent rapid Chuo-line trains in about an hour.

It is located in the upstream area of the Tama River that forms the boundary between Tokyo and Kanagawa Prefecture, and it offers an opportunity for leisurely hiking and other nature-oriented sports. It is appreciated by Tokyo's residents as a place to get out of the city without having to travel too far.

Fujigoko

The "Five Lakes of Mt. Fuji" are, as the title implies, a grouping of five mountain lakes in the east foothills of Japan's most famous mountain, Fuji. The resort-studded area of the five lakes is accessible from Tokyo even for day trips, although there are also many comfortable lodgings

森に覆われています。

日光

日光は、東京から北に2時間ほどのところにある山岳リゾートで、浅草から東武線の特急でいくことができます。日光の麓には徳川家康を祀った日光東照宮があり、その豪華な伽藍は世界遺産に指定されています。

東照宮から車に乗って、曲がりくねった山道を抜け、滝を過ぎたところに、中禅寺湖という湖があり、有名な男山が穏やかな湖面を見下ろしています。湖からは美しい高原が広がり、ハイキングコースや湿地帯を通る遊歩道があります。森には、快適な宿泊施設があり、東京の雑踏から一夜の逃避ができます。

伊豆

伊豆半島は、富士山の麓から太平洋に突き出した半島で、温泉と海とを同時に楽しむことができ、半

available if you want to get out of the city for longer. The vistas of Mt. Fuji from the shores of each of the lakes are quite spectacular, and you will find yourself surrounded by lush forests when you visit the area.

Nikko

Located about two hours north of Tokyo via the Tobu rapid train from Asakusa, Nikko is an accessible mountainous resort area. At the base of the Nikko highlands is the World Heritage Site of the ornate Nikko Toshogu Shrine, built to memorialize Tokugawa Ieyasu, the founding ruler of the long line of Tokugawa Shoguns.

A drive from the Toshogu Shrine up the many-curved road past waterfalls will bring you to Lake Chuzenji, with the famous Otoko-yama mountain looking down on the placid lake's water. Stretching out from the lake is a beautiful highland plateau with hiking paths and a boardwalk through natural wetlands, and nestled in the woods are pleasant lodgings for an overnight stay away from the bustle of Tokyo.

Izu

The Izu Peninsula juts out into the Pacific Ocean from the foothills of Mt. Fuji, and from its geographic position lets

島の両側にはひなびた漁村が点在しています。昔から別荘地としても有名で、東京から週末を過ごす人でいつも賑わっています。

半島の地形は多様で、1000メートルを超える天城連山の尾根が連なり、河谷が走り、中腹には見事な浄蓮の滝がかかり、穏やかな入り江には海岸沿いに静かなビーチが広がっています。

半島南端の下田は、1853年にペリー提督が「黒船」を着けたところで、日本は長い鎖国を終えることになったのです。東京から伊豆踊り子号に乗れば、快適に景色を楽しみながら旅ができます。

箱根

箱根は、東京から電車で西へ1時間行ったところで、富士山の近くにある山岳リゾート地です。晴れた日には湖面に富士山が映る芦ノ湖から足を伸ばすと、多くのリゾート施設が谷を下るように箱根湯本まで連なります。ここには東京へ発着する電車のターミナル駅があります。

箱根は大自然に囲まれた温泉地で、湯治と新鮮な山の空気を楽しむにはうってつけの場所です。強羅

you enjoy both the seaside and hot springs, while being dotted with rustic fishing villages on both sides of the peninsula. It has long been popular as a place to have a second home, so it is an active destination for those wishing to get away for some rest and relaxation on weekends.

The peninsula's terrain is quite varied, with the 1,000-meter-high Amagi Mountain range running down its spine, a river valley and the beautiful Joren Falls in the middle, and quiet inlets with secluded beaches on its shores.

Shimoda at the southern end is where Commodore Perry's "Black Ships" first put ashore in 1853, helping open up Japan from its long isolation, and the *Izu no Odoriko* express train from Tokyo makes your journey there a pleasant and scenic trip.

Hakone

Hakone, located to the west of Tokyo just over an hour away by train, is a popular mountainous resort area close to Mt. Fuji. Stretching from Ashi-no-ko Lake, with its nicely framed view of Mt. Fuji over the lake waters on a clear day, there are many resort facilities down the valleys to the Hakone Yumoto town where the train lines from Tokyo terminate.

This is a hot-spring resort area, surrounded by nature and known as a perfect place to enjoy both the healing baths

の渓谷をつづら折りに走る電車に乗って、必ず彫刻の森美術館を訪れましょう。そこには、ヘンリー・ムーアや他の世界でも有名なアーティストたちの彫刻作品が屋外に展示されています。

　江戸時代には、ここは江戸と今日の都とを結ぶ東海道の関所がおかれた場所で、江戸に入る人、出て行く人をチェックしていました。この関所は修復され、江戸幕府の監視システムを確実に知ることができます。

熱海

　熱海は、東京から東海道新幹線で40分ほどのところにある名高い温泉地です。東京に近い温泉地として数百年前から知られており、多くの温泉旅館がたっています。旅館では、温泉につかってリラックスできるだけでなく、食通もうならせる料理が出され、それも宿泊代に含まれています。また、熱海は箱根や伊豆への玄関口としても知られています

and the fresh mountain air. On the switch-back train up the Gora Valley, be sure to visit the Chokoku-no-mori Open-air Museum, with its outdoor collection of sculptures by Henry Moore and other world-class artists.

During the Edo era the Tokaido Road connecting Edo with the historical capital, Kyoto, ran through Hakone, and a checkpoint was situated here, monitoring the identities of all who would enter or leave Edo. The historical checkpoint has been restored, and it gives an authentic sense of the way access was guarded by the Edo regime.

Atami

Just a 40-minute ride on the Tokaido Shinkansen from Tokyo lies Atami, a famed hot-spring resort area. Known for its hot springs for hundreds of years, and being so close to Tokyo, it hosts many Japanese *ryokan* inns that provide not only relaxing hot spring baths, but gourmet-class meals that are included in the price for an overnight stay. Atami is also known as the gateway to some other destination areas mentioned here, including the Izu Peninsula and the Hakone hot-spring resort area.

伊豆・小笠原諸島

東京といえば、大都会をイメージします。しかし、東京都という行政上の地域には、伊豆諸島だけでなく、東京から南にかなり離れた小笠原諸島まで含まれます。

伊豆諸島の多くは火山島です。そんな島のうち、伊豆大島(伊豆諸島最大の島)、八丈島はリゾート地として知られていますが、八丈島は江戸時代には流刑地でもあったのです。さらに小笠原諸島は、東京から1000キロ以上離れた南海の島々で、硫黄島を含むいくつかの島は、第二次世界大戦時に激戦地となりました。

川越

川越は、東京の北側、埼玉県にある都市で、小江戸の愛称で知られています。その名前の通り、江戸時代には城下町として栄え、昔の街並みが保存されている観光地です。川越には、池袋から東武東上線で40分ほどで行くことができます。

Izu, Ogasawara island chain

When we think of Tokyo, we normally imagine the large metropolitan area of Japan's capital city. However, in the administrative district managed by Tokyo lie not only the string of Izu Islands, but the Ogasawara island chain much farther away from the city, to the south.

Most of the islands in the Izu Island chain are volcanoes, and among these are Izu Oshima (the largest) and nearby Hachijojima. Both known for their getaway resorts, and Hachijojima is known for former penal colony to which criminals were banished during the Edo era. Beyond these, the Ogasawara Islands stretch more than 1,000 kilometers to the south of Tokyo City, and a number of islands — including the famous Iwojima — were hard-fought battlefields during World War II.

Kawagoe

Kawagoe, a city in Saitama Prefecture located north of Tokyo, is known for its nickname "Little Edo." Its name alludes to the fact that it flourished as a castle town during the Edo era, and today it is a tourist destination where many old streets have been preserved. You can reach Kawagoe in about forty minutes via the Tobu Tojo train line from Ikebukuro.

近郊へのアクセス

小田急線は、新宿駅から小田原を経て箱根まで延びる鉄道です。

- [ ] The Odakyu Line is a railway line that runs from Shinjuku via Odawara to Hakone.

箱根は、東京や富士山の近くにある行楽地です。

- [ ] Hakone is a resort area near Tokyo and Mt. Fuji.

新宿からは、京王線が東京の西側に延び、八王子や高尾、多摩センターなどへつながっています。

- [ ] From Shinjuku, the Keio Line runs through western Tokyo neighborhoods such as Hachioji, Takao, and Tama Center.

西武池袋線は、池袋駅から秩父まで延びる鉄道です。

- [ ] The Seibu Ikebukuro Line is a railway line that runs from Ikebukuro Station to Chichibu.

秩父は、東京郊外の古い町で、山でのレジャーも楽しめます。

- [ ] Chichibu is an old town in the suburbs of Tokyo where you can enjoy leisure activities in the mountains.

東武線は浅草と日光、さらに関東各地を繋ぐ鉄道です。

- [ ] The Tobu Line is a railway line that connects Asakusa and Nikko, along with other destinations in the Kanto area.

Tokyo in Single Sentences

東横線は、横浜と首都圏を結ぶ鉄道で、その発着駅である渋谷駅には山手線も乗り入れています。

☐ The Toyoko Line is a railway line that connects the Tokyo Metropolitan Area and Yokohama. It departs from Shibuya Station, which is also a station on the Yamanote Line.

東京から横浜へ行くには、東京駅や品川に発着するJR線か、東横線が便利です。

☐ JR trains from Tokyo Station and Shinagawa and trains on the Toyoko Line are convenient ways to travel to Yokohama from Tokyo.

品川駅は、山手線の駅で、新幹線や横浜、鎌倉方面への列車への乗り換え駅でもあります。

☐ Shinagawa Station is a stop on the Yamanote Line where you can transfer to the bullet train and to trains for Yokohama and Kamakura.

軽井沢

Track 84

軽井沢は長野県の山地にあるリゾート地です。

☐ Karuizawa is a resort town in the mountains of Nagano.

KEY WORD ✓

☐ resort area　　　　行楽地

▶▶▶ ワンセンテンスで説明する東京

軽井沢は標高 2568 メートルの浅間山のふもとに位置しています。

- [ ] Karuizawa is located at the base of Mt. Asama at an altitude of 2,568 meters.

東京の人々は夏の暑さから逃れるために軽井沢を訪れます。

- [ ] People in Tokyo go to Karuizawa to escape the summer heat.

軽井沢は 19 世紀から避暑地として有名になりました。

- [ ] Karuizawa has been a popular summer resort since the nineteenth century.

軽井沢には裕福な人々の別荘が建てられています。

- [ ] Some wealthy people have second homes in Karuizawa.

東京から軽井沢までは、新幹線で 70 分ほどかかります。

- [ ] It takes 70 minutes by Shinkansen from Tokyo Station to get to Karuizawa.

軽井沢に古くからある大通りは「軽井沢銀座」と呼ばれ、郷愁にあふれ、ロマンチックな雰囲気があります。

- [ ] Karuizawa's old main street, called "Karuizawa Ginza," has a nostalgic, romantic feel.

軽井沢銀座沿いには、レストランや商店、カフェなどがたくさん並んでいます。

- [ ] There are many restaurants, shops and cafés along Karuizawa Ginza.

Tokyo in Single Sentences

ロマンチックな休暇を過ごしたいなら軽井沢がおすすめです。

☐ Karuizawa is a good spot for a romantic getaway.

温泉

日本には温泉と呼ばれる天然の熱水泉が何千と湧いています。

☐ Japan has thousands of natural hot springs, called *onsen*.

日本には火山がたくさんあるので、温泉がたくさん湧き出るのです。

☐ Because Japan has many volcanoes, it also has many hot springs.

数千年を通して、温泉は日本の重要な文化の一つです。

☐ Hot springs have been an important part of Japanese culture for thousands of years.

日本を旅するとき、温泉は欠かせません。

☐ You cannot visit Japan without visiting a hot spring.

東京の生活はストレスがたまるので、人々はくつろぎのひとときを温泉地に求めるのです。

☐ Because life in Tokyo is so stressful, people like to visit hot-spring resorts to relax.

▶▶▶ ワンセンテンスで説明する東京

東京の近くには、箱根や熱海、草津といった有名な温泉地がいくつもあります。

☐ There are several famous hot-spring resorts near Tokyo, such as Hakone, Atami and Kusatsu.

東京にも、大江戸温泉物語やラクーアといった温泉施設があります。

☐ There are some hot springs in Tokyo too, such as Oedo Onsen Monogatari and LaQua.

東京の銭湯には、天然温泉のところがあります。

☐ Some public bathhouses in Tokyo have natural hot-spring water.

温泉につかるのは健康や肌によいといわれています。

☐ Many people believe that bathing in hot-spring water is good for your health and your skin.

のんびりと湯につかると非常にくつろいだ気分になれます。

☐ Taking a long, hot bath is very relaxing.

温泉に入った日はよく眠れるはずです。

☐ After bathing in a hot spring you will sleep very well.

温泉は共用ですが、男湯と女湯は分かれています。

☐ Hot-spring baths are communal, but divided by gender.

Tokyo in Single Sentences

日本人は恥ずかしがり屋に見えるでしょうが、見知らぬ人と裸同士になるのは平気です。

☐ Japanese people may seem shy, but they are not shy about getting naked with strangers.

湯に入る前に体を洗うことを忘れないでください。

☐ It is important to wash your body before getting into the bath.

東京から日帰りできる観光名所

温泉

3部 江戸と東京の歴史と文化
History and Culture of Edo and Tokyo

江戸時代
江戸幕府
明暦の大火
ペリー来航
明治維新
義理と人情・勧善懲悪
将軍
旗本・御家人
士農工商
文明開化
関東大震災
東京大空襲
高度成長
バブル景気

江戸と東京の歴史と文化

江戸時代

　東京の豊かな文化は、江戸時代に育ち、熟成されたものです。東京は江戸時代の行政の中心として知られ、江戸に幕府を確立した将軍家のお膝元でした。18世紀には100万人の人口を数え、当時としては世界一の過密都市として繁栄したのです。

　江戸は身分の高い武士(さむらい)が居を構える権力の中心でしたが、同時にその日常生活や経済を支える多くの商人や職人が活躍していたところとして知られています。

　また、そうした庶民の娯楽として、芝居や出版などの活動も盛んにおこなわれていました。例えば、浮世絵などは、そうした出版活動を代表する媒体物として、当時作成され、人気になったのです。

　江戸時代は、東京のみならず、現在の日本の精神風土の原点ともいえるさまざまな価値観や風俗、しきたりなどが培われた時代だったのです。

History and Culture of Edo and Tokyo

Edo Era

The cultural richness of Tokyo can be said to have flourished during the Edo era. Known as the seat of administrative power during the Edo era, what is now Tokyo was the stronghold of the family that established the Shogunate in Edo. With a population of a million residents in the eighteenth century, Edo prospered as perhaps the world's largest and most densely populated city at that time.

Not only was it the center of power, with the samurai elite resident in the city, but to sustain their lifestyle and the vibrant economy as a whole, Edo also bustled with the activity of merchants and craftsmen in great numbers.

Imagine, too, the flourishing theater and publishing scene that thrived as entertainment for these commoners. Such art forms as ukiyo-e that originated and became popular during the Edo era are good examples of genres catering to the masses.

Not limited to the Tokyo of today, but for the whole of Japan, we can see that the origins of what it means to be Japanese — the cultural values, manners and customs — largely have their roots in the Edo era.

江戸と東京の歴史と文化

江戸幕府

　15世紀から16世紀の日本に起こった内戦・内乱の歴史は、あまりにも長すぎてとてもここに要約しきれないほどですが、多くの領国が力を失った結果、織田信長(1534–1582)、豊臣秀吉(1536–1598)、徳川家康(1543–1616)という3名の強力な武将が頭角を現し、日本統一に大きな功績をあげました。

　最終的には、徳川氏が首尾よく権力を手中に収め、軍部支配の政権(幕府)を樹立し、1603年に日本の行政上の首都を江戸、つまり今日の東京へと移しました。
　厳格な社会制度が導入され(p.394参照)、大名たちの忠誠を維持するために参勤交代を行わせ、1858年に徳川幕府が倒されるまでの250年間にわたって、その権力を維持したのです。

明暦の大火

　首都が江戸に移されて約50年後、1657年に起きた明暦の大火は市街の3分の2を破壊しました。大名や将軍家の家臣たちの住居の多くも焼けましたが、江戸城自体は被害を免れました。乾燥した天気が長く続いたあとに起こった火の手は、強風にあおられ、木造建築の街中を荒れ狂いながら過ぎて行きました。

Edo Bakufu

Japan's history of internal strife and civil war during the fifteenth and sixteenth centuries is too long to summarize here, but the resulting weakness of many of the feudal domains led to three great figures to emerge who are credited with unifying Japan — Oda Nobunaga (1534–1582), Toyotomi Hideyoshi (1536–1598), and Tokugawa Ieyasu (1543–1616).

It was the last of these, Tokugawa, who successfully consolidated power in a military-dominated government (the Bakufu), and moved the administrative capital of Japan to Edo, present-day Tokyo, in 1603.

The rigid social structures put in place (see p.395) and the *Sankin-kotai* system of maintaining the allegiance of the feudal *daimyo* lords enabled the Tokugawa Bakufu to remain in power until it was overthrown in 1858, fully 250 years later.

Great fire of Meireki

Just over fifty years after the capital moved to Edo, the Great Fire of Meireki destroyed over two-thirds of the city in 1657, including the homes of many feudal lords and retainers of the Shogunate, but spared Edo Castle itself. Fanned by strong winds after a long, dry period, the fire raged through the city's wooden structures.

この火事の原因は、仏僧が「呪いの着物」を燃やそうとした際の事故だという説があります。その着物に袖を通したことのある三人の若い女性が亡くなり、その呪いはさらに10万件以上ともいわれる家屋を焼き尽くした明暦の大火を引き起こしたというのです。

再建された江戸の町は、再びの災禍に見舞われぬよう、道を広げ、家々の密集度を下げました。しかしながら町は、1923年の関東大震災で再び焼かれ、1945年には第二次世界大戦の空襲によって手ひどく破壊されてしまうのです。

ペリー来航

1853年7月、マシュー・C・ペリー提督率いるアメリカ海軍の船団が、東京湾の浦賀の町に、蒸気を噴き上げて入港しました。彼は、フィルモア大統領の発した、日本に貿易港を開港させるべしとの使命を帯びていました。

日本は鎖国政策のために、それまでの220年間を世界から大きく隔絶されてきました。九州の長崎にある一港で行われていたオランダ貿易のみが例外(ほかに中国・韓国との貿易使節団もありました)だったので、ペリー提督の来航は徳川幕府に危機的状況をもたらしました。

武力を誇示する使節団はときに「砲艦外交」とも呼

The fire is said to have been started accidentally when a Buddhist priest tried to burn a "cursed kimono." Three young women had each died before they had a chance to even wear the kimono once, and the curse continued, as more than 100,000 residents are said to have perished in the Meireki fire.

Edo was rebuilt with wider streets and houses less tightly packed together, in hopes of preventing another disaster, though the city burned again in the 1923 Great Kanto Earthquake, and was heavily destroyed in the WWII bombing of Tokyo in 1945.

Arrival of Commodore Perry

In July 1853 a fleet of American ships under the command of Matthew C. Perry, Commodore of the U.S. Navy, steamed into Edo Bay as far as the town of Uraga, sent on a mission by U.S. President Fillmore to force Japan to open its ports to trade.

A seclusion policy had largely cut Japan off from the rest of the world for 220 years, with the exception of Dutch traders through the single port of Nagasaki in Kyushu (and diplomatic missions between Korea, China, and Japan), so Commodore Perry's arrival created a crisis for the Tokugawa Shogunate.

Through a show of force — sometimes known as "gun-

ばれました。このときは「ペリーの黒船」と呼ばれた彼らは、日本に孤立をやめて貿易とアメリカ船への燃料の補給を認めるように要求しました。ペリーは要求をはっきりと表明したあと、一年以内に回答を受け取りに戻ると約束して去りました。

2度目の来日は、1854年2月、ちょうど半年後でした。そして3月、神奈川（現在の横浜）での条約締結にこぎつけました。この条約に基づき函館と下田の二港が開かれ、他の西洋諸国にも日本と通商条約を結ぶ足がかりができ、日本の長きにわたる鎖国政策は事実上、終わりました。このことがきっかけで、国内には徳川体制への反対勢力が育ち、わずか14年後に起こる、1868年の明治維新へとつながっていきます。

明治維新

1603年から1868年までの日本は、徳川家による武力政権によって統治されており、1603年に首都が京都から江戸（今日の東京）に移されたため、この時代は江戸時代として知られています。

この時代の特色の一つは、平和な時期が長く続いたため、日本文化が花を開き、歌舞伎など数多くの伝統芸能や、世界中から賞賛を受けた木版画の浮世絵といった芸術が生まれたことです。

もう一つは、日本が長期間の鎖国政策によって海

boat diplomacy," and in this case as "Perry's Black Ships" — the mission demanded that Japan end its isolation and permit trade and the refueling of American ships. After making these demands clear, Perry promised to return within a year to learn Japan's response, and left.

His second arrival in February 1854, just half a year later, led in March to the Treaty of Kanagawa (in today's Yokohama). The treaty's opening of two ports, Hakodate and Shimoda, effectively ended Japan's long seclusion, opening the way for other Western nations' treaties with Japan, and it set the stage for internal opposition to the Tokugawa's rule that led to the Meiji Restoration in 1868, just fourteen years later.

Meiji Restoration

From 1603 until 1868, Japan had been ruled by the Tokugawa family's dominance of power in what is known as the Edo era, as the capital had been moved from Kyoto to Edo (today's Tokyo) in 1603.

On one hand this was a period of prolonged peace, enabling the flowering of Japanese culture and the birth of many traditional theater and art forms admired the world over, including kabuki and ukiyo-e woodblock printing.

On the other hand, Japan had sealed itself off from

外の出来事から国を閉ざしている間、世界は西洋の植民地帝国によって切り分けられ、帝国は貿易に(そしてときには支配に)熱心だったということです。ペリー提督の「黒船」が1853年と翌54年に現れ、日本に脅威が迫っていること、幕府の国防能力と統率力が低下していることを知らしめるまでは、中央政権への反対勢力は少しずつ強まっていたもののきちんと鎮圧されていました。

長州藩と薩摩藩による、徳川体制の終了と天皇への政権の「返還」を求める正式な異議申し立てによって(1866年に始まった内戦を経て)、1868年1月、明治天皇が天皇の名のもとに公式の権力を行使するという宣言を出しました。

この明治維新によって、政権の大変革が起こり、大名と武士の封建体制が解体され、士農工商制が廃止され、国際的な貿易関係を持つ産業国家への転換が起こりました。

義理と人情・勧善懲悪

「義理」と「人情」は、日本文化の2つの原則であると言われていますが、この2つは矛盾して描かれることがあります。

江戸時代には、歌舞伎や浄瑠璃でさまざまな物語が上演されました。物語の題材の多くが、社会的な

developments overseas through its long seclusion policy, as the world was carved up by Western colonial powers eager for trade (and, often, domination). Domestic opposition had gradually arisen but had been effectively quelled, until the arrival of Commodore Perry's "Black Ships" in 1853 and 1854 signaled a threat to Japan and a weakening of the central government's ability to protect the nation and provide leadership.

Formal opposition from the domains of Choshu and Satsuma, calling for an end to the Tokugawa family's rule and a restoration of power to the Emperor, led (after internal warfare from 1866) to a declaration in January 1868 by Emperor Meiji to have formal power exercised in the name of the Emperor.

Major changes in government, an end to the feudal order of *daimyo*, samurai, and the four-part class system, and a shift both to industrialization and international trade relations resulted from the Meiji Restoration.

Giri and Ninjo, duty & human feelings

"*Giri*" and "*ninjo*" refer to a pair of important principles in Japanese culture, translated as "duty" and "human feelings," with these principles depicted in conflict with each other.

During the Edo era, a wide range of content was conveyed through kabuki theater and the ballad-styled

義務である「義理」と、人としての情である「人情」との間で苦しむ人の生き様が取り上げられます。

例えば、武士の娘が身分が違い結婚することのできない商人の息子と恋におちるといったストーリーがそれにあたります。また、主君へお恩を感じる武士が、自らの家族を犠牲にして主君の仇を討とうと葛藤するストーリーなどもそれに該当します。一方、権力をもつ者が悪役となり、庶民をいじめ、そこに正義の味方が立ち向かうという悪を懲らしめる勧善懲悪の物語も庶民の支持を集めました。

当時、いわゆる版権についての考えがない中、面白い物語は、どんどん脚色され、色々な作家によってストーリーに変化が加えられました。江戸時代は舞台芸術が花開いた時代でもあったのです。

performances known as *joruri.* The theme of many of these theatrical productions was the internal conflict in people's lives between carrying out their social obligations, on the one hand, summarized in the term *giri* (duty), and on the other hand being true to their feelings as humans, captured in the Japanese word *ninjo*.

For instance, stories about a samurai's daughter falling in love with a merchant's son who is not permitted to marry her despite their passionate love for each other. Another story that fits this genre might be of a samurai's moral quandary, as he feels indebted to his feudal lord, on the one hand, but in order to repay his loyal debt to his lord he must sacrifice his very own family. Similarly, stories that gained great support from the public often focused on people in power who abused their office, inflicting suffering on the common people under their control. The hero in such stories would take the side of those suffering injustices, and seek to bring the villainous abusers of power to justice.

In those days the whole idea of copyrights was not yet in place, so interesting stories were adapted and presented in a variety of new ways. Edo culture, as we see here, saw a flowering of theatrical arts.

将軍

将軍とは、古代から近世にかけて軍隊の最高司令官のことを意味する言葉です。正式には征夷大将軍といいます。つまり、蛮族を平らげる軍の最高司令官という意味です。

1192年以降、日本に軍事政権が生まれると、この称号は行政の長の意味で使用されるようになりました。将軍は天皇より任命される位ですが、ほとんどの時代、それは世襲されたのです。

1600年に徳川家康が日本でもっとも影響力のある独裁者となり、その本拠地を江戸に開きました。そして1603年に将軍に任命されたことで、江戸は日本の行政の中心となったのです。ちなみに、天皇は

最後の将軍、徳川慶喜

794年以降、ずっと京都に宮廷を維持していました。

徳川家は、その後15代にわたって1868年まで将軍の地位を世襲し、徳川幕府を維持したのです。1868年に明治維新という大改革があり、江戸は東京となり、天皇も京都から江戸城に移ります。その後江戸城は皇居となって現在に至っているのです。

Shogun

The word "Shogun" has referred, from olden times to more recent history, to the highest possible military office. To be fully accurate, the title in Japanese would be "*Sei-i Tai shogun*," going back to when the military chief oversaw the "subjugation of barbarians" in ancient times.

Ever since 1192, when a military regime first ruled Japan, the title of Shogun has been used to signify the very top administrator's position. In theory, Shogun is a rank that would be appointed by the emperor, but in practical terms the office has usually been hereditary, passed on within the Shogun's family or chosen successor.

Tokugawa Ieyasu became Japan's most powerful dictator in 1600, and established Edo as his central command. Shortly thereafter, he was formally confirmed as Shogun in 1603, and from that year Edo effectively became the new capital of Japan. We should mention that the Imperial Court had been maintained over the centuries in Kyoto, from the year 794.

The Tokugawa family retained the position of Shogun for fifteen generations from 1603 to 1868, passing on both the title and power through heredity. With the Meiji Restoration of 1868 came a major reform of governmental structure; the capital's name was changed from Edo to Tokyo, and the Imperial Court was moved from Kyoto to Edo Castle. From

旗本・御家人

江戸幕府は、日本中に拡散していた大名と呼ばれる藩王を統率する最高権力機関でした。江戸幕府は天領と呼ばれる直轄領を各地に所有し、経済力を維持していました。

また、江戸幕府は旗本・御家人のシステムを用いていました。旗本・御家人は、幕府の直属の家臣団で、全国の藩の統治をするための軍事力の要としていたのです。旗本は将軍に謁見できる身分の高い家臣で、御家人はそれ以下の下級官吏を指しています。

旗本と御家人、そしてその家来を含めると8万名が政治的にも軍事的にも幕府を守護する直営軍となっていたのです。しかし、皮肉なことに江戸時代は現行の政治体制よりも平和な時代でした。重職の旗本や御家人ですが、実際は武人というよりは官吏として幕府の様々な役職についていたのです。

that time to the present, what had been the castle has been known as the Imperial Palace, and the nation's emperors have resided there.

Hatamoto, Gokenin, the Shogun's Retainers

Although every province of the nation was under the control of the local *daimyo*, in fact the Bakufu in Edo became the supreme command for all of Japan. The Bakufu exerted direct control over some property called *Tenryo*, and was able to maintain its control over the nation's economy.

In addition, it used the "*Hatamoto*" and "*Gokenin*" system of designating those who were direct retainers of the Shogun, to maintain crucial military control over all of the feudal domains. The *Hatamoto* were retainers of a high social status, permitted to have direct audiences with the Shogun; the *Gokenin*, on the other hand, held the lower-level status of minor government officials.

The *Hatamoto* and *Gokenin*, 80,000 in all including their retainers, served as the military government's mechanism to ensure political and military dominance. Ironically, this system of control also meant that the Edo era was quite peaceful, without any serious threats to the existing political order. Despite their lofty titles of *Hatamoto* and *Gokenin*, then, the samurai class actually served as bureaucratic administrators rather than in a martial function, serving the

士農工商

　江戸時代には、厳しい身分制度がありました。天皇や貴族を除き、将軍や大名に直接に仕える武士は、最も身分が高いとされました。武士の次のランクが農民、そして手先で物品を製造する手工業者、一番下のランクが、商人という順番でした。この身分制度を「士農工商」といいます。各ランクの漢字から一文字を上から、武士の「士」、農民の「農」、工業の「工」、そして商人の「商」をとったのです。

　しかし、商人は社会的には、最も身分が低いとされたものの、江戸時代に貨幣経済が浸透すると、経済をにぎる商人の力が強くなります。

　逆に武士の中には、自らの主人である大名が将軍に罰せられ改易されたりした場合、職を失うことがよくありました。失業した武士のことを浪人といいます。彼らの困窮は、江戸時代が進むにつれ、社会問題にもなったのです。

Bakufu in a variety of posts.

Shi-no-ko-sho, Four Social Classes

A very strict social class structure was enforced during the Edo era. With the exception of the Emperor and Nobility, the highest class were the samurai, who could be direct retainers of either the Bakufu or the feudal *daimyo* lords. Next below the samurai were farmers, then artisans who crafted things with their hands, and at the lowest status were merchants. This status system was referred to as "*Shi-no-ko-sho*," taking one character from each status in descending order, as "*bushi*" for samurai, "*nomin*" for farmers, "*kogyo*" for artisans, and "*shonin*" for the merchant class.

However, even though the merchant class were at the bottom of the social ladder, their strength actually increased over time, as the economy was increasingly a monetary one, and they held the economic reins of the country.

In contrast, among the samurai class there were many cases in which they lost their economic means of survival, such as when their feudal lords, the *daimyo*, were punished by the Bakufu and made to forfeit their feudal domains and all their property. Samurai who had lost their lord were referred to as "*ronin*," and their poverty became a social issue as the Edo era progressed.

We need to acknowledge the reality that there was a

なお、「士農工商」のさらに下のランクがあったことも忘れてはなりません。賤民とされたその人々は、激しい差別を受けました。明治維新が起こり、江戸幕府が滅びたその後も、差別の意識が根強く残り、以降、今日まで社会問題であり続けているのです。

文明開化

250年間におよぶ鎖国によって、日本は世界の技術進歩から大きく隔てられてきました。中国・韓国の貿易使節団と、長崎のある一港だけから入ってくる「蘭学」のみが例外でした。

しかし1868年に明治維新が起こると、外交官や視察団たちがヨーロッパやアメリカを訪れました。彼らはそこで多大なる影響を受け、産業、工学技術、医療、社会学、哲学などに関する莫大な量の情報を持ち帰り、日本は西洋文明に開化したのです。

日本は「近代化」を国策とし、新しいテクノロジーを速やかに取り入れました。西洋諸国の植民地政策がアジア地域にも広がっていることや、アヘン戦争（1839年と1856年）で中国の主権が損なわれたことを懸念して、西洋と肩を並べ、植民地化を回避し、さらには1850年代に西洋列強と結んだ不平等通商条約を破棄するために、日本は大急ぎで産業化を推し進めたのです。

social class held down even lower than the *Shi-no-ko-sho*. These "*senmin*," or "lowly people" as they were called, were discriminated against, and the deep roots of that discriminatory behavior have persisted as a social problem even after the Edo Bakufu was dismantled at the time of the Meiji Restoration, to this day.

"Civilization and Enlightenment"

Japan's 250 years of official seclusion (*Sakoku*) had largely cut the nation off from developments elsewhere in the world except through trade missions with Korea and China, and the "Dutch Learning" through the single port of Nagasaki.

With the Meiji Restoration in 1868 came, however, official diplomatic and study missions to Europe and the U.S. which brought back multiple impressions and an enormous amount of information — industrial, technical, medical, social, and philosophical — about "civilization" in the West.

As official policy, Japan sought to modernize by swiftly absorbing new technologies. Mindful of Western colonial expansion, including in Asia and particularly the loss of Chinese sovereignty in the Opium Wars (1839 and 1856), Japan sought to rapidly industrialize, "catch up," avert colonization, and overturn the unequal treaties imposed by Western powers in the 1850s.

関東大震災

　1923年9月1日の正午少し前、東京の相模湾沿岸を震源とする巨大地震が、横浜と東京近郊の市街ほぼ全域を破壊しました。マグニチュード7.9の地震は、たくさんの家々やビルを損傷させ、そして地震発生時刻には、家々の台所で昼食の用意が進められていたために、地震そのものより、引き起こされた火災によって亡くなった被害者のほうが多く出ました。

　14万人が犠牲になったと見られており、その25パーセント以上は火災によるもので、3万8千人が集まる避難場所が焼き尽くされるということも起こりました。東京と横浜にはより広い道路や公園が再建され、建築物の安全規定が見直されました。それでも関東は活動的な断層線上にあって地震がちな地域であることから、1960年、9月1日は防災の日と制定されました。

　防災の日には、学校や会社などさまざまな組織が、避難訓練や、いつの日か首都を襲う地震に備えるよう呼びかけを行います。

Great Kanto Earthquake

Shortly before noon on September 1, 1923, a major earthquake centered on Sagami Bay southeast of Tokyo destroyed much of Yokohama, Tokyo and surrounding towns. With a magnitude of 7.9 on the Richter Scale, the earthquake damaged many homes and buildings, but the timing of the quake — as lunch was being prepared in countless kitchens — led to fires that killed more than the quake's shaking itself.

Of the estimated 140,000 who perished, over 25% were killed in a firestorm that consumed an evacuation grounds in Tokyo where 38,000 people had taken refuge. Tokyo and Yokohama were rebuilt with wider roads, parks, and building safety codes, but mindful that the area sits on active fault lines and is prone to more earthquakes, September 1 has been designated since 1960 as Disaster Prevention Day.

On that day in particular, schools, offices and many organizations conduct drills to remind and prepare the public for when future earthquakes will take place beneath the nation's capital.

東京大空襲

　第二次世界大戦（日本では太平洋戦争とも）では、1941年から1945年8月15日にかけて、日本とアメリカ及びその同盟諸国とが、アジアで戦火を交えました。

　この長く悲劇的な戦争は、軍人・民間人を問わない広範囲の犠牲者を出しました。アメリカとその同盟諸国の進出により、日本は支配下におく領土をどんどん失い、1944年7月にサイパンの北マリアナ諸島をアメリカに制圧されたことが戦局を分けました。これによって、新しく開発されたB-29爆撃機の基地がサイパンと近くのテニアン島に配備され、日本全域がその航続範囲内に入りました。

　1944年11月、日本の首都であり工業都市である東京への爆撃が始まりました。百を超える空襲のあと、1945年3月、のちに「史上最大規模の壊滅的空襲」といわれた、334機のB-29爆撃機による空襲が決行されました。その一度の空襲作戦で、8万人から10万人が亡くなったと見積もられています。主に焼夷弾が使われ、市街のほとんどが焼かれました。

　東京の空襲と、続いて広島と長崎に投下された原子爆弾は現在も賛否が分かれる問題ですが、ともかくそれによって日本は戦争を続けていく力を失いました。3月9日から10日の「東京大空襲」の日は毎年、首都東京では特別な追悼の日となっています。

Great Tokyo Air Raid

World War II (often called the "Pacific War" in Japan), fought in Asia between Japan and the U.S. and its allies between 1941 and August 15, 1945, was a long and tragic war that caused widespread military and civilian casualties.

As Japan lost more and more territory under its control to advancing U.S. and Allied forces, a key turning point in the war took place in July 1944, when Saipan in the Northern Marianas fell under U.S. control. This placed all of Japan within flying range of the newly developed B-29 bombers stationed on Saipan and nearby Tinian.

Bombing raids on Tokyo, Japan's capital and manufacturing city, began in November 1944, but out of hundreds of raids, the bombing of March 9–10, 1945, carried out by 334 B-29s, has been called "the single most destructive bombing raid in history." An estimated 80,000 to 100,000 deaths were caused by this one bombing raid, which primarily used incendiary bombs to burn most of the city.

The bombings of Tokyo, and the subsequent atomic bombings of Hiroshima and Nagasaki, remain controversial, but weakened Japan's ability to continue the war. The March 9–10 fire-bombing of Tokyo, in particular, is memorialized each year in the capital city.

高度成長

　第二次世界大戦後の日本は、戦争によって甚大な損害を受けた経済と社会基盤の復興に着手しました。「復興」という言葉は、19世紀後半から20世紀前半にかけて急速に工業化した日本にとってキーワードです。

　1950年代の中頃から、日本政府は速やかな戦後復興を何よりも優先し、猛烈な勢いで建設工事が始まりました。日本でオリンピックが開催された1964年には、東京と大阪間を結ぶ新幹線が開通しました。

　1960年から1980年にかけての20年間は、日本の「高度成長期」として知られています(続く1980年から1990年までは「バブル経済期」)。ハイテク分野、自動車産業、鉄鋼業、造船業、製造業などが急激に成長し、さかんに輸出が行われると、世界市場の日本への視点に変化が生じました。現在では「メイド・イン・ジャパン」は、世界に認められた高品質製品の証です。

バブル景気

　高度成長期後の1960年から1970年にかけての10年間、日本製品は国内でも海外市場でも売れに売れ、日本経済は「天井知らず」と目されていました。日本企業と日本人の利益性が高まり収入が増加すると、

High-speed growth

Following WWII, Japan set out to rebuild from the enormous damage to its economy and infrastructure caused by the war. "Rebuild" is an important word, though, as Japan had already industrialized rapidly in the late 1800s and first half of the 1900s.

Priority was given by the Japanese government to a speedy recovery from the mid-1950s, and a frenetic pace of construction began when the country was awarded the Olympic Games in 1964 — the year the Shinkansen linking Tokyo and Osaka was opened.

The two decades from 1960 to 1980 are known as Japan's "high-speed growth" years (followed by the 1980–1990 period known as Japan's "bubble economy" years). High-tech areas, automotives, steel, shipbuilding, manufacturing, and exports all grew quite rapidly, and saw a shift in perspective in global markets, now regarding "Made in Japan" as a sign of world-class, high-quality products.

Bubble economy

Following the high-speed growth decades of the 1960s and 1970s, Japan's economy was perceived as almost unstoppable, with so many successes in manufactured products for domestic and export markets. With high

経済学者が「バブル経済」と呼ぶ、商品・サービス・土地などの価格が、実際と見合わない高値に急激に上昇するという現象が起こりました。物価が上昇しつづけているのに、企業や人々がお金に余裕があるかのように感じると、狂乱的な購買と投資が行われるという悪循環へ転じます。日本は「ナンバーワン」の座についたかと思われました。日本企業によって、アメリカの有名な不動産物件や企業が買収されました。日本の地価も株式評価も高騰し、それも大変な高騰だったので、大勢の人が株式市場で大口投資を行いました。バブル（泡）はあまりにも大きくなりすぎると、破裂してしまうというリスクがあります。

　日本のバブル経済は、1990年1月初頭に破綻しました。日本経済は、今日に至ってもそのショックからは立ち直れていないと、多くの経済アナリストたちが分析しています。

profitability and increased earnings by many Japanese companies and individuals, however, came a phenomenon economists call a "bubble economy" — when the price of goods, services, stocks, and real estate grows faster than the real value. When it appears that prices will continue to rise, however, and companies or people feel that they have extra money to spend, there is a frenzy of buying and investing that can turn into a dangerous cycle. Japan appeared to be "number one," Japanese firms bought famous properties and companies in the U.S., land prices grew very high, and the stock valuation of Japanese companies, too, was so high that many invested heavily in the stock market. When a bubble gets too big, however, the risk is that it will burst.

The bubble economy of Japan burst in early January 1990, and many analysts say that the economy has not fully recovered from that shock even today.

江戸と東京の歴史と文化

江戸時代以前

東京は、1868年まで江戸と呼ばれていました。
- Until 1868, Tokyo was called Edo.

東京は昔は江戸と呼ばれていました。
- In the past, Tokyo was called Edo.

江戸という地名は、11世紀に江戸氏という豪族が城を築いたことが起源といわれています。
- The name Edo comes from the Edo clan who built a castle here in the eleventh century.

江戸氏が没落したあと、太田道灌が江戸を整備し、城を築きました。
- After the fall of the Edo clan, Ota Dokan took over Edo and built a castle there.

15世紀から16世紀にかけて、日本が戦国時代になると、江戸一帯は北条氏という有力な豪族が支配しました。
- From the fifteenth through the sixteenth century, during Japan's warring period, the Edo region was controlled by the powerful Hojo clan.

北条氏は東京の西、箱根に近い小田原に本拠を置きました。
- The Hojo clan had their stronghold in Odawara, near Hakone.

Tokyo in Single Sentences

北条氏は1590年に、日本を統一した戦国大名、豊臣秀吉によって滅ぼされました。

☐ In 1590, the Hojo clan was crushed by Toyotomi Hideyoshi, the warlord who united Japan.

豊臣秀吉の最も有力な家臣、徳川家康が北条氏の領地を受け取り、江戸に本拠を置きました。

☐ Toyotomi Hideyoshi gave his most powerful vassal, Tokugawa Ieyasu, the Hojo clan's territory. Tokugawa Ieyasu made Edo his home base.

豊臣秀吉が死ぬと、徳川家康が江戸を拠点に勢力を伸ばしました。

☐ After Toyotomi Hideyoshi's death, Tokugawa Ieyasu used Edo as his base of power.

江戸時代

Track 87

1603年に徳川家康が将軍になり、江戸は日本の行政の中心となりました。

☐ In 1603, Tokugawa Ieyasu became Shogun and Edo became the political center of Japan.

KEY WORD ✓

☐ warring period	戦国時代
☐ warlord	戦国大名
☐ vassal	家臣

江戸と東京の歴史と文化

江戸時代以前 ● 江戸時代

▶▶▶ ワンセンテンスで説明する東京

1603年以降、天皇の御所のある京都が日本の首都で、将軍のいる江戸が日本の行政の中心となりました。

☐ From 1603, Kyoto, the home of the Emperor, remained the capital while Edo became the political center.

徳川家康が江戸に開いた政権を徳川幕府といいます。

☐ The administration Tokugawa Ieyasu established in Edo was known as the Tokugawa Shogunate.

徳川幕府は1603年から1868年まで日本を統治しました。

☐ The Tokugawa Shoganate ruled Japan from 1603 to 1868.

徳川家康は、1615年に大阪城にいた豊臣秀吉の子供、豊臣秀頼を滅ぼしました。

☐ In 1615, Tokugawa Ieyasu overthrew Toyotomi Hideyoshi's son, Toyotomi Hideyori, who was in Osaka Castle.

三代目の将軍、徳川家光の時に、日本は鎖国をし、それは1854年まで続きました。

☐ The third shogun, Tokugawa Iemitsu, closed Japan to foreigners and the country remained closed until 1854.

徳川幕府は身分制度を設け、武士がその頂点にたち、その下に農民、職人、そして商人の順に身分を定めました。

☐ The Tokugawa Shogunate established a class system with warriors on the top, followed by farmers, artisans, and merchants.

Tokyo in Single Sentences

江戸時代には身分の異なる者は、基本的に別々の地域に住んでいました。

☐ During the Edo era, people of different classes were generally segregated.

全国の大名は、定期的に江戸に住むことを義務づけられ、江戸に大きな屋敷をもっていました。

☐ All of the feudal lords were required to live in Edo for a certain period, so there were many big estates.

江戸はベニスのように、川と運河を船が行き来した水運の都市でした。

☐ Like Venice, Tokyo was a city of rivers and canals traversed by boat.

江戸時代、赤坂、麹町など江戸城のそばには身分の高い武士や大名の家がありました。

☐ During the Edo Period neighborhoods alongside Edo Castle, such as Akasaka and Kojimachi, were where the highest ranking warriors and feudal lords lived.

江戸時代、町人の住んでいた地域は、下町と呼ばれていました。

☐ During the Edo era the area where the townspeople lived was called *Shitamachi*.

KEY WORD ✓

☐ administration	政権
☐ rule	統治する
☐ overthrow	滅ぼす
☐ class system	身分制度

江戸と東京の歴史と文化

江戸時代

江戸時代、日本橋あたりには裕福な商人が店を構えていました。

☐ During the Edo era the wealthiest merchants had their shops around Nihonbashi.

江戸時代、深川や浅草といった地域には、町人が住んでいました。

☐ During the Edo era the townspeople lived in neighborhoods like Fukagawa and Asakusa.

江戸は17世紀から18世紀に繁栄し、人口も100万人を超えるようになりました。

☐ Edo prospered between the seventeenth and eighteenth centuries, with a population reaching one million people.

18世紀の江戸の人口は100万人を超え、世界で最も規模の大きな街になりました。

☐ When the population of Edo reached one million people in the eighteenth century it was the largest city in the world.

都心の一部になっている品川や新宿は、江戸時代は江戸の外の宿場町でした。

☐ Neighborhoods that are now considered to be part of central Tokyo, such as Shinagawa and Shinjuku, were post stations outside the city limits during the Edo era.

東京を代表する繁華街である渋谷は、江戸時代は村のひとつにすぎませんでした。

☐ Shibuya, known today as one of Tokyo's biggest shopping districts, was a village during the Edo era.

Tokyo in Single Sentences

江戸時代、江戸は何度も火事に見舞われました。

☐ Edo saw many fires during the Edo era.

火消しは、現在の消防士にあたり、江戸の人々を火事から守りました。

☐ Firefighters, called *hikeshi*, protected the people of Edo.

町人は社会的な身分は低いものの、江戸の文化を担った人々です。

☐ Even though the townspeople were low on the social ladder, they were Edo's cultural leaders.

江戸時代、江戸の経済を動かした商人は身分は低いものの、実際は社会に大きな影響力を持っていました。

☐ The merchants who drove Edo's economy were low on the social ladder; however, in reality they had a big influence over society.

江戸の治安は、現在の警察にあたる奉行所が担っていました。

☐ Order in Edo was kept by magistrates who functioned like today's police force.

江戸と東京の歴史と文化

江戸時代

KEY WORD ✓

☐ townspeople　　　　　　町人
☐ post station　　　　　　宿場
☐ magistrate　　　　　　　奉行所

江戸の火消しや目明かしを題材にした推理小説は、今でも人気があり、テレビドラマなどにもなっています。

☐ Novels about Edo-period firefighters (*hikeshi*) and detectives (*meakashi*) are popular even today, and sometimes are turned into television dramas.

徳川幕府は、1853年にアメリカからペリー提督が開国を求めて来日した頃から衰退し、1868年に滅びました。

☐ The Tokugawa Shogunate, which was weakened from demands by American Commodore Perry to open the country in 1853, collapsed in 1868.

幕末には、江戸のそばの横浜に、外国人の居留区が設けられました。

☐ During the closing days of the Edo era a residential district for foreigners was created near Edo, in Yokohama.

徳川幕府が衰退し、滅びるまでを幕末といい、政治、そして社会がとても混乱しました。

☐ The period of the Tokugawa Shogunate's decline is called *bakumatsu*, and it was a period of political and societal turmoil.

幕末には、天皇を中心に国をまとめようという人々と、徳川幕府の体制を維持しようとする人々との間で激しい戦いがありました。

☐ During the closing days of the Edo era, those who supported a movement to restore the Emperor to power and those who supported the Tokugawa regime fought a bitter war.

明治時代

江戸時代が終わり、天皇を中心とした新しい政権ができたことは、明治維新として知られています。

- [ ] At the end of the Edo era a new government was formed and the Emperor was restored to power; this is known as the Meiji Restoration.

1868年に徳川幕府が滅びると、江戸は東京と名前を変え、日本の首都となりました。

- [ ] In 1868, when the Tokugawa Shogunate collapsed, Edo was renamed Tokyo and became the official capital of Japan.

1868年に徳川幕府が滅びると、天皇は京都から江戸城に移り、これが明治時代の幕開けとなりました。

- [ ] In 1868, after the collapse of the Tokugawa Shogunate, the Emperor moved from Kyoto to Edo Castle. This marked the beginning of the Meiji period.

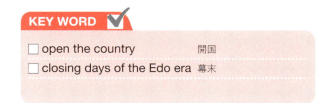

KEY WORD
- [ ] open the country　開国
- [ ] closing days of the Edo era　幕末

▶▶▶ ワンセンテンスで説明する東京

天皇が将軍のいた江戸城に移ると、江戸城は今日でも使われている皇居と呼ばれるようになりました。

☐ When the Emperor moved into Edo Castle it was renamed the Imperial Palace, the name used today.

徳川幕府に代わる新しい政府は、西欧の文化を積極的に取り入れました。

☐ The new government that took over from the Tokugawa Shogunate aggressively promoted Western culture.

1872年には、東京から横浜まで日本で初めての鉄道が開通しました。

☐ In 1872 Japan's first railroad, which connected Tokyo and Yokohama, opened.

明治時代、1889年に東京と神戸の間が鉄道で結ばれました。列車は現在の新橋がある駅から出ていました。

☐ During the Meiji Period, in 1889, a train line connecting Tokyo and Kobe was completed, and trains departed from a station located where Shinbashi is today.

明治政府は江戸時代の身分制度を廃止した後、1871年に大名のタイトルも地位も廃止されました。

☐ The Meiji administration abolished the Tokugawa-era class system and in 1871 the titles and ranks of the feudal lords were repealed.

明治政府は、徳川幕府の封建的な制度を全て廃止し、近代国家を造ろうとしました。

☐ The Meiji administration abolished the Tokugawa-era feudal system and in its place established a modern nation state.

Tokyo in Single Sentences

明治政府による、旧来の制度を廃止し、西欧文明を導入してゆく方針は文明開化として知られ人気がありました。

- [ ] The Meiji administration abolished the previous systems and established policies to introduce Western civilization; this campaign was popularly known as "Civilization and Enlightenment."

明治時代に日本は近代国家として急速に発展し、東京はそんな日本の首都として国とともに成長しました。

- [ ] During the Meiji Period Japan quickly developed into a modern nation state and Tokyo, as its capital, developed along with it.

明治天皇が1910年に亡くなるころには、日本は極東の強国に成長し、東京には中国などから多くの留学生が集まりました。

- [ ] By the time of the death of the Meiji Emperor in 1910, Japan had become one of the leading powers in the Far East and attracted many foreign students from China and other countries.

KEY WORD ✓

☐ Meiji administration	明治政府
☐ feudal system	封建制
☐ Civilization and Enlightenment	文明開化

江戸と東京の歴史と文化

明治時代

大正から昭和

現在の東京駅は 1914 年に完成しました。

☐ The current Tokyo Station was built in 1914.

大正天皇の時代、1923 年に東京は大地震とその後の火事に見舞われ、甚大な被害を受けました。この地震を関東大震災と呼んでいます。

☐ During the reign of the Taisho Emperor, in 1923, Tokyo was hit by a big earthquake, followed by a fire, which caused enormous damage; this earthquake was called the Great Kanto Earthquake.

関東大震災による火事のために、江戸時代以来の古い町並みの多くが失われました。

☐ Most of what remained of the city of the Edo era was destroyed in the fires following the Great Kanto Earthquake.

1925 年には、現在の山手線が完成し、東京の主要地区が環状線によって結ばれました。

☐ In 1925, the current Yamanote Line was completed, creating a loop line linking Tokyo's major districts.

第二次世界大戦がはじまると、東京は空襲によって大きな被害を受けました。

☐ During the air raids of World War II, Tokyo was heavily damaged.

幾度かの空襲の中でも、1945年3月11日の東京大空襲は最大の被害をもたらし、約10万人が犠牲になり、東京は壊滅的な打撃を受けました。

☐ In the air raids, the most damaging of which was the Great Tokyo Air Raid of March 11, 1945, around 100,000 people died and the city was devastated.

戦後から現在

第二次世界大戦の終結後、日本は連合軍に占領され、その本部が東京に置かれました。

☐ At the end of World War II, Japan was occupied by the Allied Forces, and Tokyo was their headquarters.

戦後の混乱期、東京は食料や住宅が不足し、闇市が街中にできました。今東京の商店街として賑わうアメヤ横町も、闇市がその起こりでした。

☐ During the chaotic days after the war, when Tokyo lacked food and housing, black markets appeared around the city; Ameya Yokocho, which today is a lively shopping street, was one of these black markets.

KEY WORD

☐ reign	御代
☐ air raid	空襲
☐ black market	闇市

▶▶▶ ワンセンテンスで説明する東京

1964年、戦後の混乱期を乗り越え復興した東京は、オリンピックを開催しました。

☐ In 1964, after Tokyo had recovered from the chaotic post-war years, the Olympics were held.

1964年の東京オリンピックは、アジアで最初のオリンピックでした。

☐ The 1964 Tokyo Olympics were the first Olympic Games held in Asia.

1964年のオリンピック開催に間に合うように、東京では首都高と呼ばれる自動車専用道路など、さまざまなインフラが整備されました。

☐ Tokyo's highway system, called *shutoko*, and other infrastructure projects were completed in time for the 1964 Olympics.

1980年代、東京の物価や地価は世界で最も高いものでした。

☐ In the 1980s, Tokyo had the world's highest cost of living and real-estate prices.

1990年代になり、いわゆるバブル景気が崩壊すると、東京は長く苦しい不況に突入しました。

☐ At the beginning of the 1990s the so-called bubble economy burst, and Tokyo entered a long, painful recession.

現在、東京は日本文化を世界に向けて発信しようとしています。

☐ Today, Tokyo aims to transmit Japanese culture to the world.

Tokyo in Single Sentences

2020年

東京は、2020年に夏季のオリンピックを開催します。

- [ ] Tokyo will host the 2020 Summer Olympics.

東京は1964年について2020年に夏季のオリンピックを開催します。

- [ ] Tokyo hosted the Summer Olympics in 1964 and will do so again in 2020.

2020年東京オリンピックは都心におけるコンパクトな大会を目指しています。

- [ ] The 2020 Tokyo Olympics is planned as a compact event in the heart of the city.

2020年の東京オリンピックは、現在の国立競技場を建て替えた新国立競技場をメインスタジアムに使用します。

- [ ] The main venue for the 2020 Tokyo Olympics will be the New National Stadium, a reconstruction of the existing National Stadium.

KEY WORD ✓

☐ cost of living	物価
☐ real-estate price	地価
☐ bubble economy	バブル景気
☐ venue	会場

江戸と東京の歴史と文化

戦後から現在●2020年

英文 東京紹介事典

2016年9月4日　第1刷発行

編　者　IBCパブリッシング編

発行者　浦晋亮

発行所　IBCパブリッシング株式会社
〒162-0804
東京都新宿区中里町29番3号
菱秀神楽坂ビル9F
Tel. 03-3513-4511
Fax. 03-3513-4512
www.ibcpub.co.jp

印刷所　中央精版印刷株式会社

© IBC Publishing 2016
Printed in Japan

落丁本・乱丁本は、小社宛にお送りください。
送料小社負担にてお取り替えいたします。
本書の無断複写（コピー）は
著作権法上での例外を除き禁じられています。

ISBN978-4-7946-0433-0